Philo's Place in Judaism:

A Study of Conceptions of Abraham in Jewish Literature

The original publication of this book was
made possible through a gift by the late
SIDNEY NEUMANN,
of Philadelphia, in memory of his parents,
ABRAHAM and EMMA NEUMANN.

Philo's Place in Judaism:

A Study of Conceptions of Abraham
in Jewish Literature

SAMUEL SANDMEL

Professor of Bible and Hellenistic Literature
Hebrew Union College - Jewish Institute of Religion

AUGMENTED EDITION

KTAV PUBLISHING HOUSE, Inc.

NEW YORK

1971

To

F. F. S.

The rabbis call Sarah a Woman of Valor
and Philo allegorizes her as Virtue.
Both qualities blend in you.

Table of Contents

INTRODUCTION TO THE REPRINT

The reprinting of this volume provides opportunity for (1) a brief bibliographical note; (2) some extended comments on Philo and Gnosticism, and, at the end of the book, (3) a new subject index to the Philonic material.

* * *

1.

In *Scholarship on Philo and Josephus (1937-1962)*, New York (undated), Louis Feldman provides (pp. 1-26) a systematic listing with annotations of studies in Philo, these arranged in reasonable topics. It closes with an enlightening summary entitled "Desiderata in the Study of Philo" (p. 24-26). Feldman's annotations are well balanced, reasonable, and apropos.

Gerhard Delling (with Gerhard Zachhuber and Heinz Berthold) has provided an extensive *Bibliographie zur jüdisch-hellenistischen und Intertestmentarischen Literatur 1800-1865* (*Texte und Untersuchungen zur Geschichte der Altchristlichen Literatur*, Band 106), Berlin, 1969, with pages 34-50 devoted to Philo. After a review of various editions of Philo (items 629-649), there appears section a, "Gesamtdarstellungen" (items 650-689); section b, "Arbeiten zu einzelnen Schriften" (items 690-720), and section c, Arbeiten zu einzelnen Themen" (items 725-981). Such classification is always difficult; items classified in other sections of the *Bibliographie* are indicated through extensive cross-references; some of the items listed under Philo might well have been listed elsewhere, as Professor Delling notes in his foreword. Such matters, though, are inherent in the very nature of things. An alphabetical index of authors is provided.

The French translation of Philo is progressing but is as yet incomplete. Volume I, *De Opificio Mundi*, 1961, contains a worthy essay by the translator, Roger Arnaldez; he, Jean Pouilloux and Claude Mondésert, are editing this series of volumes. Arnaldez has not made the effort in his essay to supply a complete bibliography, but he supplies a rather handy review of various trends in the study of Philo, commenting on my study, on pp. 110-111. There are the natural differences in the quality of the translations and annotations in the volumes I have seen; I found especially admirable the essay by Marguerite Harl in Vol. 15, on *Quis Rerum Divinarum Heres Sit*. I reviewed Volumes 4, 15, 20, 22, and 31 in *Erasmus*, XXII, 1970, pp. 679-683.

The inauguration of the McCormick Philo Institute at McCormick Seminary is greatly to be welcomed. I have been informed that the initial project, to be directed by Robert Hamerton-Kelly, will concentrate on the sources of Philo. Also, an updated bibliography on Philo is being undertaken at McCormick by Earle Helgert. Professor Heinrich Rengstorf of Münster announced in 1966 the proposed publication by the Institutum Judaicum Delitzschianum of some Philo fragments, not Armenian, and the presence at Münster of Ludwig Früchtel's testamentary collection which can lead to a complete index or concordance to Philo. The following volumes which have come to my attention appeared after Professor Feldman's list: Klaus Otte, *Das Sprachverständnis bei Philo von Alexandrien,* Tübingen, 1968; *Philon d'Alexandrie,* Lyon, 1967; Ursula Früchtel, *Die Kosmologischen Vorstellungen bei Philo von Alexandrien,* Leiden, 1968. Mention might be made here of G. Guirovich, "Bibliografia sullo Gnosticismo," in *Scuola Cattolica* 97 (Supplement I, 1970), pp. 39*-54*.

*   *   *

2.

As to Philo and Gnosticism, perhaps one might begin with the abrupt question, Was Philo a Gnostic? The answer will lead us into a veritable maze, and, hopefully but not certainly, out of it. We shall need to deal, as others to be cited have done, with definition, and, beyond the bare definition, with attendant assumptions.

In studies in "the history of religions" towards the end of the 19th century, the term Gnosticism had begun to be used in a new way. Antecedently, especially in studies in the New Testament and early Christianity, the term was used to denominate a specifically Christian manifestation of the second century. Normally it was assumed that this Christian Gnosticism was an outgrowth of earlier, inchoate beginnings. The newer usage, however, supposed that these admitted antecedents were much more than merely inchoate, and that Gnosticism was already something of a developed and flourishing movement well before the birth of Christianity. Moreover, Gnosticism, whether early or late, was broader than Christianity, having *entered* into Judaism too, as attested by passages in the later rabbinic literature which mention "two dominions" and the elusive *minim*.

There abide into our time residues of the diversity in defining Gnosticism. Robert M. Grant, "Gnosticism," (*Interpreter's Dictionary of the Bible*, 1962) begins his article by defining Gnosticism as "a constellation of religious phenomena found during the second century and later." (In the concluding section of his article, after speaking of a "proto-Gnostic" influence on New Testament writings as "fairly probable," he goes on, "It is fairly clear that much of the debate . . . is a matter of definition.")

On the other hand, one can cite the approach of Rudolf Bultmann in "Gnosis," in *Theologisches Wörterbuch zum Neuen Testament,* 1933; the essay appeared in an English translation by J. R. Coates, *Bible Key Words: Gnosis,* London, 1952. Bultmann, both in this article and in his other writings, treats Gnosticism as if it was definitively an early and broad pre-Christian phenomenon.

Still another facet of the difference in definition is reflected in the symposium on Gnosticism at the 100th meeting of the Society of Biblical Literature in December, 1964. The papers by G. Quispel, R. M. Wilson, and Hans Jonas are published in J. Philip Hyatt, editor, *The Bible in Modern Scholarship*, Nashville, 1965. The debate there centered primarily around the issue of the origin of Gnosticism as related to Judaism. G. Quispel, "Gnosticism and the New Testament," (Hyatt, pp. 252-271) argues that Gnosticism "owes not a little to Judaism" (that is, it came from Judaism, rather than entering into it). He proceeded to distinguish, cautiously, among three Jewish milieux as sources for Gnosticism: (1) the "outskirts of Judaism, namely in Samaria"; (2) "the milieu of esoteric lore transmitted within the very heart of Palestinian Pharisaism"; and (3) "certain baptist sects in Palestine which seem to have had some relation to the Jewish religion." (Passingly, Quispel added, "The Hellenistic Judaism of Alexandria as represented by Philo, however, does not seem to have the same relevance to our subject.") Thereafter in his essay Quispel made the effort to establish a connection between "Wisdom" in Judaism and "the female counterpart of the Godhead in Gnosticism." Quispel went on to say that " the most important Jewish contribution, however, both to Gnosticism and to early Christianity, seems to have come from esoteric circles *in the heart of Palestinian Judaism*" (the italics are mine).

Quispel is in accord with the researches of Gershom Scholem, citing especially the latter's *Jewish Gnosticism, Merkabah Mysticism, and Talmudic Tradition*, New York, 1960. Scholem has been among those willing to use Gnosticism as the "convenient term for the religious movement that proclaimed a mystical esotericism for the elect based on illumination and the acquisition of a higher knowledge of things heavenly and divine." In his book Scholem propounded two questions. The first was, Did there exist a pre-Christian Jewish Gnosticism that served as a point of departure for early Christian heresies? To this Scholem gives a reserved affirmation. His second question was, Had such Jewish Gnostic teaching already acquired a dualistic and heretical character? The answer to the second question, according to Scholem, is to be found, not in apocalyptic literature or Talmudic passages, but in the esoteric tradition, exemplified in the "Hekaloth Books," some complete, and some only "fragments and amorphous material scattered widely through Hebrew manuscripts"; Scholem listed these sources specifically (pp. 5-7). Significantly, Scholem stated that this Hekaloth material is much older than a fourth or fifth century dating which he had earlier proposed. Now he was even prepared to speak of a first or early second century origin; his evidence, so he contended, "makes a case for connecting the Hekaloth strata of the late second or early third century with this even earlier stage of Jewish Gnosticism, one which was striving equally hard to maintain a strictly monotheistic character" (p. 42). (That is to say, it is baseless, according to Scholem, always to equate Gnosticism with heresy.) Scholem went on to scorn researchers whose knowledge of Judaism in the first Christian century is limited to what is found in Strack-Billerbeck, *Kommentar zum Neuen Testament aus Talmud und Midrash;* the hekaloth material goes uncited there. Scholem regards his *Jewish Gnosticism* (p. 8) as "deepening, and in some cases, supplementing" his earlier presentation in his *Major Trends in Jewish Mysticism. The Hilda Stich Strook Lectures, 1938,* published in 1941. In this earlier volume, Philo is mentioned three times, once (p. 14) passingly in relation to the Therapeutae; a second time in connection with the medieval *Hasidim,* whose doctrine of *Kavod* ("divine glory"), as something created, "had little more significance than the notion of a created logos . . . had for Philo" (p. 111); and a third time, still another passing allusion to Philo's logos, as creator, which idea "was developed by . . . sectarians, who for a long time moved on the fringe of Rabbinic Judaism . . ." (p. 113). Scholem presents no exposition of Philo himself, possibly because the definition of the scope of his lectures (pp. 18-19) excludes Philo from consideration. But one nevertheless wonders why.

Back to Quispel and the symposium, Robert McLachlan Wilson's paper was not a direct response to Quispel (Hyatt, *The Bible in Modern Scholarship*, pp. 272-278). Wilson's paper included some exceedingly apt statements especially on the terminological problem; he also warned against "superficial and facile solutions" to the inherently complex problems, as he had done in his highly illuminating and important study, *The Gnostic Problem,* London, 1958. Proceeding further, in his "Gnosis,

Gnosticism, and the New Testament," in *Le Origini dello Gnosticismo*, Leiden, 1967, pp. 511-527, Wilson attempts to provide a terminological distinction, as between gnosis, the early broad movement, and Gnosticism, the second century heresy. He terms his effort as not altogether successful; he is here much too modest. Indeed, the conference in Messina of which *Le Origini* is the published version, promulgated a "Proposal for a Terminological and Conceptual Agreement with regard to the theme of the Colloquim"; the proposal appears in Italian, French, German, and English (pp. xx-xxxii). The matter of clarifying definition is reverted to in the same volume, pp. 1-27, by Ugo Bianchi, "Le problème des origines du gnosticisme," with allusions to others (J. Danielou and H.-M. Schenke) who also have written on the subject, and as I have, quite independently, myself, in *The First Christian Century in Judaism and Christianity*, New York, 1969, pp. 98-99. But granted that some of the confusion could be eliminated by using the word gnosis for the early, broad movement, and Gnosticism for the second century Christian manifestation, residual problems and issues abide, to which we presently turn.

The comment by Hans Jonas on Quispel (Hyatt, pp. 279-293) was divided into two sections, the second of which (pp. 286-293) is about "the alleged Jewish origins of Gnosticism." In it Jonas charged Quispel[1] with overstatement and poor logic; he lamented that Scholem had done "a semantic disservice to clarity" in call-

---

1. Quispel's rejoinder to Jonas, "The Origins of the Gnostic Demi-
· urge," is found in Patrick Granfield and Josef A. Jungmann, ed.,
Kyriakon: Festschrift Johannes Quastum, I, Münster (no date),
pp. 271–276. I am indebted to Professor Quispel for this and
other welcome offprints. Antecedently, Quispel had published
Gnosis als Weltreligion, Zurich, 1951, and "Der gnostische Antropos und die jüdische Tradition," in *Eranos-Yearbook* XXII
(1953), Zurich, 1954, pp. 195-234. His views are challenged by
K. Schubert, "Problem und Wesen der jüdischen Gnosis," *Kairos,*
1961, pp. 2 ff., and K. Stürmer, "Judentum, Griechentum und
Gnosis," *Theologische Literaturzeitung* 73 (1948), sp. 581.

ing Palestinian Hekaloth mysticism a Gnosis. He concluded that in a "loose and non-committal sense" one may ascribe the origins of Gnosticism "at the fringes of Judaism," though he nevertheless did not hestitate to object to, or even to scorn much of Quispel's presentation. This latter was especially the case in respect to a matter raised by Quispel (and by others). Second century Christian Gnosticism was, as is admitted on all sides, "anti-Semitic." If early, pre-Christian or non-Christian Gnosticism provided the matrix for this later "anti-Semitic" aspect, and, if indeed early Gnosticism was generated or else influenced by Judaism, was early Gnosticism likewise "anti-Semitic"? That is, did Judaism not only spur or even spawn early Gnosticism, but did it also promptly generate anti-Semitism? How would the case be with hekaloth Gnosticism, if it were a non-heretical product of Palestinian Pharisaism? Jonas himself preferred, however, to describe the Jewish share in the origin of Gnosticism as "catalytic and provoking." He went on (p. 293); "To the breathtaking possibility of its [Judaism] even being positive begetter of the essence [of Gnosticism], I keep an open mind but will not lower my price. A Gnosticism without a fallen god, without benighted creator and sinister creation, without alien soul, cosmic captivity and acosmic salvation, without the self-redeeming of the Deity—in short: a Gnosis without divine tragedy will not meet specification." This Jonas view, as is evident, adopts a definition, and a set of assumptions, almost directly the reverse of the Scholem view, and laments Scholem's term "Jewish Gnosticism." Rather curiously, there is a certain counter-balance to Scholem's avoidance of Philo: the Colloquium on Le Origini pays little attention to Scholem's "Jewish Gnosticism," possibly, as note 1, page 746 implies, because Scholem's Jewish Gnosticism was not dualistic.

It seems to me that beyond the terminological differences, we encounter in the Scholem-Quispel and Jonas differences a reflection of genuine ancient parallel tendencies, one more or less Palestinian and Semitic, and the other diaspora and hellenistic, and that these two tendencies require some measure of scholarly distinction, despite the possible partial overlap.

*   *   *

The question of Philo as a Gnostic, or a Jewish Gnostic, or a representative of Gnosis, is not reflected in my ensuing study; hence some explanation for the omission there, and now the present inquiry, seems called for. I do not intend by this explanation to atone for some supposed trespass; indeed the purpose of the explanation is to reflect some of the problems inherent in the research in the troubled waters of hellenistic Judaism and early Christianity.

My first studies in Philo were influenced or even shaped by my teacher, Erwin Goodenough. My work on Abraham was undertaken to try in some way to measure the extent of hellenization in Philo. Goodenough had come to Philonic studies and to hellenistic Judaism as a digression; in his seeking to understand the rapid hellenization of early Christianity, he supposed that an antecedently hellenized, non-normative hellenistic Judaism had paved the way for such rapid hellenization. He had found it necessary for his purposes to try to establish that a hellenistic Judaism markedly different from normative Palestinian Judaism had indeed existed, since such a distinction went, and still goes, unacknowledged. Philo, *properly understood* (as according to Goodenough, he was not by those who denied any hellenization in Philo), was a witness to his hellenistic Judaism. Subsequently Goodenough carried his researches far beyond Philo, as in his massive 13-volume *Jewish Symbols in the Greco-Roman Period*; initially, however, the center of his research was Philo. His effort in his various studies in Philo was to discover what he termed the bridges between Philo and the Hellenistic pagan religions, especially the Mysteries, as indicated by the sub-title of his first significant Philonic study, *By Light, Light: The Mystic Gospel of Hellenistic Judaism*. Goodenough's thesis, in brief, was that Philo represented a hellenization of Judaism in the sense that he interpreted his inherited Judaism as if it were like the Greek mystery religions—whose proliferation and ascendancy are later than Philo. Philo scorned the pagan mysteries on the assumption that Judaism was the one and only true mystery, with the pagan mysteries palpably false. While passingly Goodenough did suggest that cultic changes were involved, he held for the most part

that the ancestral religion was retained by Philo relatively un-
changed, but its import and nuances had become modified as
these latter were viewed intellectually. Goodenough supposed
that there was a sort of analogue between Philo and such Greek
intellectuals as Plutarch, with Philo having done for Judaism
what Plutarch later did for the cult of Isis and Osiris. By implication, if Philo had, in his intellectual approach, converted
Judaism into a mystery religion, the cultic ceremonies necessarily
acquired mystery significance. Goodenough asserted that it would
be outside Philo, and not within the corpus of his writings, that
non-intellectual, practical syncretism, usually termed magic,
would be reflected, for not only was Philo an intellectual, but he
was a rationalist; hence neither myth nor magic could reasonably
be expected in his pages.

At no time was there any acute awareness that I can recall
on the part of Goodenough of Gnosticism. In *By Light, Light*,
there is a single entry in the index on Gnosticism, this to his page
119; there Goodenough says: Philo "could . . . have had no
sympathy with that travesty of philosophy, the type of mythological presentation to which we give the collective name of Gnosticism." There is another entry, "gnosis (sic!), in Liturgy," with
inconsequential references to seven diverse pages (308, 313, 317,
326, 330, 351, and 355; he should have added 356), all to the
one chapter, "The Mystic Liturgy," and to citations from the publication by Bousset, "Eine jüdische Gebetssamlung in siebenten
Buch der apostolic Konstitutionen," *Nachrichten von der König-
liche Gesellschraft der Wissenschaft zu Göttingen, 1915* (1916),
pp. 435-485. In any event, even these comments on Jewish
prayers did not impel Goodenough in this book to any discussion
of any consequence of Philo and Gnosticism. In the imposing, "A
General Bibliography of Philo," which Goodenough compiled
with Howard L. Goodhart (in *The Politics of Philo Judaeus,* New
Haven 1938, pp. 125-348), there are thirty-eight entries under
"XVIII. Mystery, Mysticism, Salvation, Faith, and Religious
Experience"; in "XXIV: Philo's Relation to Gnosticism," the
entries are nine, only one of which seems directly to relate to the
heading; indeed, many of the entries in XXIV seem to me as

readily suitable for XVIII. That is to say, Goodenough had published almost nothing relative to Gnosticism; in my close relations
with him—how I cherish these!—I recall not a single oral
mention even of the word.

I now explain this omission in the following way: Goodenough, despite his intention to write a new history of early Christianity, had neither the time nor at that juncture any deep interest in New Testament scholarship. For example, in my recollection, he was quite unaware of Rudolf Bultmann in general and
of Bultmann's theory that the logos hymn at the beginning of
the Gospel According to John was a pre-Christian gnostic composition borrowed and adapted by the evangelist. I think, too,
that Goodenough, for all the unique breadth of his remarkable
scholarship in other areas, continued to view Gnosticism primarily as the Christian heresy of the second century.

Goodenough did not raise for me, nor did I for myself at that
time, the pregnant question of the possible relationship between
gnosis in the broader sense and the hellenistic mysteries. I am
not sure that enough information on either the mysteries or gnosis
is available to do more than indicate a possible thread of relationship. I know of no literature directly on the subject. There
are some stray hints in Paul Schmitt, "Ancient Mysteries in the
Society of Their Time, and Their Transformation," in *Eranos
Yearbook* (Bollingen Series XXX.2), pp. 93-118, especially
note 4, page 95: "I am convinced that Hellenistic Gnosis was
pre-formed in the Hellenic mysteries. . . ." Bultmann, in his
article, "Gnosis," speaks passingly of the Mystery Religions
"which impart the secret learning for salvation" as "one of the
sources of Gnosticism" (p. 7). Perhaps a tentative formulation
might be this, that the mysteries were organized cults, *thiasoi*,
whereas gnosis was, instead, a mode of thinking or feeling, which
both overlapped with the mysteries and transcended the mere
thiasoi. Here is one of many related areas which calls for investigation.

*   *   *

We might, now, review some of the associations of Philo and Gnosticism. The older literature on Philo, from such eminent scholars as Carl Siegfried and James Drummond, seldom used the term Gnosticism; for example, the total attention paid by Siegfried in *Philo von Alexandria als Ausleger des Alten Testaments*, 1875, is very brief. He provides an *Abhang*, pp. 341-342 called "Philo und die Gnostiker," to his discussion of the early Christian apologists. He begins: "Philo's influence on the Gnostics is unmistakable, and is so generally admitted." Like a great many succeeding commentators on Philo, Siegfried cites a number of Philonic passages, echoed in later ancient writers, which seem Gnostic. Like others, Siegfried provides no direct inquiry into Philo and Gnosticism, this for the reason that at that stage in scholarship, the question had not arisen.

Ludwig Blau, in his fine survey, "Gnosticism," in *Jewish Encyclopedia* (p. 683, column 3), cites a single passage from "The Allegory of the Laws," #52, commenting, "It is evident that this is the language of gnosis" (p. 683, column B).

Bultmann in his "Gnosis" devotes his section V, 2 to Philo; it runs about two pages. It is oriented to Philo's epistomology: "Philo's idea of knowledge and use of *gignoskein* are thoroughly Hellenistic, i.e., either rationalist or Gnostic." Presently he comments further: "There is a knowledge of God . . . an immediate vision of God, described by Philo as an ecstasy. . . . This is the Gnostic view." Bultmann's last point is that at places "Philo mixes up Greek philosophy, Gnosticism, and the Old Testament." That is, Bultmann provides in his context a small quantity of excerpts from Philo, but does not provide an encompassing assessment.

C. H. Dodd (in *The Bible and the Greeks*, London, 1935, p. 246) regarded Philo as "a teacher on the Jewish side of the dividing line, who is glad to use all the resources of pagan philosophy to elucidate the mysteries of his own Scriptures"; and (in *The Interpretation of the Fourth Gospel*, London, 1953) commented that "there is a sense in which . . . Hellenistic Jews like Philo . . . could be called gnostics." R. M. Wilson, *The Gnostic Problem*, p. 161, speaking of Gnosis as "an atmosphere, not a system," and using Gnosticism in the newer, broader way, states that "Philo could in a sense be called a Gnostic, much as Paul or Clement of Alexandria, but in the narrower sense . . . he is not a Gnostic." J. Doresse (in "Gnosticism," pp. 544-579, in C. J. Bleeker and G. Widengren, *Historia Religionum: Handbook for the History of Religions*, Vol. I: *Religions of the Past*, writes (p. 544), "We can however state . . . that the essential part of the Greek philosophic vocabulary of which the [Gnostic] sects were to make full use of their treatises appears with Philo . . ." Similarly, it is not difficult to find in many a modern scholar an allusion to a Philonic passage which is described as having some gnostic overtone or substance. This is the case with Marcel Simon's excellent "Eléments gnostique chez Philon," in *Le Origini*, pp. 360-374. Simon asks, shall we call Philo a "*gnosticisant*," or a "*pré-gnostique*"? Or "free him of any connection?" The answers, he says, depend on definitions and basic views of the origins of gnosis and Gnosticism.

But is there something more than such bits or rather random matters, something quite fundamental? Such is my conviction. From my continued study of Philo there has crystallized a viewpoint adumbrated here and there in the scholars, but not to my knowledge fully developed. The viewpoint is already present in the present study, as Arnaldez (I, pp. 110-111) noted in his work cited above. This viewpoint now seems to me to be related to Gnosticism, or gnosis, rather than to the mysteries. It derives from my interpretation of Philo's basic approach to Scripture; by basic approach I mean something quite apart from the mechanics of his biblical allegory. In presenting this interpretation now, I do so deliberately briefly; it now anticipates material found in subsequent pages and there documented.

For Philo, the Bible is not so much the history of the human race or of the Hebrews as it is the potential or actual religious experience of every man. Each of us is in part Adam, or Enoch, or Noah, or Abraham; or, to say the same thing in another way, in us too there are to be found Adam, Enoch, Noah, or Abraham. Just as the scriptural account moves on from the opening pages of Genesis to the high point of Moses, so we too can move on from the most lowly state of human living to the highest, from living in the delusive world of appearances into living in the world of immaterial reality. We can move away from bondage to our body and into freedom from it. Scripture teaches us about every phrase of this movement, of which we can partake; hence we can understand every phase intellectually, philosophically. Beyond such understanding, Scripture enables us to take the actual steps which this movement requires. Scripture has a purpose beyond merely informing us, and that purpose is to guide our steps and to encourage us and exhort us to move on.

History, the past, and existential guidance, the present, are one and the same, and they spur us on. The Adam of Genesis I was the idea of man, and hence this ideal man never appeared on earth; it was the Adam of Genesis II, fashioned out of material dust and immaterial spirit, who was the ancestor of the race. Fashioned as he was of antithetical materials, he lived as all men live, under the tension in which the material aspect of him tugged in one direction, the immaterial aspect in the opposite. Allegorically, though, Adam is a mind, any mind, including yours and mine. The mind functions through the senses; Eve allegorically is sense perception, without which our minds do not function. The serpent is pleasure; when the mind or the senses become bent on pleasure, the result is the loss of virtue. Generic, ideal virtue is the Garden of Eden, whose four rivers are the particular four virtues, justice, manliness, bravery, and temperance, of which the Stoics speak. The human race lost virtue, and hence man could be in great despair. Happily there is a road for him, and for us, to travel, for man differs from the animal through possessing hope, symbolized by Enos. Hope leads to the stage of repentance, Enoch, the symbol of the wiping out of a man's past. In turn, repentance leads to tranquility, symbolized by Noah; tranquility is only a relative righteousness, not the ultimate righteousness.

That individual who has progressed as far as Noah can conceivably go even further, depending on his personal gifts. The continued progression is attainable through teaching, intuition, and practice, symbolized respectively by Abraham, Isaac, and Jacob. The historical ancient patriarchs each achieved his righte-

ousness through these gifts; the characterizing quality of each
partiarch was the particular one of the three qualities which
predominated in him. Existentially each of us can achieve in his
own life what the historical patriarchs achieved in theirs, provided we have the gifts and capacities of learning, intuition, and
practice comparable to those which they possessed and symbolize. Thus, there both was a historical Abraham, and there is also
an existential Abraham-capacity in us. As Abraham migrated
from Ur, astrology, so we too can migrate from improper and
untenable belief. As he, at Harran, turned from meterology to
introspection, so can we.

Like Abraham, we all traverse a Canaan, the vice of adolescence; we traverse the period of wavering between choosing material things or spiritual things, as symbolized by Lot. Like Abraham we all face the dilemma of whether our five senses and four
passions (symbolized by the nine kings of Genesis XIV) will
rule our progressing mind, or whether our mind will rule them,
regimenting them to their appropriate functions. Our training
involves education, the encyclical studies symbolized by Hagar,
which are preliminary to virtue, Sarah, and indeed, require the
strictest discipline, as symbolized by Sarah's punishing discipline
of Hagar. If we move through these proper preliminaries, and
prepare our inward being in the way that Abraham organized
and prepared his household, in Genesis XVIII, then we can be
vouchsafed the best possible vision of the divine (the three
visitors). Lesser minds apprehend of this vision at most either
the creative power of God, symbolized by *theos,* or else the ruling power, symbolized by *kyrios,* or even both of them; better
minds proceed to the third of the three, the *logos.* To the best
minds (such as that of the historical Abraham), the three are in
reality a vision of a one, a one which goes beyond all other
unitary conceptions.

Comparably, one may achieve righteousness in sharing, existentially, in the experience of Isaac and Jacob—provided one
has gifts comparable to the endowments of the patriarchs. The
possessor of such gifts coincidentally possesses *orthos logos,*
"right thinking," and can, on his own, in terms of these high gifts,

achieve the ultimate. But suppose his gifts are less, is he debarred from the ultimate righteousness?

Not at all. Provision has been made for the less gifted. This provision is the body of particular laws ordained through Moses (beginning in Exodus XX). These laws are no more than a recording of what the patriarchs did. He who conforms with the Mosaic laws is thereby coincidentally living like the patriarchs. If his gifts of mind are so poor that he has no perception beyond the literal requirements, then he lives like the patriarchs but without awareness that he is doing so; this is the level of the "mystery of Aaron." The laws, however, are susceptible of allegory, and they too are symbols of the progression of the soul to perfection. He who lives by the allegory òf the laws is to be on the level of the "mystery of Moses." In the "mystery of Moses," circumcision, for example, symbolically prunes passion from the body; Passover symbolizes the passing of the soul out of domination by the body. Moses himself is the allegory of the divine logos, while Aaron bears to Moses the relationship which uttered speech, necessarily impure, bears to true reason, which is pure.

* * *

The very many things which Philo says in his leisurely, often prolix, manner, are reflections of Pythogoreanism, Platonism, and Stoicism, as the scholars have amply noted. What must not escape attention on the part of those whose primary interest in Philo rotates about these philosophical matters is that they are only secondary in Philo, illustrative or expository material to buttress his principal purpose. That purpose was to exhort his readers to live the holy life, actually to travel on the "royal road" to perfection. The philosophy enters in as a justification, as it were, of the reliability of Philo's exhortations. Indeed, were his treatises briefer, and prepared for the ear rather than the eye, it would not be amiss to term Philo a preacher—a preacher who made constant reference to philosophy—but a preacher he remains.

Philo's treatises are a guide to the way of God. He already knows the way; he sets the task for himself to guide others. He is an "illumined" man.

*   *   *

Now is all this gnosis or Gnosticism, or what is it? Which of Jonas' prerequisites for Gnosticism are present, and which are missing? I see no trace of a fallen god; I see, however, fallen man, in Eden. I see no benighted creator; I see, however, the logos as the creator. As to a sinister creation, I see in Philo the view that this world of appearance is rather sinister, and that the sage is indeed an alien soul in this world. I do not see cosmic captivity or acosmic salvation; I do see salvation of the soul from the prison of the body. I do not wonder at the absence of a fallen god, for Philo was a staunch Jew; in light of Genesis I, and the repeated refrain of "God saw and it was good," Philo could scarcely admit of a benighted creator. Philo was a dualist, antagonistic to the body with its senses and passions; how extreme a dualist is he? Compared with Christian gnostics, his dualism was not extreme; compared with the rabbis in the normative tradition, it was extreme.

If for the moment we venture to use the word Gnostic for Philo, then we must quickly supply the necessary qualifications. Philo contains no myths (indeed, except for *Legatio* and *In Flaccum,* he is devoid of all narrative); he reflects no magic such as is known to have characterized other marginal Jews of his age; he believes in prophecy, but in so exalted a form that apocalyptic, so frequent in his age, is totally missing from his writings. He is a God-intoxicated rationalist, and an austere, and sometimes modest, sometimes arrogant, illumined man. What shall we call Philo? A philosopher? A philosophic mystic, as I do in the succeeding pages? An ecstatic, as Michel Nicolas ("Etudes sur Philon D'Alexandre," *Revue de l'Histoire des Religions* V (1882), pp. 318-339, VII (1883), pp. 145-164, VIII (1884), pp. 468-601; 757-771 repeatedly does? Professor Harl speaks of Philo as reflecting an "interiorization of the Jewish religion . . . He is the first representative of a new type of religious man" (*op. cit.*, p. 153). Might one go on to speak of him as an early Gnostic, either as a Jewish Gnostic, or else a Gnostic Jew?

What gain would there be in affixing the label of Gnostic onto Philo? In essence, none, for the content of Philo is not altered thereby. But in implication there is much.

An understanding of the two surviving forms of first-century Judaism, namely, Rabbinic Judaism and Christianity, in their own context, is possible only when the fullest attainable perspective on the total religious situation of that era is utilized. Both in Jewish and in Christian studies there have prevailed certain theories which can be termed isolationist, when each of these manifestations is presented as if it was free from all context, rivalry, and challenge. Traditionalist scholars in particular seem to incline towards interpretations which suppose that because something of consequence emerged in the second century, this was a providentially guided straight-line development out of the past, free from any "taint." Thus, rabbinic Judaism was the natural outgrowth of Pharisaism, which alone was a dominant trend, and the subordinate trends were peripheral to the point of justifying either a neglect of them, or of their being forced into the simple mold of variants of Pharisaism. According to such a frequent view, Philo was little different from the rabbis; he only put their doctrines into a Grecian dress, but clothes are, after all, of no significance.

In the case of studies in Christianity, the same sort of thing prevails, not only because it is to traditionalists a gratifying pattern, but also because of the influence of Acts of the Apostles. Paul is repeatedly interpreted by Christian traditionalists in almost exactly the same way that Philo is by Jewish traditionalists. The age-old debates in Christian New Testament scholarship about the Paul of Acts and the Paul of the Epistles turn out to be reflections of isolationists and their interpretive opponents. Isolationists take Paul to be a typical Pharisee, to the point of seeing in him no significant echo, or echo at all, of the hellenistic world. To the contrary, quite a different case can be made, and has. According to this other view, gnosis appears in Paul's

Epistles not only in viewpoints that are his own, but also in other gnostic viewpoints which he alludes to that he feels he must combat. Without an assumption that Paul's letters deeply and broadly reflect gnosis, in Paul and in his background, the Epistles make relatively little sense as authentic documents. On the other hand, an effort to understand Pauline Christianity against a background of gnosis illuminates many a passage which would otherwise be obscure. Such I would regard as the significant contribution of Walter Schmithal's scholarship, as in *Die Gnosis in Korinth* (Göttingen, 1956) and other important studies. If Gnosticism arose only in the second century, then we can scarcely understand I and II Corinthians or even facets of Galatians. (See, for example, Robert Jewett, "The Agitators and the Galatian Congregation," in *New Testament Studies,* XVII (1970), pp. 198-212.)

Perhaps those who charge Schmithal with overstatement in this or that detail are right. But in my judgment he is nearer to the realities of Paul's age than are those who have been unaware of the complexities and cross-currents and synretisms of the age of Philo and early Christianity. I much prefer Schmithal's view to the abiding reliance on Harnack's dictum that Gnosticism was the *result* of the hellenization of the Gospel. It seems to me more apt to suppose that gnosis *caused* the profound hellenization of Christianity.

*   *   *

Is there some danger that Gnosticism may become the fad, the passing fad, of current scholarship? There is a tendency among academicians to create these fads. Some years always need to pass before the permanent values rise out of, and over, the exaggerations and the extremes. But that an unchallengeable residue will abide seems likely to me.

*   *   *

A particular phase of the study of Christianity which good friends have spoken to me of excites my interest, but not yet my agreement. As is well known, there is almost nothing of the substance of the Gospels to be found in the Epistles of Paul. In my *The Genius of Paul* (reprint), New York, 1970, pp. 107-109, I set forth the opinion that Paul knew more Gospel materials than he reproduces, but was disinterested. Consistent with my total view of Paul and Paulinism, I also expressed the judgment that Paul, a hellenistic Jew, represented a deviation from the unfolding early Christendom, with the Gospel materials, absent from his letters, being the norm. One friend, Professor Lindsey Pherigo, if I understand him, is testing a thesis that Paul and quasi-Gnostic Paulinism represent "normative" Christianity, while the Gospel traditions represent the later deviation. I await his future publication of the results of his inquiry. Another friend, Howard Teeple, has published his contention that there never was an early legacy of an oral tradition from Jesus and his immediate followers ("The Oral Tradition That Never Existed," *Journal of Biblical Literature,* (LXXXIX, 1970, pp. 56-68)). Teeple, while he speaks passingly of "semi-gnostic thought in John," makes no comment on Paul and Paulinism; he contends that "the spirit, not historical tradition," instructed the apostles in their preaching. Perhaps one might again cite Bultmann, *Gnosis* (p. 42):

> "Paul admits (I Cor. ii, 6 ff.) that the Christian also possesses a form of wisdom, which enables him to know the divine plan of salvation that is hidden from the 'rulers' of this age, a knowledge penetrating into the deep things of God because it depends on his gift of the Spirit; and he admits that the spiritual man is superior to the psychic, and is judged of no man. But such knowledge has for its content nothing but God's saving act (I Cor. ii, 12); it is no vague speculation. It is a reality only in one whose way of life is in accordance with the Spirit (iii, 1 ff.).

Perhaps some combination of the views of Pherigo and Teeple may be examined together, for whatever future light may be revealed.

*   *   *

I express my gratitude to my student, Reverend D. Peter Burrows, for the largest part of the work in preparing the new index. To my secretary, Mrs. Sam November, I grow into increasing debt.

Preface

MY doctoral dissertation at Yale University was called *Abraham in Normative and Hellenistic Jewish Tradition.* This present work, initially published in two installments of the *Hebrew Union College Annual,* Vols. XXV and XXVI, is based on that effort. The arrangement has been altered, especially so as to sharpen the focus on Philo, and I have omitted a section which dealt with the New Testament. In the earlier work I gave a characteristic sampling of Philo's material on Abraham; here I have striven for completeness. Since indices to Philo do not assure completeness, I have utilized Ryle, *Philo and Holy Scripture* as a quasi-index. Even so, I am not certain that these aids and elaborate re-reading, especially of the Exposition, have assembled all the Philonic passages; I should welcome having brought to my notice any significant passages which I may have missed.

The annotations are so numerous that the possibility of inadvertent error is omnipresent. Mr. Martin Cohen, a student at the Hebrew Union College - Jewish Institute of Religion, has double checked the references; he has also helped on the index. His services were provided through the College Placement Bureau. Mr. Cohen went far beyond the routine requirements, and I am deeply grateful to him.

President Nelson Glueck has made resources of stenographic help available to me. Without his warm interest and support, the sheer mechanics involved might have deferred publication for some time.

I record with pleasure and gratitude my academic and personal debt to Professor Erwin R. Goodenough, for his guidance and his many acts of kindness.

Philo's Place in Judaism:

A Study of Conceptions of Abraham in Jewish Literature

CHAPTER ONE

The Problem

I

LOUIS GINZBERG says in the introduction to the Notes of his *Legends of the Jews* (Vol. V, viii–ix): "There are few Jewish authors about whom so much has been written as about Philo. And yet the most important problem connected with Philo is not yet solved. Was he a Jewish thinker with a Greek education, or a Greek philosopher with Jewish learning? I hope that the very numerous references in the Notes to the frequent similarity of the views held by the Rabbis and by Philo will contribute something towards the solution of this problem."

In the twenty-five years that have elapsed since these words were printed, there has been considerably more written about Philo, and there have been more efforts made to solve the problem. The differences of opinion still exist, however, so that the conclusion is inevitable that the proposed solutions have failed to satisfy all the workers in the field.

The present study attempts to clarify some of the issues at stake; if it may be no more persuasive in the solution which it proposes than previous efforts, it may at least reduce the area of controversy. Some of the scholarly disagreement seems to me to partake of the semantic. Some of it seems to me to stem from substitutions of the whole for a part. A review of the efforts made to delineate Philo's relations to the rabbis, such as over-lappings in haggada and halaka, considerations of chronology of the witnessing literature, and some observations on procedures utilized in the past precede the main body of my essay. It can

1

well be that seeing the problem in its true light, with a consideration both of certainties and also of imponderables, may of itself
suggest the direction towards solution.

These are the external facts about Philo. His dates are roughly
20 B. C.–40 A. D. He has bequeathed to us enough of his writings
to fill eleven volumes in the Loeb Classics; these writings are
in Greek, though a few of them are today preserved only in
translation. A native and resident of Alexandria in Egypt, he
was a prominent leader in the Jewish community.

Philo was a later contemporary of Hillel and Shammai, and
of Jesus and Paul. The Temple in Jerusalem was a flourishing
institution in his time; we know that Philo visited it at least once.

It is well known and universally agreed that by and large
Philo's writings represent, at least coincidentally, a reconciliation
of Jewish revelation and Greek philosophy. The nature of Philo's
treatises is such, however, that one could make out the case
either that he is a philosopher, or else that the philosophy,
conceded on all hands to be present, is only incidental.

The assessments of his philosophy as to its quality have
been varied. Wolfson[1] declares that Philo is an original philosopher, and the true father of religious philosophy as it prevailed
from his own day down to the time of Spinoza. At another
extreme, Reitzenstein[2] dismisses Philo's philosophical writings
with the scornful comment that to term Philo an eclectic is
unduly to praise him. Schuerer[3] speaks of Philo as primarily a
psychologist and moralist. A good many workers in the history
of religion consider the work of Philo as of no value in itself,
but as a rich mine of the varied religious and philosophical
opinions prevalent in the first Christian century. Indeed, for
some researchers Philo's sole value is the light he is supposed
to shed on other and weightier literatures, such as the New
Testament or Patrology.

[1] *Philo*, I, especially p. 114.

[2] *Studien zum antiken Synkretismus, aus Iran und Griechenland*, 30. Other
such negative judgments are cited in Völker, *Fortschritt und Vollendung bei
Philo von Alexandrien*, 44, note 2.

[3] *The History of the Jewish People in the Time of Jesus Christ*, Eng. Translation, Second Division, III, 330.

A considerable literature exists on the question, what was Philo's relationship to rabbinic Judaism? A complex of difficult problems precludes an easy answer, though some such have been offered. These we shall note below. To anticipate an item, it is an almost insuperable task of delicacy to recover from the Pharisaic literature exactly what the state of Pharisaism was in Philo's time, when the Temple was still functioning and when the fervent rivals of Pharisaism had as yet not virtually disappeared. The attestation of Paul in Philippians 3.5, that he was a "Pharisee" suggests that possibly diaspora Pharisaism was not completely identical with the Palestinian variety;[4] if this is so, the presence of varieties within Pharisaism makes it even more difficult to describe the relationship between Philo and his Jewish contemporaries.

Moreover, there are overlappings in the Philonic and rabbinic traditions; related or identical items of haggada appear in both. For example, that Noah was righteous in his own generation means that only by a relatively low standard was Noah righteous. Such items are, on the one hand, sufficiently numerous that by substituting a whole for the part, the commentator can infer from the random congruent facets a total congruency. But such a conclusion would rest on selective evidence, for it would perforce omit an abundance of points at which extreme disparity prevails. On the other hand, the commentator who would deny totally any relationship between Philo and the rabbis necessarily disregards the manifest identities and the need of assessing them. The circumstance of the mixture of both congruency and disparity leads naturally to diverse weighings among the scholars of either the one or of the other.

The admittedly different form of the Philonic writings and the rabbinic pericopes provides its own unique complication. The rabbis are neither philosophical in manner nor are their "writings" rhetorical; the disparities between them and Philo might conceivably be due to what ensues when non-philosophical

---

[4] Cf. Goguel, *La Naissance du Christianisme*, 232, note 6. For more thorough-going scepticism on the passage see "Saul", *JE*, XI, 79, by Kohler. The genuineness of the passage has been questioned by a minority, though a respectable one, of Protestant scholars; cf. *Dictionary of the Bible*, III, 844.

statements, of a laconic, epigrammatic character, are metamorphosed into philosophy, embodied in Stoic "diatribes." Accordingly, the disparities between Philo and the rabbis could
conceivably be not a matter of content but only that of form.
We shall see that this contention is made with some frequency
and insistence.

The ubiquitous semantic problem, as it applies to Philonic
research, is partly as follows. The commentators who agree in
noticing specific disparities between Philo and the rabbis can
express their observations in correct but misleading fashion. One
could say: though Philo deviates from the rabbis, he is not much
different from them, or: though Philo agrees with the rabbis, he
is notably different from them. The word "different," through
its vagueness, fits nicely into either of these sentences. Judgments such as these in the scholarly literature are not deliberately
evasive, nor are they untrue to the Philonic material. The
difficulty is the form in which they are couched; and it is the
obligation of the researcher in describing the phenomena in
Philo's writings to select as precise and unmistakable language
as he can.

What is there measurable in a judgment that Philo writing
in Greek, in the Alexandrian scholastic tradition, reflects a
"maximum hellenization of Judaism"? Or, that the hellenization
in Philo is simply that of the use of language and phrases of that
language, and indicates no profound hellenization at all?

Or, Wolfson's phrase[5] that Philo represents a "collateral
branch of Pharisaic Judaism." If it is "collateral" on which we
focus, then we should infer that Philo's Judaism was in significant
measure different from the Pharisaism of the *direct* ancestry,
yet if we focus instead on "Pharisaism" in the phrase, then we
can readily overlook the significant qualifying words, "collateral
branch."

That is to say, the form of the description of the observed
phenomena can imply either much more or much less than the
commentator intends. Or a reader can infer something at variance
with that which the scholar has meant to imply. In the problem of

[5] *Philo*, I, 56.

Philo and the rabbis, all too often the area of disagreements among scholars could be reduced by a consideration on the part of the reader of what a particular colleague's intent is.

Not that thereby all disagreement would fade (and thereby the fun of scholarly research lost). Divergency of interpretation can exist even after the clearest communication exists among scholars.

To my mind, it is appropriate to alter the question from either "Is Philo hellenized?" or "How much is Philo hellenized?" to this, "Granting some hellenization, how *measurably* much is Philo hellenized?" One needs always to recall that the little or greatly hellenized Philo is in his own light a loyal Jew, and that the philosophy, or anything else which he used in his writings, seemed to him either congruent with his Judaism or even derived from it. This latter is true, even when we modern pedants can demonstrate that his true source is a non-Jewish one.

Finally, in comparing Philo and the rabbis, it is often overlooked that Philo is but a single man, of a rather restricted time and place; the rabbis are many, and of both wider time and diverse places. For the comparison to be the most reliable, it would need to assess the imponderable measure of heterogeneity within the milieu of the rabbis. It scarcely needs demonstration, in the light of different currents within rabbinic thought, that an assumption of total, all-embracing homogeneity among the rabbis is gratuitous. One needs recourse to generalizations, in which one depicts the overwhelming central and typical rabbinic sentiments, to arrive at a body of material with which Philo may then be cautiously compared.

II

The rabbinic literature, as is well known, is later in redaction than the time of Philo, but some material, both haggada and halaka, contained in the later collections, is undoubtedly earlier than Philo. This is known to us through the incidence of such material in the Apocrypha and Pseudepigrapha, especially in

the Book of Jubilees; and Josephus, who is slightly later than
Philo but earlier than the rabbinic collections, is a further witness
to the fact that some rabbinic material is considerably older
than the date of the compilation of the rabbinic collections which
have also preserved the material. That the rabbinic compilations
are later than Philo is no obstacle to the possibility that Philo
could be utilizing early rabbinic material. The question is not,
could Philo have used early rabbinic material, but rather, did
Philo actually do so.

The context of the problem in relationships is highlighted
in our day in two lines of antithetic interpretation. To digress
to them may clarify the issue. Wolfson is the most recent representative of a distinguished line of interpreters whose position
can be summarized in Wolfson's words, that we encounter in
Philo, "a Hellenization in language only, not in religious belief
or cult."[6] Philo is a fairly good representative of "native Palestinian Judaism."

On the other hand, Goodenough[7] is the most recent representative of an equally distinguished succession of interpreters
who see evidence in Philo of hellenization that is more than
surface. Indeed, Goodenough goes so far as to say, primarily
on the basis of Philo, that "Judaism in the Greek Diaspora did,
for at least an important minority, become a mystery . . . . .
Since a Jew could not simply become an initiate of Isis or
Orpheus and remain a Jew as well, the amazingly clever trick
was devised, we do not know when or by whom, of identifying
the personalities of the Bible with those of Greek mystery religions, and accordingly 'Judaism was transformed into the
greatest, the only true Mystery.' "

In part the issue between Wolfson and Goodenough (as symbols of the conflicting approaches) rests on the import of certain
words, phrases, and conceptions in Philo. These are admittedly
terms of the mystery religions; and Wolfson and Goodenough
unite in seeing Philo a denouncer of Greek mysteries. But Good-

---

[6] *Philo*, I, 13. Cf. Wikgren, Colwell, and Marcus, *Hellenistic Greek Texts*,
xxi and 81.

[7] *By Light, Light*, and numerous scattered essays.

enough asserts that the terms have an authentic mystery connotation for Philo's one true Mystery, while Wolfson dismisses
them as no more than the slang or vocabulary of the day.

A somewhat similar issue has existed in scholarly circles
respecting the Septuagint. How hellenized is the Greek Bible?
Ralph Marcus[8] has written some words of acute observation
which have a decided relevance for our problem respecting
Philo. "Every translation is a compromise between two civiliza-
tions. Neither spoken nor written word is a series of one-to-one
correspondences between word and idea. The various words of
a language have a delicate contextual relation to other words,
and this relation cannot be exactly reproduced in another language. This inadequacy of contextual reproduction is especially
marked in the confrontation of two such distinct and histori-
cally unrelated languages as Hebrew and Greek. Beyond or
beneath the linguistic incongruities there are all kinds of cultural
incongruities . . ." Marcus notes that there are definite hellenizations in the Septuagint, but these, properly, he calls "surface."
They include providing Greek case endings for Hebrew proper
nouns, and accomodations in the rendering of technical terms.
Still another surface form is the employment of Greek metrical
forms, as in the LXX Proverbs. Also, certain mythological terms
appear in the LXX, such as allusions to Titans; but Marcus
adopts Redpath's explanation that the name Titan would occur
as a natural word of translation.

But the allegation of hellenization deeper than surface was
made many generations ago. Gförer, in 1831, and Dähne, in
1835, advanced such views; the most adequate refutation, says
Marcus, is Freudenthal's, whose "examination of the various
passages where such psychological, ethical, and metaphysical
terms are used . . . makes it certain that they have no philosophical connotation in the LXX."

The problem of Hellenization, then, is anterior, to Philo.
But it is an acute problem in Philo (and in Paul too) for the
definitely philosophical cast of the Philonic writings provides

---

[8] "Jewish and Greek Elements in the Septuagint," *Louis Ginzberg Jubilee
Volume*, 227–245.

an array of hellenizations which though possibly still only surface, yet go beyond the merely grammatical or lexical details mentioned above. The fact that Philo is in some sense a philosopher means that he owes some debt to the Greeks.[9]

Marcus[10] points to another important fact, "A sober analysis of the literary and archeological materials . . . will reveal the inadequacy of the contrast between Greek intellectualism and Jewish morality. The Greek philosophers were interested in morality . . . The Jewish teachers of the Hellenistic and Roman periods . . . consistently tried to prove a rational basis for their doctrines of revealed morality . . . certainly Greek polytheism is categorically opposed to Jewish monotheism. But this opposition would be greatly lessened if one compared Greek religious philosophy rather than popular Greek religion with Judaism."

When in Philo we encounter some rationalization of a moral teaching, it can with equal likelihood be *a priori* Greek in origin or Jewish in origin. The fact is that Philo frequently cites his Greek source. But more often he does not. It is not impossible, then, when the source is not specifically indicated as Greek, and when it coincides with a doctrine found in rabbinic literature, that it may stem from a Jewish source.

To revert to the main line of argument, that Philo writes in Greek, and not in Hebrew or Aramaic and that his writings are philosophic in form are not inescapable obstacles to Philonic dependence on, and thorough-going agreement with, Palestinian Judaism. It is possible to suppose that Philo transfers a Hebrew or Aramaic sentiment into a Grecian philosophical form. It is possible, *a priori*, that this and no more is what Philo has done. Since dependency could have existed, the question is this, did it exist?

---

[9] An excellent review of Philonic scholarship from the end of the eighteenth century through the middle 1930's is to be found in Völker, *op. cit.*, 15–47. Völker is properly critical of the methods used by some researchers, especially those who have tried to fit Philo into some strait-jacket of exclusive classification, such as Stoic, Platonist, and the like. Völker has good things to say on the Jewish and Greek sides of Philo. He seems to me ultimately to fall into the same kind of pit which he has dug for others. His review of the literature is the best which I have seen.

[10] *Op. cit.*, 231–232.

Abstractly, there are three possible patterns into which an oversimplified statement of the possible relations between Philo and the rabbis can fall.

Pattern A would depict Palestinian Jewry, especially rabbinic Judaism, as the acknowledged leader and authority in religious matters for Alexandria, as early as 20 B. C.–40 A. D. Whatever local or regional developments, peculiar to Alexandria, are discernible, are small and insignificant. Frequent communication took place; and rabbinic sentiments and even utterances passed from Palestine to Egypt; Philo received these, and turned them into philosophical form. Whatever hellenization is present is only surface.

This pattern implies that the language difference between Palestine and Egypt was little or no barrier. The rabbinic exegesis, indeed even subtleties founded on the Hebrew text, were readily absorbed in the Greek-speaking community; moreover, Hebrew in this pattern must have been known among the Greek Jews, and in good measure. While those who bring Palestinian views to Egypt occasionally bring back Alexandrian views to Palestine, it is a rather unequal exchange, since Palestine is the place of the primary intellectual activity, while Alexandria is almost thoroughly dependent on Palestine. By and large Klausner,[11] Belkin,[12] and Marmorstein,[13] as we shall see specifically, seem to fit either completely or almost so into Pattern A.

[11] *Pilosofim v'Hoge De'ot* I, especially 68. Klausner repeats his observations in a number of other books, *Historia Yisre'elit*, IV, 50–67, and *Mi-Yeshu 'ad Paulos*, 166–193; in the latter Klausner alludes on p. 116 to his more complete essay in the former. One notes the relative smallness of the grist and the surprising plurality of the mills.

[12] *Philo and the Oral Law*, 25. Note Belkin's fine survey there of the work of Ritter, *Philo und die Halacha* and of I. Heinemann, *Philons griechische und jüdische Bildung*. That Belkin has demonstrated more abundant parallels and overlappings between Philonic and rabbinic halaka is to be conceded; that he has searchingly considered the implications of the work he has done is much less evident.

[13] One hesitates to apply the damning epithet of dilettante to a scholar, but such a judgment does not seem too harsh respecting the facets of his work on Philo in two articles: *The Old Rabbinic Doctrine of God*, I, 45 ff. and a reply, in *JQR* (NS) XXII (1932), 295 ff., to a criticism of the latter.

Pattern B, on the other hand, would suppose that communication is at a minimum and that independence rather than dependency is the key-note of the relationship. Whatever Hebrew was known in Alexandria was by Philo's time a bare and therefore useless minimum. Alexandrian Jewry was not a cultural suburb of Palestine, but self-contained and almost self-sufficient. Identity in or similarity of doctrines is explainable as either through co-incidence or the result of limited communication. *Mutatis mutandis*, Goodenough,[14] Lewy,[15] and Stein[16] would represent pattern B. A large dependency of Palestine on Alexandria is argued for by Weinstein, *Zur Genesis der Agada*; the position of Daube[17] would tend to support Weinstein.

Pattern C would differ from the other two in that it would subordinate neither Palestinian Judaism to Alexandrian, nor Alexandrian Judaism to the Palestinian, but would affirm that each developed along its own lines of creativity but without the complete loss of communication. In this pattern, there is room in a common broad base for the idiosyncrasies of each Judaism to develop, and for each to exercise some limited influence over the other. It might be said that Albeck[18] and Wilfred Knox[19] represent this pattern C.

These three positions are only theoretical and over-simplified, and objections could be raised at classifying some of the scholars as I have done; rigidly to insist on this classification is foreign to my purpose. But it needs to be noted that in scholarly circles one finds usually the occupation, or an endorsement, of some extreme position, and all too seldom an intermediate or moderate one. It does not follow that a position is wrong because it

---

[14] *By Light, Light.*

[15] *Philo Selections*, 20–21 and 108.

[16] *Die allegorische Exegese des Philo aus Alexandrien*, 1929, 20–26, and *Philo und der Midrasch*, 1931.

[17] "Rabbinic Methods of Interpretation and Hellenistic Rhetoric," *HUCA*, XXII, 239–264.

[18] See his *Mabo* to Theodor, *Genesis Rabba*, 84–85. Albeck points out that coincidence between Philo and the rabbis does not necessarily imply dependency, and even if it should, the problem of who depended on whom is beyond solution; similarly Bernfeld, *Da'at Elohim*, I, 51–52.

[19] Cf. *St. Paul and the Church at Jerusalem*, 1939.

is extreme. What is relevant is that much of the writing on Philo has begun with strong "Either-Or" assumptions, with the result that one-sidedness extends too pervasively throughout entire articles and books.

Assumption leads to a corollary. Thus, for example, there is a correlation between the view of Philo as an exponent of quasi-Pharisaic Judaism and the answer to the question, did Philo know Hebrew. Almost every scholar who espouses Philo as a quasi-Pharisee affirms that Philo knew Hebrew; those who see Philo as primarily a Greek deny that he knew Hebrew.

This question, however, could conceivably be approached independently of larger issues. Conceivably (though not probably) Philo could have known Hebrew and yet have been thoroughly hellenized. Contrariwise, Philo might have been unfamiliar with Hebrew but yet have had mediated to him the essential doctrines of the Pharisees.

It chances, moreover, that the question of Philo's knowledge of Hebrew is one instance of many in the scholarly world where some datum, acknowledged by both sides, is assessed in diametrically opposed ways. Specifically, Philo finds the allegorical quantities, which he uses, in the supposed etymology of the proper names of the Hebrew Bible; time after time, Philo, interpreting the name, tells us what the supposed Hebrew meaning is. These etymologies are sometimes capricious and even totally "unscientific"; but at other times they are close enough to the Hebrew to be tolerably acceptable. Those who focus on the correct Hebrew in Philo have substance for affirming his knowledge of it; and those who focus on the errors have basis for denying his knowledge. Siegfried wrote a very long essay[20] on the problem in 1872; I read a paper[21] on the subject to the Society of Biblical Literature in December, 1952.

---

[20] In *Archiv für wissenschaftliche Erforschung des alten Testaments*, II Bd., II Heft, 143–163.

[21] My conclusions then, as here, were that Philo exhibits no decisive first-hand knowledge of Hebrew.

But the etymologies may not themselves be decisive; Philo says plainly on many occasions that the etymologies are not his own, but that he has heard them. Accordingly, whatever knowledge of Hebrew the etymologes show need not have been the personal possession of Philo. Both Lewy and Goodenough have suggested that Philo had available to him a kind of *notarikon* of etymologies of names; and a fragment of such a list, from a period later than Philo, has been published by Deissmann.[22] Secondly, not all of Philo's etymologies are based on the Hebrew text. Following the Septuagint, he finds an allegorical quantity in Masek, read as a proper name, for the *ben-mesheq* of the Massoretic Text; and the etymological quantity for Enos is "hope," because LXX renders Gen. 4.26 (אז הוחל לקרא) as "he *hoped* to call" etc. Whatever knowledge of Hebrew these etymologies reveal, it does not necessarily follow that Philo himself knew the Hebrew text.

Still another argument in favor of his knowing Hebrew, used by Wolfson, is that occasionally Philo displays a knowledge of a Greek version closer to the Hebrew than our Septuagint. But Wolfson himself admits that this argument is not a decisive one, since it is quite possible that Philo's Greek Bible was not our Septuagint, but a version different in details and closer to the Hebrew.[23]

There is, then, no compelling evidence that Philo himself knew Hebrew, even though his writings reflect some knowledge

---

[22] In *Veröffentlichungen aus der Heidelberger Papyrus-Sammlung*, I, *Die Septuaginta-Papyri* etc., Heidelberg, 1905, 86–93. Both Origen and Eusebius attribute such a list to Philo. The present list has many overlappings with Philo, but enough diversity to establish authorship by some other hand. The evidence is too scanty for definitive judgment, but the inference tends to be that Philo had recourse to material such as this third or fourth century Christian list later provided.

[23] *Philo*, I, 89, based on Ryle, *Philo and Holy Scripture*, xxxix. Katz, in *Philo's Bible*, tries to account for the circumstance that the citations which precede Philo's allegorical treatises, the *lemmata*, vary from the text cited within the treatises; the *lemmata*, coming first in the essays and being readily separable, were made to conform to the usual LXX reading; within the body of the essays, the text preserved would tend to show that in Philo's time there was as yet no standard LXX.

of it. Wolfson contends that despite this absence of positive evidence, the burden of proof is on those who would deny it. Why this should be so is quite beyond me; it seems a most illogical contention. Philo gives abundant information about his Greek education, but none about his Hebrew education;[24] to my mind the burden of proof would rest on the affirmers.

At any rate, if one will take another statement of Wolfson's out of context, the true issue will stand out: "The question is not really whether Philo knew Hebrew but rather to what extent he knew it."[25] That is indeed the true issue.

But Wolfson should not be followed when he goes on to say[26] that while Philo "did not know enough of the language to write his interpretations of Scriptures in Hebrew, he knew enough of it to read Scripture in the original and to check up on the Greek translations whenever he found it necessary." I shall show below that the chief characteristic of Philo in this matter is his indifference to Hebrew; and he used it, if at all, so little that his knowledge of it was at best useless. If this conclusion seems startling, let it be borne in mind that Philo affirms that the Septuagint is in every sense a completely inspired work; and we must not forget that Alexandrian Jews made a *yom tob* of the supposed anniversary of the translation.

Does Philo use the *middot* of rabbinic exegesis? He alludes to "canons of allegory," but does not reproduce any of these.

Siegfried[27] gives a long list of Philo's hermeneutic methods,

[24] Cf. Marcus, "Rashe P'rakim be-Shittat Ha-Hinuch shel Pilon Ha-Alexandroni," in *Touroff Jubilee Volume*, 3–11.

[25] *Philo*, I, 90.

[26] *Ibid*. Wolfson cites there, in note 27, some of the later studies on this divisive problem.

[27] In *Philo von Alexandria als Ausleger des alten Testaments*, Siegfried not only studies the types of hermeneutics but believes that certain allegories preserved in rabbinic literature are traceable to Philo; these alleged similarities are in tone but not in content, and Wolfson is right in saying (I, 134–135). "Altogether too much importance is attached by students of allegory to the kind of things which allegorists read into texts . . . The main thing is that by the time of Philo the principle was established in native Judaism that one is not bound to take every scriptural text literally."

which can be studied for comparison and contrast with the various lists of *middot* attributed to Hillel, Ishmael, and others. Of these only the list of Hillel would presumably be prior in time.

The conclusions are that a loose similarity in effect emerges, but there are differences in details. Philo certainly seems to anticipate some specific norms which Jewish tradition ascribes to rabbis later than Philo, and Philo uses some norms which are not paralleled in extant rabbinic collections.[28]

By and large scholarship has followed Zechariah Frankel[29] in the view that Palestinian exegesis has influenced the Alexandrian, and though a minority view, promulgated by Weinstein,[30] sees the influence of Alexandria on Palestine; Weinstein's views have been dismissed by Strack as only an arbitrary hypothesis. My own reading of Weinstein forces me to the same conclusion as to Weinstein's method.

Very recently, David Daube addressed himself to the problem of the development of rabbinic exegesis, and offered the theory that "Rabbinic methods of interpretation derive from Hellenistic rhetoric." Along with his main case, which rests on an effort to fit the developing rabbinic exegesis in the larger frame-work of the first pre-Christian century, Daube notes that the oldest list of *middot* is ascribed to Hillel; and Hillel was a student of Shemaiah and Abtalion; these latter are the first to be called by the later rabbis *darshanim*; and while doubt has been thrown on their alleged descent from proselytes, Daube believes that Graetz has amply shown that they were either Alexandrians by birth or else had lived there and studied there.

The effect of this statement by Daube, if it is correct, is to

---

[28] This conclusion emerges unmistakably when one compares what Siegfried has collected with Strack's summaries, *Introduction to the Talmud*, 93–98. Whatever may be Philo's "canons of allegory," he shows no acquaintance with the particulars of the rabbinic *middot*.

[29] *Vorstudien zur Septuaginta*, 1841; *Ueber den Einfluss der palästinischen Exegese auf die alexandrinische Hermeneutik*, 1851; *Ueber palästinischen und alexandrinischen Schriftforschung*, 1854, and in numerous articles. Other literature in this field is assembled in Prijs, *Jüdische Tradition in der Septuaginta*, 1948, xiii–xiv, and 105.

[30] *Zur Genesis der Agada* II: *Die alexandrinische Agada*, 190. See Strack, *op. cit.*, p. 166 and other references there given.

go beyond suggesting general hellenistic influence on the rabbis, and to insist that this influence is specifically Alexandrian. This may be so. But one wonders at the necessity of discerning an Alexandrian origin; were there no possible hellenistic influences within Palestine? Is it not just as likely, granted for the moment that rabbinic exegesis is hellenistic in origin, that this exegesis derived from an impetus felt within Palestine[31] long before the Alexandrian community had become exegetically creative? Moreover, is exegesis such an artificial human pursuit that its origin and development need to be traced to "influences"? Both on general and on specific grounds, Daube has failed to persuade me.

Respecting Philo, Daube has the following to say: "Philo was acquainted with them (sc. hellenistic rhetorical categories), and the conclusion has been drawn that he was influenced by Palestinian Rabbinism. But it is far more likely that he came across them in the course of his general studies at Alexandria . . . It (such embellishment) recurs in Cicero, Hillel and Philo — with enormous differences in detail, yet *au fond* the same. Cicero did not sit at the feet of Hillel, nor Hillel at the feet of Cicero; and there was no need for Philo to go to Palestinian sources for this kind of teaching. As we saw, there are indeed signs that Hillel's ideas were partly imported from Egypt. The true explanation lies in the common background."[32]

Daube's effort seems to me to be still another instance in which scholarship is not content simply to notice similarities, but feels called on to answer unanswerable questions of influence and dependency. It is out of the caprice of such efforts that there emerge the heated differences in scholarly interpretations, as the researcher insists, in a context of scanty evidence, on one and only one possibility in the midst of multiple choices.

Similarly, the allegorical method of Philo might be limited in its derivation either to hellenistic influence or to a rabbinic influence. Such futile pursuits are on record in the scholarly research. Allegory was even before Philo's time a well-known

---

[31] Cf. Lieberman's excellent studies, *Greek in Jewish Palestine*, New York, 1942, and *Hellenism in Jewish Palestine*, New York, 1950.

[32] "Rabbinic Methods of Interpretation and Hellenistic Rhetoric," *HUCA*, XXII, 239–264.

device among both Gentile and Jewish Greeks;[33] there is the probability that Philo's allegory stems from the hellenistic background.

Not that, on the other hand, allegorical interpretation is unknown among the rabbis. To the contrary. It begins, indeed, within the Bible.[34] The rabbinic literature preserves a good amount of allegory, in scattered instances, almost submerged in the non-allegorical.[35] The ancient Jewish allegorists, according to Lauterbach,[36] consisted of two classes. The *dorshe reshumot* were simple allegorists, while the *dorshe hamurot* were extreme. Lauterbach sees the former as living in Palestine, and the latter as Alexandrians. Belkin,[37] however, allocates both classes to Palestine. Ultimately an opposition to allegorizing crystallized itself among the rabbis, and while recollections of it were retained, the practice fell into relaitve desuetude.

Possibly Philo owes a debt to such rabbinic allegorizers. There seems little doubt, however, that the major debt is to his hellenistic background. However, the study of Philo's allegories is unyielding for a decisive fixing of Philo's relationships, positive and negative, with the rabbis. I shall discuss below a question related to the allegories, namely whether they are, as alleged, Philo's device for turning rabbinic dicta into philosophic form.

The theory is advanced respecting Josephus by Hölscher[38] that there existed hellenistic compilations of scriptural interpretations from which Josephus and Philo drew. Rappaport[39] seems correct in his assertion that to presuppose a written com-

---

[33] The best study is Decharme, *Critique des traditions religieuses chez les Grecs*, 1905. See "La méthode allégorique chez les Juifs avant Philon," in Bréhier, 45–61, for Judeo-Greek efforts.

[34] Isa. 5, Ezek. 15.17, and elsewhere. These are, of course, allegories in Scripture, not allegorical interpretations of Scripture.

[35] Cf. *JE*, I, "Allegorical Interpretation"; and Heinemann, *Altjüdische Allegoristik*.

[36] "Ancient Jewish Allegorists," *JQR* (NS) 1910, 291–333 and 503–31.

[37] *Op. cit.*, 13.

[38] In Pauly Wissowa, Sp. 1955 and 1961.

[39] *Agada und Exegese bei Flavius Josephus*, xvii.

pilation of this kind is hazardous, since it tends to replace, respecting Josephus, known oral sources with unknown and presumably lost written sources. Perhaps Hölscher's theory rests on an extension of Freudenthal's term,[40] hellenistic "midrash"; Freudenthal says nothing about a written compilation; the term might have been happier had it been "haggada"; but the traces of haggada among Judeo-Greek writers would scarcely lead one to think along the lines of a stabilized collection of pericopes.

Philo speaks some eighteen times of the sources of his exegesis.[41] Moreover, Philonic material reappears in patristic writings. Hence Bousset[42] and Bréhier[43] have written about a scholastic tradition, largely Stoic in character, which influenced Philo and carried Philo's influence to later generations. The notion commends itself if one will not press "school" too rigidly,[44] as Bousset does infelicitously.

Where Daube saw Alexandrian influence on the rabbis, Wolfson proceeds in a direction that is almost the opposite. In matters of haggada, and indeed of halaka, Philo is for him dependent on "native Palestinian tradition." A review of some of that case which Wolfson builds up may reveal its own inadequacy.

Philo speaks with great frequency of "unwritten law." Heinemann[45] argued that the term "unwritten law" in Philo never

[40] *Hellenistische Studien*, I, 76–77.

[41] Siegfried, *op. cit.*, 26–27. These sources are mostly "natural philosophers," a vague and unspecified group. The most significant passage is *V. C.*; the Therapeutae "have also writings of men of old, the founders of their way of thinking, who left many memorials of the form used in allegorical interpretation . . ." No further light exists on the alleged written sources than is contained in this passage; conclusions based on it are perforce conjectural.

[42] *Jüdisch-christlicher Schulbetrieb in Alexandria und Rom*, 14.

[43] *Op. cit.*, 45–61.

[44] Völker, *op. cit.*, pp. 3–4, note 1, makes some telling criticisms of Bousset, and cites also the authority of Cohn and of Heinemann. The divisive word here is "school," with its overtones of formality and channeled transmission. Perhaps "scholastic tradition" expresses the idea more properly; I see no reason to deny the continuity of transmission of materials.

[45] "Die Lehre vom ungeschrieben Gesetz im jüdischen Schrifttum," *HUCA*, IV, 1927, 149–171.

means the *torah she-b'al pe*. Wolfson believes that it occasionally does; hence he sets out to refute Heinemann in part. This is Wolfson's procedure: I. H. Weiss is his authority for the view that the early exponents of oral law were technically (note the word technically) called "elders." Wolfson connects these "elders" with the elders mentioned in Philo's prelude to his life of Moses. But the question was never, does Philo have some "elders" from whom he received things; the question is, *who* are these elders? There is nothing in the passage in Philo to justify the necessary identity of these elders.

Further, Wolfson connects the ἔθη of Spec. IV, 149–150 with *halakot* and Philo's "unwritten law" with the halaka. His demonstration consists of saying that in the passage, the "unwritten law" does not exist before Moses, but exists side by side with it, and therefore this is one of the passages in which unwritten law means the halaka. Now a glance at the passage reveals the following: ἔθη are customs, not *halakot*, and Philo is saying that customs are "unwritten laws, the decisions approved by men of old (παλαιῶν ἀνδρῶν), not inscribed on monuments nor on leaves of paper which the moth destroys, but on those partners in the same citizenship." As we shall see in the body of this study, the patriarchs are regarded by Philo as the "men of old" who did not live by the written Torah, since it has as yet not been recorded; these men, however, lived by the unwritten law of nature, and those men were themselves "laws", in that the law of Moses is the set of positive enactments of those things which the ancients did. "Unwritten law" in this passage does not and cannot mean the *Torah she-b'al pe*, and the "men of old" are the patriarchs, whose lives Philo commends to his generation for emulation, and they are not the "elders" who give the rabbinic oral tradition.

Next, Philo says that praise cannot be given to him who obeys the written law, since that is compulsory, but that he who observes the unwritten law deserves commendation. Wolfson finds a rabbinic parallel in the dictum, *habibim dibre sofrim midibre torah*, "the words of the scribes are more precious than the words of the Torah." This "parallelism" is for Wolfson another link in the chain binding Philo to the rabbinic halaka.

But let anyone examine Aristotle's *Rhetoric*, i 14,7, and he will see that Philo is quoting that passage almost verbatim, and that the parallelism is not with the rabbis but with Aristotle. Or, more precisely, Aristotelianism is Philo's source, not rabbinic literature. And it may be added that the two passages do not mean anything at all in the same vein. The rabbinic dictum is a reflection of the tone and regard that tradition had for the work of the scribes, but the tradition nevertheless grants a priority to the Torah, even while elevating the soferim.[46] Philo (and Aristotle) are discussing the law of nature as contrasted with "positive" law.

Wolfson regards as parallel Philo's statement in *Mig.* 90 that one should not do away with the established customs which divinely empowered men, greater than those of our time, have laid down, and the statement of *Eduyot* I, 5, "No assembly of scholars can repeal the words of another assembly of scholars unless it is greater in learning and in numbers." Philo's statement is an exhortation to preserve customs; the *Mishna* is a device for regulating the relationship of a later legislative (or quasi-legislative) body to an earlier one.

Returning to the question, did Philo know the *torah she-b'al pe*, one must recognize that the manner in which Wolfson answers this question in the affirmative is hardly tenable. One need not infer from a casual similarity in one or more facets of Philonic and rabbinic statements that such similarity amounts to total identity, nor that that dubious identity requires Philo to be dependent on the rabbis. Were the case to rest only on the proof which Wolfson offers, then the rejection of his proof would entail the rejection of the notion.

I doubt that looseness in method or in thinking exists in more pronounced form than in the quests for parallels and dependencies between bits or bodies of literature. The parallels between Jesus and the rabbis, between the rabbis and Paul, between Paul and the Stoics, and the like, are all too often marked by two curious aberrations. First, the alleged parallels are almost always

---

[46] Cf. R. H. 19a, *v'en dibre Torah tzerikim hizzuk . . . dibre sofrim tzerikim hizzuk*; and Num. R. XIV. *Hiqshu dibre Torah le-dibre sofrim she-hem 'amitim k'motam.*

noted only in the facets in which sentiments or words coincide, but are not searched for words and facets which differ. Wolfson seems to me to be notable in asserting, over and over again, that two statements which in reality touch no more than tangential circles, are to be considered as completely coinciding. Second, it becomes a standard step to move from the supposed parallelism of two statements to an insistence on a particular kind of direct dependency of the one on the other; hence Wolfson unfailingly makes Philo dependent on a rabbinic dictum, of uncertain or even later provenance, almost as if to deny Philo and his fellow Alexandrians any creativity at all. His book, which has many merits, abounds in absurdities in which the existence of parallelisms is grossly overstated and the inference of direct dependency belabored. If one followed Wolfson's method, he could go beyond Bergmann, who compared Stoic philosophy and Judaism[47] and make the rabbis dependent not on the Bible, but on the Stoics; or the Stoics dependent on the rabbis. Jewish scholarship has often had to note that to illuminate the New Testament by collections of excerpted material from rabbinic literature is hazardous, because the all important context is thereby lost. Similarly in other areas of comparative study facile conclusions are reached about similar sentiments which are not adequately weighed.

As still another sample of a somewhat misguided effort to dovetail Philo and the rabbis, we turn to Marmorstein and the question of the attributes of God. Zechariah Frankel was among the first to note, about a hundred years ago, that the rabbis coincide in interpreting each of the usual two Scriptural names of God, YHWH and *Elohim*, and *Theos* and *Kyrios*, with the qualities of mercy and justice. But the rabbis equate YHWH with mercy, while Philo interprets its LXX equivalent *Kyrios*,[48] with justice; and Philo ascribes mercy to the rendering *Theos* for *Elohim*, to which the rabbis assign justice. Frankel,[49] whom

[47] In *Judaica. Festschrift zu Hermann Cohens Siebzigstem Geburtstage*, 145–166.

[48] Cf. Siegfried, *op. cit.*, 142.

[49] Cf. *Vorstudien*, 189 ff.; *Einfluss*, 84 ff.; and *Ueber palästinische und alexandrische Schriftforschung*, 23 ff.

George Foot Moore[50] follows, suggests that behind these similar but divergent views lies a common *type* of exegesis, but which diverged naturally in the shift of language from Hebrew to Greek; the Greek interpreters, using Greek etymological bases, were led to connect *Theos* with mercy and *Kyrios* with judgment, while the Palestinians, using their own equivalent bases, made their expected connection. Frankel is among those who denied that Philo knew Hebrew, and thereby he explains Philo's divergence from the Palestinian form of the common exegesis. This view, however, is unacceptable to Marmorstein.

"Philo," says Marmorstein, "never invented these terms, but took them from Palestinian sources. There never was a discrepancy between Philo and the Rabbis in this respect." Then how account for the at least apparent divergency? The fact is, says Marmorstein, that for the earliest Palestinian teachers the quantities existed as assigned by Philo. It is only with the time of Meir and Simon ben Yohai that the terms *middat ha-din* and *middat ha-rahamim* occur. Before their time these terms were not used. "Instead we read the terms *middah tobah* and *middah pur'anut*, the measure of goodness and the measure of punishment . . . The tannaitic Midrash usually adopts these earlier terms. None of these, however, enables us to glance at the inner meaning of the use of the divine name. One can see in YHWH the *middat pur'anut*, and in *Elohim* the measure of goodness, or *vice versa*." The older sources, then, agree with Philo, but later rabbinic usage made a deliberate and calculated change. We may momentarily defer Marmorstein's explanation of this change to consider the basis by which he arrives at his proof for the older usage; it depends primarily on a manuscript reading of the Mekilta, rejected on the basis of other manuscripts as a simple copyist's error by both Friedmann and Lauterbach. Finkelstein expressed the judgment that Marmorstein's case rested on the basis of a single doubtful passage which runs counter to well-authenticated rabbinic sources.

The change was made, says Marmorstein, in the second century, in response to the use by gnostics of the divine names;

[50] *Judaism*, III, note 123.

since gnostics regarded *Kyrios* as the God of the Jews and lower than *Elohim*, the Highest God, "the teachers of the second century changed the order."[51]

The point to be noted is that rather than posit Philo's capacity to adapt a rabbinic viewpoint to Philo's own needs, of language, of philosophy, and of homily, Marmorstein creates this artificial pattern of a rabbinic attitude abruptly reversing itself. It is a curious example of choosing a complex explanation for a relatively simple one.[52a]

I discuss this particular point at length in connection with Philo's exegesis of Gen. xviii, and it is unnecessary at this moment to go into the details. I am here trying to show only that the character of the alleged dependency by Philo on the rabbis, among some scholars, is far-fetched and untenable in method and in result.

Wolfson has given some attention to the relation between the parallel traditions. These, he says, may be assumed to be of a fourfold nature. "First, some of them undoubtedly emanate from a common source, the traditions of early Palestinian Judaism which the Alexandrian Jews had brought with them from their home country. Second, some of them are later innovations independently arrived at by the rabbis and Philo, owing to the common method of interpretation employed by them. Third, some of them may have been borrowed by Alexandrian Jews from their contemporary Palestinian Jews through the various channels of intellectual communication that existed between them. Fourth, some of them were probably borrowed by Palestinian Jews from the works of Philo." And again, "the rabbinic parallels quoted would serve their purpose to whichever of these

---

[51] See Marmorstein, *The Old Rabbinic Doctrine of God*, I, 45 ff., and Finkelstein's review in "Recent Progress in Jewish Theology," *JQR* (NS), XX (1930), especially pp. 363–364.

[52a] Marmorstein, in response to Finkelstein, admits the justice of the latter's criticism, but tries to restate the previous position with some tortuous citation. The new terms, says Marmorstein, were not found in the older authorities; but, on the other hand, "I am perfectly aware that owing to the deplorable condition of our texts it may happen that the new term crept into an older saying or that amoraic teachings contain the old form." "Philo and the Names of God," *JQR* (NS) XXII, 1931–32, 295 ff.

four types of parallels they belonged." This statement is altogether reasonable as a pattern; it is a sad fact that Wolfson fails to follow this pattern of his own, but sees Philo at every turn dependent on the rabbis.

For it is taken for granted by Wolfson, throughout his book, that a rabbinic statement, of whatever provenience, is often a source for Philo's alleged parallel statement. Goodenough, in a searching review of Wolfson's book,[52b] pointed out that often the rabbinic authority cited in a given instance lived in a period long after Philo. In context, Goodenough laments that Wolfson excludes as sources for clarifying Philo's thought the mystic philosophers of the period after Philo. His question amounts to this, if rabbis later than Philo can serve as sources for the knowledge of Judaism at Philo's time, why cannot later hellenistic writers serve for Philo's hellenistic background? Goodenough makes it abundantly clear that he is not doubting that late rabbinic collections, "even the medieval ones, contain material, some of which must even antedate Philo." Goodenough then concedes that rabbinic tradition goes back to the period before Philo.

In a reply to Goodenough, and in defense of Wolfson's method, Bamberger[52c] makes the following points. The ascription of a statement to a particular rabbi gives us only a *terminus ad quem*, since the rabbi may actually be quoting much more ancient material. We know from Jubilees and Josephus that material contained in the rabbinic sources are much, much more ancient than the date of compilation of a rabbinic collection. Pharisaic rabbinic thought remained largely homogeneous over a period of many centuries. The pre-Philonic character of some Pharisaic tradition shows that "Wolfson is justified, by and large, in the use he has made of Talmudic parallels." Bamberger does not stop to note whether an alleged parallel exists in similar or identical form, shape, and significance; Bamberger says that "though one may cavil at one instance or another, it is not illegitimate . . . to quote later teachers as if they were sources of Philo's thought."

[52b] *JBL*, LXVII (1948), 87–109.
[52c] *JBL*, LXVIII (1949), 115–123.

The conclusion here is a little startling, in that it suggests that all of the oral law was contained not in the revelation to Moses at Sinai but in the earliest *tannaim*. But it is Bamberger's intent which needs to be focused on rather than the the implications of his words. He is exactly right in insisting that rabbinic literature contains material older than Philo. In a conversation, when I asked him if he meant thereafter to imply Philo's unfailing dependency on the rabbis, his reply was, of course, in the negative. Accordingly, some of the language and some of the conclusions in Bamberger's article do not completely or adequately portray his viewpoint. The printed words, however, are not accompanied by the clarifying commentary. Marmorstein, showing Philo's lack of knowledge of Hebrew and dependency on the rabbis, insists that the second century rabbis deliberately altered the doctrine of attributes, while Bamberger's article imputes an unfailing homogeneity to the rabbis.

Obviously, the Biblical laws required interpretation and application in Alexandria as elsewhere. Philo recapitulates quite an extensive body of post-biblical Jewish law. As scholars have studied the matter, they have come to diverse conclusions. Ritter[53] is sure that there is a direct connection between the rabbinic halaka and these laws in Philo, and he assumes that these laws were the decisions of Jewish courts in Alexandria. Juster[54] and Bréhier,[55] however, deny the existence of independent Jewish courts. Lauterbach[56] argued for a direct relationship between the Palestinian and the Philonic halaka, but he conceded that in certain instances Philo's laws rest on Alexandrian decisions rather than on Palestinian: indeed, Lauterbach finds that in occasional instances Philo's halaka made its way into rabbinic halaka.

Heinemann,[57] on the other hand, maintains Philo's basis to be Greek and Roman laws and traditions, and many similarities between Philo and the halaka would be coincidence. Good-

---

[53] *Op. cit.*, 15–16.
[54] *Les Juifs dans l'empire romain*, I, 4 ff.; II, 157 ff.
[55] *Op. cit.*, 33 ff.
[56] In *JE*, X, 15–18.
[57] *Philons griechische und jüdische Bildung* is largely devoted to this topic.

enough[58] restates the position that Philo's halaka are the decisions of courts in Alexandria. These decisions are for the most part traceable to Greek and Roman law; and such Philonic law as is not traceable to the Greeks and the Romans must be Jewish. Goodenough leaves it to rabbinists to determine whether these Jewish laws are the rabbinic halaka, or an independent Alexandrian halaka.

Belkin agrees with Goodenough that the legal decisions in Philo are based on actual court practices of Jewish courts in Alexandria. He agrees in this measure with Goodenough and Heinemann that for some of Philo's *halakot* a Greek or Roman basis is to be supposed. But for any laws not directly traceable to Greek or Roman origins, a Palestinian source is to be supposed. The Palestinian halaka was "known and practiced among the Jews who lived outside of Palestine . . . Philo's halakah is based upon the Palestinian Oral Law as it was known in Alexandria . . . No longer may a sharp line of distinction be drawn between Palestinian and Hellenistic Judaism."[59]

Goodenough, however, seems to remain unconvinced by this last statement of Belkin's. In a review,[60] he credits Belkin with finding more rabbinic parallels than Heinemann supposed existed, but Goodenough insists that the increase in the number of parallels does not invalidate the claim that the Alexandrian courts developed their own halaka, independently of Palestine. We reach accordingly a stalemate.

For my part, in the measure in which I have gone into the matter, I find that the scholars tend to omit from consideration the fact that the source common to Philo and the rabbis was the Bible, and that the common source could yield relatively common deductions, especially in something so fixed as law. Similarity between the Philonic and the rabbinic halaka could thus easily be the result simply of coincidence. I see no reason to deny Lauterbach's assertion of cross fertilization: Philo both receives and gives; he both accords in general principles, and presents differences in specific details. It is certainly not to be ruled out

---

[58] *The Jurisprudence of the Jewish Courts in Egypt,* 16–29.
[59] Cf. S. Belkin, *Philo and the Oral Law,* p. 29.
[60] *JBL,* LIX, (1940), p. 413.

that Philo was acquainted with Roman and Greek law.[61] I should therefore neither assert the complete independence of Philo on the halaka, nor his complete dependence on it.

But I should be prepared to disagree sharply with the notion that identity of halakic observance (which is not really the situation) would obliterate the line of distinction between Palestinian and Hellenistic Judaism.

III

In my own presuppositions, I find the presence of common items in Philo and the rabbis indicative of the existence of communication; at the same time, I believe that each Jewry developed its own idiosyncrasies. I believe that it is quite futile to try to determine in the common items where precedence lies and where dependency exists.

Indeed, for me such matters are scarcely the main issue. With the Bible as their common heritage, with halakic inferences natural from the Bible, with communication present, with intensive Jewish loyalty common to both, I do not see any need for asserting and trying to prove total difference or chicken-and-egg dependency.

Rather, I believe the essential difference between Philo and the rabbis can be discerned in noting such things as their different use of a common item, or their different inferences from a common Biblical basis. For example, the rabbis, Philo, and Josephus, all agree that Abraham began in astrology but moved from the observation of heavenly bodies into the discovery of the existence of God. This the rabbis relate in their usual narrative manner. Josephus, however, in writing for Gentiles, and in wishing to portray Abraham as a mathematician and a philosopher, declares that it was his notice of the aberrations in the movements of heavenly bodies that led Abraham to his

---

[61] In a conversation, Professor Sonne suggested that possibly rabbinic halaka is itself partially dependent on Greek or Roman law. If so, the overlappings between Philo and the rabbis do not necessarily involve direct dependency of the one upon the other.

momentous discovery. Philo, however, describes a totally different process; Abraham did not proceed from the heavenly bodies to God, but turned completely away from astrology and turned within himself; Philo, as we shall see in detail, has some contempt for the method of the Abraham of the rabbis and of Josephus!

It is in such items in which a common motif is used in a strikingly diverse form that the clearest distinctions between Philo and the rabbis emerge. These items, when coupled with the consistent idiosyncrasies of Philo's interpretation accumulate to provide the restricted but highly significant area in which Philo's religious experience and orientation — let us call it his religiosity — is marked off from the rabbis.

It is often overlooked in religious history that the distinctions which mark off "sectaries" from each other are largely intensive in details but simultaneously limited in scope. It is the rare Jew who knows the distinction between a Methodist and a Baptist. Even on knowing the distinctions, theological, ecclesiastical, and historical, the Jew can wonder why these, to him, unimportant factors should occasion competing denominational structures, in light of such shared items as a common Scripture and a supposedly common ritual calendar. To a religious sectary, however, ancient or modern, the specific items in which divergency of belief or practice exists are the important ones; the overlappings and commonly held attitudes recede from importance and even notice.

The differences between the Hassidim and the Mitnagdim can be set forth with some precision and clarity. The modern commentator, convinced of the Jewish loyalty of both, would not suggest that loyalty to Judaism, or disloyalty, was germane to a study of the differences. Nor would he be apt to suggest that either group lacked the Bible, the Talmud, and the more or less common halaka. In much they were the same; in a little, they were at variance with each other, and engaged in controversy which at times became bitter. To put it in an arbitrary mathematical formula, one could conclude here that the relevant differences represent possibly only five per cent, but that over-

lapping or congruency marks the other ninety-five per cent.
In the case of the Karaites and the Rabbanites, the mathematical
formula might be altered to, let us say, fifty per cent of congruency and fifty per cent of difference. Between Reform Jews and
Orthodox Jews he might list the figures respectively as forty
and sixty.

The scope of difference between an orthodox group and a
deviating one varies in time and in place, but the specific restricted difference inevitably exists within a framework of general
or extensive agreement. What Baptists and Methodists share
makes them both Christian; what they have parted on makes
them Baptists or Methodists, Conformists or non-Conformists,
Protestants or Catholics. Accordingly, as it applies to Philo
and the rabbis, the significant differences can conceivably be
rather limited in scope, but decisive in intensity. All too often
the commentators have overlooked this elementary consideration.

The specific differences between Philo and the rabbis which
I shall point out are not such as those of cult practice, but differences in the assessment of what the identical cult practices would
mean. To select an extreme example so as to clarify my meaning,
Jews are well acquainted with the ceremony of the *kiddush* and
the *motzi*. A similar observance obtains among the Christians,
mutatis mutandis, in the Holy Communion.[62] Assuming that the
Eucharist developed from these ceremonies, the words of Knox[63]
are apt: "There is nothing in Jewish literature which provides
any parallel for the conception of a ritual meal in which bread
and wine are the means by which the believers are able to enter
into communion with the life of the deity." Externals of ritual
may be identical, but their internal significance may be at
variance. Hence the historic and continuing disputations within
Christendom on the significance of the Eucharist. Accordingly,
the significant divergence between Philo and the rabbis respecting Passover, for example, could revolve not on the external
observance but on the internal meaning.

No, it is not the identity of halakic practice or haggadic

---

[62] An extensive literature on the antecedents of the Eucharist exists. For
our purposes it is not germane whether it is a ceremony of Jewish or of pagan
origin; cf. Kennedy, *St. Paul and the Mystery Religions*, 256–279.

[63] *St. Paul and the Church of Jerusalem*, 376.

fancies which is the issue, as I see it, between Philo and the rabbis. Halakic observance may well have been uniform, or only minimally diverse. The true issue is what the one or the other sees in these practices, in the Bible, and in the nature of man and the nature of God. We shall see that Philo, the Jew, despite basic congruency, diverges almost as significantly from the rabbis as the Eucharist does from the *kos* and the *leḥem*.

The medium through which I set forth my case is an exposition of what Philo tells us about Abraham. Both Beer, in his *Leben Abrahams, nach Auffassung der jüdischen Sage*, Leipzig, 1859, and Ginzberg, *Legends of the Jews*, I, 183–308 and notes, V, 207–269, have most competently assembled the narrative material. This they each work into a connected account, reserving for their annotations relevant comments on overlappings and differences. I have been greatly helped by both studies.[64]

But to see Philo's Abraham most clearly, it is necessary to keep the different conceptions of Abraham separate from each other. The patriarch serves authors of non-canonical literature and limited parts of the New Testament (Synoptic Gospels, Paul, and James) as the exemplar of that which the writer is arguing for. To see what the writer makes of Abraham is often to see most clearly what the writer is trying to say. Accordingly, I try to keep the various Abrahams separate from each other, though in the apparatus I frequently indicate common or strikingly variant items.

A French publication, *Cahiers Sioniens*, devotes its June, 1951 issue (Vol. V, No. 2) to "Abraham, Père des Croyants." The nine essays cover the range from the history of the biblical patriarch through Kierkegaard; a scant eight pages encompass the "Traditions juives sur Abraham." The interesting essays on Abraham in the New Testament and in the Christian liturgy are outside the present investigation. The separate treatment in the *Cahiers Sioniens* of the different Abrahams is quite commendable.

In the ensuing chapters I discuss the various traditions about Abraham in Jewish haggadic material. Thereafter I present a detailed treatment of Abraham in Philo.

[64] See below, Chapter Three, note 9, a comment on Philo's Abraham as depicted in Goodenough, *By Light, Light.*

CHAPTER TWO

Some Conceptions of Abraham

THE uniqueness of Abraham in Philo is the more readily
seen, I have said, when other conceptions of him are
contrasted with it. Accordingly, I present briefly some of the
material from Apocrypha, Pseudepigrapha, Josephus, Graeco-
Jewish writers, and rabbinic literature. I have deemed it unnecessary to repeat all the legendary narratives; Philo tells us
no narratives about Abraham; moreover, Ginzberg and Beer
have assembled this material so that it is unnecessary here to
reproduce it. I have culled from rabbinic literature some leading
motifs about Abraham of a non-narrative character, derived
often from the ingenuities of biblical interpretation.

First, one needs to recall that material about Abraham is
found throughout the Bible beyond Gen. 12–25. The earliest
mention in the literary prophets seems to be in Deutero-Isaiah.

A summary of earlier history in Josh. 24 tells that Terah,
Abraham's father, was a worshiper of strange gods but Abraham
worshiped God.[1] Neh. 9.7 states that it was God (not, as in
Gen. 11.31, Terah) who brought Abraham out of Ur of the
Chaldees. A very obscure allusion, Isa. 29.22, speaks of God's
redeeming Abraham; the phrase is regarded by Marti,[2] and
probably correctly, as a very late gloss based on material subsequently developed elaborately in rabbinic writings: LXX

[1] Josh. 24.2.
[2] *Das Buch Jesaja*, 1900, 218.

renders פדה by ἀφώρισεν and supplies a preposition ἐξ making the phrase mean the house of Jacob "which He separated out out of Abraham."[3]

A number of passages allude passingly to events or places associated with Abraham: the double cave;[4] the famine in Abraham's day;[5] the wells dug with Abimelech;[6] his residence in Hebron.[7]

God's covenant with Abraham and His promises to him are matters of frequent reference and allusion. Both the promises (especially of the inheritance of Canaan) and the covenant are repeated in generations after Abraham with specific recollection of Abraham. So, to Isaac;[8] to Jacob;[9] to Menasseh and Ephraim;[10] to Joseph's brothers;[11] to Moses;[12] to all Israel;[13] to Caleb and Joshua.[14] While explicit reference to the covenant or promises is not present in the case of Elijah, he is recorded as praying to the God of Abraham, Isaac and Israel.[15] The Chronicler portrays Jehoshaphat as praying to the "God of our fathers"[16] who gave the land to "Abraham Thy beloved."[17] The Psalmist terms the covenant an eternal one, commanded to the thousandth generation, made with Abraham, sworn to Isaac, established as a statute to Jacob, and an eternal covenant with Israel.[18]

---

[3] This is probably a tendentious rendering, designed to exclude Esau and his descendants from the benefits of descent from Abraham. Such sentiments are voiced in rabbinic writings and in Jubilees, as we shall see.

[4] Gen. 49.30–31 and 50.13.

[5] Gen. 26.1.

[6] Gen. 26.15, 18.

[7] Gen. 35.27.

[8] Gen. 26.3.

[9] Gen. 28.4, 35.12.

[10] Gen. 48.16.

[11] Gen. 50.24.

[12] Ex. 33.1 and Deut. 1.8. Deut. 34.4 records God's showing to Moses the land promised to Abraham, Isaac and Jacob which Moses now sees but will not enter.

[13] Deut. 29.12; 30.20; 1.8; 6.10.

[14] Num. 32.11–12.

[15] I Kings 18.36.

[16] II Chron. 20.6.

[17] Ibid., 7.

[18] Ps. 105.8–10; cf. I Chron. 16.15–17.

The covenant and the promises, then, given originally to Abraham, are renewed at frequent intervals and become a perpetual covenant to the offspring of Abraham.

The recollection of this covenant prompts God to save Israel. The prelude to the calling of Moses is God's hearing the outcry of the children of Israel and His recollection of His covenant with Abraham, Isaac, and Jacob.[19] After the golden calf incident, God proposes to Moses that He destroy Israel and raise a new people out of Moses; Moses' reply in part is to remind God of His servants Abraham, Isaac, and Jacob, and the promises to them; accordingly God withholds the evil He had spoken of.[20] When Israel was in the wilderness, God remembered Abraham His servant, and brought out Israel in joy and singing.[21] The conquest of Palestine came not as a result of the righteousness of Israel, but because of the unrighteousness of the Canaanites and because of God's desire to fulfill his promise to Abraham, Isaac, and Jacob.[22] In the days of Jehoaz God graciously has mercy on Israel for the sake of the covenant with Abraham, Isaac, and Jacob.[23]

God is identifiable by being spoken of as the God of Abraham. God so identifies Himself to Isaac[24] and to Jacob.[25] It was the God of Abraham and Isaac who prevented Laban from defrauding Jacob.[26] The covenant between Jacob and Laban is sealed by the "heap of stones"; we are told [27] that "the God of Abraham and the God of Nahor will judge between us, the God of their fathers." The passage has troubled the modern commentators almost as much as it has the rabbinic interpreters.[28] It seems to accord equal rank to both Nahor's God and to Abraham's. MT reads "judge" as a plural; LXX renders it as a singular,

---

[19] Ex. 2.23–24.
[20] Ex. 32.13; similarly, Deut. 9.25–29.
[21] Ps. 105.42.
[22] Deut. 9.5.
[23] II Kings 13.22–25.
[24] Gen. 26.24.
[25] Gen. 28.13.
[26] Gen. 31.42.
[27] Gen. 31.53.
[28] Cf. Morgenstern, *A Jewish Interpretation of the Book of Genesis*, 263.

undoubtedly a deliberate alteration. The *Targumim* retain the plural. Rabbinic interpreters struggle with the verse.[29]

God identifies Himself to Moses as the God of Moses' fathers, Abraham, Isaac, and Jacob,[30] and instructs Moses to identify Him to the children of Israel in the same way.[31] So, too, Ex. 6.3 which states that Abraham knew God as El Shaddai and not as Yahweh.

Jacob, in prayer, addresses God as the God of Abraham and of Isaac;[32] so, also, Elijah[33] and David.[34] The letters which Hezekiah sends out urging repentance instruct the readers to return to the God of Abraham, Isaac and Jacob.

The children of Israel are described as "seed of Abraham";[35] Ps. 105.6 uses the phrase which in another version, I Chron. 16.13, reads "seed of Israel."[36] Abraham is the rock whence Israel is hewn; pursuers of righteousness are bidden to look to him; God will comfort Zion.[37]

Abraham is God's beloved and Israel is his seed.[38] Abraham is God's servant.[39] Israel is the people of the God of Abraham.[40] The land of Palestine was given to the seed of Abraham, God's beloved.[41]

The summary in a passage in Neh. 9.7 ff., gives in a kind of digest form the biblical view of the career of Abraham. The one God created the universe and is the Master of it. God chose Abram, brought him out of Ur of the Chaldees, and changed his name to Abraham. God found his heart faithful

[29] Cf. Rashi and Ibn Ezra *ad loc.*
[30] Ex. 3.6.
[31] Ex. 3.15–16.
[32] Gen. 32.10.
[33] I Kings 18.36.
[34] I Chron. 29.18.
[35] Jer. 33.26 and II Chron. 20.7.
[36] Ibn Ezra to I Chron. 16.13 notes the different readings and declares that they are justified since the seed of Abraham is the same as the seed of Israel.
[37] Isa. 51.1–3.
[38] Isa. 41.8.
[39] Ps. 105.42.
[40] Ps. 47.10.
[41] II Chron. 20.7.

before Him; he made a covenant with him to give to his seed
the land of the Canaanites, Hittites, Amorites, Perizzites, Jebu-
sites, and Girgashites. In His righteousness, God had fulfilled
His word.

One additional passage remains to be cited, as if in contradiction of all that has been cited above: God is Israel's Father; Abraham has not known them, nor has the patriarch Israel recognized
them; God is the Redeemer from eternity.[42] The passage seems
to say quite clearly that neither the fatherhood of Abraham nor
that of Jacob is of any avail, for the true Fatherhood is that of
God. Ingenuity might tend to remove the apparent contradiction;
indeed, the rabbis infer from the passage that in this instance
it is the unmentioned Isaac whose merit is the saving force,[43]
while elsewhere the difficulty is removed by asserting that
Abraham did not rescue Israel from Egypt and Jacob did not
rescue Israel in the desert.[44] The presence of a discordant note
in an assemblage of biblical passages should not disturb us
unduly; it is quite easy for people to hold on to different and
contradictory attitudes; or to do what the rabbis did in this
case, to interpret the discordant verse in such a way that it
becomes concordant.

To summarize, the biblical Abraham is presented to us in a
quasi-biographical form, as in Genesis; his achievements and
character are set forth at some length. Certain clear motifs are
discernible: Abraham was chosen by God; by implication he
was the first to worship the true God; God made with him a
covenant renewed generation after generation with his seed;
Abraham was a saving force for Lot, and Abraham's merit
remained a saving force for later generations; Abraham was
an exemplar of fidelity, obedience, hospitality, and military
prowess. Abraham withstood a testing of his faith. Abraham
was a prophet, a servant and beloved of God. As the patriarch, he was a progenitor of sons, and his sons, his seed, possess the memory of what Abraham did as a saving force for
themselves.

[42] Isa. 63.16.
[43] *Shabbat* 89b.
[44] *Targum, ad loc.* Cf. also Rashi and Redaq.

Turning to the non-canonical material, the trial through which Judith and the elders were passing was not as extreme as the trials through which God put Abraham, Isaac, and Jacob.[45] The fathers[46] were Chaldeans whose neighbors cast them out because they would not worship the ancestral gods, but the God of heaven, Whom they knew. They fled into Mesopotamia.[47] Sanctification is to come upon the Messiah as God's voice[48] came from heaven to Abraham and Isaac.[49] In the present age intercession by one on behalf of another is possible, in the manner in which Abraham prayed for Sodom, but such intercession will not be possible in messianic times.[50] The acts of the Samaritans are not surprising, for they had persecuted Abraham and tried to violate Sarah.[51] The heavenly Jerusalem had been revealed to Abraham at the Covenant between the Pieces.[52]

The Law had been given to Abraham who had fulfilled it; it included the belief in the coming judgment, in the messianic age, and resurrection.[53] As Abraham was faithful in trial and reckoned righteous, so should his descendants have zeal for the Law.[54] In transmitting the Law, Benjamin followed the pattern of Abraham, Isaac, and Jacob.[55] Abraham is recorded as the friend of God,[56] because he kept the commandments of

[45] Judith, VIII, 26–27.

[46] Abraham, rather than "the fathers," is the usual hero of the conflict with Chaldean neighbors; see below, page 38. Judith gives a compressed summary here which overlooks individuals, and in the abridgement seems to coalesce the trips to Egypt by Abraham and by Jacob and his sons into one.

[47] Judith V, 5–8.

[48] Test. Levi, XVIII, 6.

[49] Gen. 22. 11.

[50] IV Ezra, VII, 102–115.

[51] Test. Levi, VI, 8–9.

[52] II Baruch, IV, 4. Charles, *Apocrypha and Pseudepigrapha of the Old Testament*, II, 482, seems correct in calling this passage a Christian interpolation.

[53] II Baruch, LVII.

[54] I Macc. II, 52.

[55] Test. Benjamin X, 4.

[56] Textual difficulties make the reading uncertain. I follow the reconstruction given in Charles, *op. cit.*, II, 806.

God and did not walk by his own spirit. He delivered the commandments to Isaac and Jacob.[57] Abraham was circumcised on
the day of his knowing the law; Mastema departs from him
who cleaves to the Law.[58] Abraham (like Noah, Isaac, and Jacob)
married in the faith.[59]

Were it not for the merit of Abraham, Isaac, and Jacob,
not one of their seed would have been left after the destruction
of Jerusalem and the temple.[60] The land into which Joshua was
leading the Israelites was the land of the fathers.[61] The tribes
prayed to the God of Abraham, Isaac and Jacob, asking Him
to remember the covenant and the oath and the promise to
give their children the land.[62] Esther prayed to the God of
Abraham.[63] Joseph prayed to the God of his fathers and to the
angel of Abraham.[64] Indeed, Isaac received his promise by virtue
of the merit of Abraham.[65] The blessing which Judah received
came ultimately from Abraham.[66] Levi was buried at Hebron with
the fathers,[67] and Dan was buried near them.[68] The messianic
ingathering will be for the sake of Abraham, Isaac, and Jacob.[69]
In the messianic times the children of Israel will be delivered
and will dwell in the land of Abraham.[70]

Abraham was a plant of righteousness, and his descendants

---

[57] *Zadokite Frag.* IV, 2–3.

[58] *Ibid.*, XX, 2–3.

[59] Tobit IV, 12–13.

[60] Test. Levi, XV, 4.

[61] Assumption of Moses, II, 1.

[62] *Ibid.* III, 8–10.

[63] Addit. to Esther, C 8 and C 30.

[64] Test. Joseph, VI, 7. Similar such allusions to prayer to the God of the
Patriarchs are found in Sirach LI, 12 ff. and Psalms of Solomon IX, 17 and
XVIII, 4.

[65] Sirach XLIV, 19–22.

[66] Test. Judah, XVII, 5. Some versions read "Isaac" in place of "Abraham."

[67] Test. Levi, XIX, 5.

[68] Test. Dan. VII, 2.

[69] Test. Asher, VII, 7.

[70] Tobit, XIV, 7. The same statement appears in Epist. Baruch II, 34
which adds Isaac and Jacob to Abraham. The Itala Tobit lacks the mention of
Abraham at this point.

became that too.[71] When Abraham chose God, Michael and seventy angels taught seventy languages to the nations of the world. Only the house of Abraham was taught Hebrew. Nimrod and others chose angels but Abraham chose God. Only the house of Abraham chose God and abided with Him.[72]

The seed of Abraham is synonymous with the word Jew.[73] Bilhah and Zilpah, the wives of Jacob, were of the family of Abraham.[74] Abraham had other descendants, such as the Spartans.[75] Abraham, Isaac, and Jacob will arise unto life in messianic times.[76] They will rejoice at the coming of the Messiah.[77]

Two allusions of a colorless variety occur in resumés of history.[78]

Abraham appears in the above sources in little more than allusions. He obeyed the Law, and commanded it to his offspring. He is an exemplar for his descendants to emulate. His merit is a reservoir of grace for them. Reunion of his seed (or, at least, his righteous seed) with him will take place in messianic times. Abraham abides in some ancestral place, awaiting that joyous moment.

[71] Enoch XCIII, 5.

[72] App. Test. Naph. VIII–X.

[73] IV Macc. VI, 17, 22; XVIII, 1, 21; Psalms of Solomon IX, 17; XVIII, 4. Test. Levi, VIII, 15; II Macc. I, 2.

[74] Test. Naphtali I, 10. This notion is found again in *Tar. Jon.* Gen. 29.24, 29.

[75] I Macc. XII, 19–23. Cf. II Macc. V, 9 which depicts Jason as fleeing to the Lacedaemonians to find shelter among kinfolk. Cf. also Charles, *op. cit.* I, 112, and Freudenthal, *Hellenistische Studien*, 1875, I, 29–30. Abraham is portrayed in the Bible, it will be recalled, as the father of many nations. The question of the "true" seed arises only when an exclusivist advantage is desired; otherwise an all-inclusive common ancestry is admissible. The rabbis (*Yal. Shim.* 904) classify Sarah as a daughter of Shem, Hagar a daughter of Ham, and Keturah a daughter of Japhet; this would mean that nations of all three races of mankind stem from Abraham.

[76] Test. Judah XXV, 1; Test. Benjamin X, 6.

[77] Test. Levi XVIII, 14. A passage in IV Ezra VI, 8 tries to establish some relationship between the Messianic age and the patriarchs, but the passage is corrupt and obscure.

[78] Enoch LXXXIX, 10 and Wisdom of Solomon X, 5.

The few details that are added, and which are peculiar to this literature, reflect contemporaneous needs and interests. The Samaritans wronged him; he did not marry outside the faith; the Hebrew language was given to him and to his seed.

These writings do not really tell about Abraham. They allude to him as though the simple allusion is sufficient for the reader's understanding. It is implicit that he is the great ancestor who abides and whose merit abides. We see that Abraham is implicit, but we do not really see Abraham. His importance to the writers, and by inference to the readers, is such that they feel no need to go into details. Abraham has become intimately part of their assumptions and pre-dispositions.

The author of Jubilees provides as the setting for the birth and wondrous youth of Abraham an agricultural crisis brought on by Mastema, the chief of the malignant spirits.[79] Ravens and birds eat all the seeds which Terah and others plant, with the result that the yield of the earth is only large enough barely to preserve life. Terah at this point married Edna, the daughter of Abram.[80] Our Abraham was named for his grandfather who died before the birth of the baby.[81]

Abraham perceives that all the world is going astray after graven images and uncleanness. His father teaches him writing. At the age of twenty[82] he separates himself from Terah so as to avoid idolatry, and he prays to be spared participation in the errors of his fellowmen.[83] In his fourteenth year Abraham has

[79] Mastema is mentioned in Hos. 9.7–8. In Jubilees X, Noah prays to God that all the evil spirits may be imprisoned so that they cannot exert their dire influence on men. Mastema protests that unless some spirits are left in his control he will be unable to lead men astray. The decision arrived at is to imprison all but a tenth of the evil spirits.

[80] Rabbinic sources name her Emtelai, *B. B.* 91a. On this name and the name Abram assigned to the grandfather, see Ginzberg, *op. cit.* V, 208–209, and Beer, *op. cit.*, 96–97. I cite these henceforth simply as Ginzberg or Beer.

[81] Jub. XI, 11–15.

[82] The rabbis allocate this event to the age one, or three, but usually forty-eight. See below, page 77.

[83] Jub. XI, 16–17.

power over the ravens, and drives them away.[84] By this action Abraham becomes famous throughout Chaldea. Abraham in the next year teaches the people how to make ploughs so that the seeds, buried in the earth, cannot be stolen by the ravens.[85] This narrative is peculiar to Jubilees and does not reappear in rabbinic literature.

In his twenty-fourth year Abraham appeals to Terah to desist from fruitless idolatry and to turn to the true God. Terah replies that he is aware of the truth that Abraham speaks, but that he fears the people who would slay him for desisting from idolatry; he warns Abraham of this danger, enjoining silence on him. When Abraham is sixty he sets fire, in the middle of the night, to the family house. Haran, his brother, rushes in to save the idols and he perishes in the flames.[86]

Terah takes his sons to Haran. When Abraham is seventy-five he sits up all the evening of the New Year to learn from the stars what the New Year would provide in the way of rain. He becomes aware that the heavenly bodies are the servants of God, and that He, not they, controls the rains. Abraham prays to be withheld from the error of going astray by worshiping the heavenly bodies. In reply, the command is delivered by the "angel of the Presence"[87] for Abraham to quit his native land.[88] At God's command the ministering angel teaches Abraham

[84] The incident seems based on Gen. 15.11, the descent of the עיט which Abraham drives away.

[85] Jub. XI, 16–20.

[86] Jub. XII, 1–14. The narrative seems to be derived from a play on 'Ur as synonymous with 'or, fire. The same play underlies a somewhat different rabbinic narrative, of Nimrod's casting Abraham into the fiery furnace from which God saves him; in the latter story Haran is undecided about throwing in his lot with Abraham until after the miraculous rescue; the forces which saved Abraham, however, permitted Haran to die in the fiery furnace. Cf. Ginzberg, I, 198–202. Jubilees does not seem to know the legend of Abraham in the fiery furnace. Possibly both of these legends circulated as expansions of the word 'Ur, and the author of Jubilees preferred the present legend to the one preserved in the rabbis; Isa. 29.22 may be an allusion to Abraham in the fiery furnace.

[87] Ostensibly the author of Jubilees; cf. Jub. I.

[88] Gen. 12.1–3 is quoted, and then there is added that God is Abraham's God and destined to be the God of Abraham's seed, Jub. XII, 24.

Hebrew, which had ceased to be the language since the Babylonian captivity. Abraham takes the books of his fathers, transcribes them, and studies them, receiving help where it is needed from the angel. Abraham busies himself with these books for the six rainy months.[89] Thereafter[90] Abraham informs Terah that he is going to Canaan. Terah blesses him, and asks him to return for him if Abraham should find some land.[91]

Abraham travels, as the biblical account narrates, to Canaan. He comes to the lofty oak[92] where he builds an altar.[93] He is delighted with the details of the agricultural richness of the land.[94] Moving to the mountain,[95] he builds an altar and offers a sacrifice[96] at the new moon of the first month, and proclaims, in calling on the name of God, "Thou, the Eternal God, art my God."[97]

His southward journey[98] is related with the addition of the mention of Hebron and Bealoth.[99]

Three years later, on the coming of famine, he goes to Egypt for five years.[100] The seizure of Sarah is passed over quickly,

[89] Jub. XII, 15–27. This portrayal of Abraham learning Hebrew is as naive a touch of depicting a contemporaneous matter by reading it into Abraham's life as I have encountered. This matter is peculiar to Jubilees. Cf. App. Test. Naph. VIII–X.

[90] The next episode took place in the fifth year of the sixth week, the departure from Haran in the seventh year. It does not seem possible to harmonize these dates with the six months mentioned in Jub. XII, 27.

[91] Jub. XII, 28–30.

[92] This description rests on LXX Gen. 12.6, which MT calls the oak of *More*. This is one of several passages in which it appears that the text we have of Jubilees in places conforms, or has been made to conform, to the LXX. Cf. Charles, II, 4–5.

[93] Jub. XIII, 1–5.

[94] Jub. XIII, 6.

[95] Gen. 12.8.

[96] The Bible says nothing about a sacrifice. Josephus also adds this statement *Ant.* I, VII, 1; see note 230 below.

[97] Jub. XIII, 6–9. The words in quotations are added by Jubilees.

[98] Gen. XII, 9.

[99] Jub. XIII, 10. The rabbis infer from the verse that he journeyed to the site of the Temple, *Gen. R.*, XXXIX.

[100] *Seder Olam* I makes the sojourn three months. Artapanus (In Eusebius, *Praep. Ev.* IX, 18, 420b) makes it twenty years.

without mention of Abraham's statement that she is his sister, and without mention of the gifts given by Pharaoh.[101] Returning to near Bethel[102] Abraham offers a sacrifice to God Who has brought him back in peace.[103]

The quarrel with Lot is skimmed over. Abraham regrets Lot's departure for wicked Sodom because Abraham has no offspring. God tells him[104] that he will have seed which will inherit the land.

The war of the kings is only partly preserved, and what is preserved shows evidence of being greatly compressed.[105] The tithe which Abraham gives Melchizedek, a tithe of first fruits, is ordained by God to Abraham's descendants eternally; the tithe is to be given of seed, wine, oil, cattle and sheep. God gives these tithes to His priests to eat in joy.[106]

Jubilees XV, 1–16 recapitulates the events of Gen. 15 with almost no variations from the biblical account. The LXX is followed in making "Masek" a handmaid.[107] Jubilees adds that the events take place near Hebron, and specifies that Abraham offers the sacrifices on an altar which he builds.[108] The singular 'ayit of MT Gen. 15.11 is replaced with the plural "birds" of the LXX;[109] the tardema of MT Gen. 15.13 is represented by the ecstasis of the LXX.[110] Jubilees portrays Abraham as awakening before the smoke and fire[111] pass between the "pieces."[112] Jubilees adds a conclusion not found in Genesis, that Abraham offers the various animals and birds and the drink offerings as a sacrifice.[113]

---

[101] Jub. XIII, 10–15.   [102] Gen. 13.3.
[103] Jub. 13.16.
[104] Gen. 13.13–17.
[105] Jub. XIII, 22–29.
[106] Jub. XIII, 25–27. The rabbis infer that Abraham gave in addition to the tithe, terumah, deriving this from the harimoti of Gen. 14.22, Gen. R. XLIII. On Abraham as the giver of tithes, see PRE XXVII and Num. R. XII.
[107] Gen. 15.2
[108] Jub. XIV, 10–11.
[109] Jub. XIV, 12.
[110] Jub. XIV, 13.
[111] Gen. 15.17.
[112] Jub. XIV, 17.
[113] Jub. XIV, 19. Jubilees seems to be portraying Abraham in terms of the

The covenant made is a renewal of the covenant made with Noah[114] on Shabuot, which the sons of Noah fail to observe[115] and which Abraham reinstitutes.[116]

Jubilees reproduces in abridged form the story of the union of Abraham with Hagar, but omits the first expulsion of Hagar.[117]

A year later, at Shabuot, Abraham makes his offerings on the altar. God appears to Abraham, enjoins him to be perfect, changes his name from Abram to Abraham, and commands him to circumcise himself and his household. Apart from allocating the incident at Shabuot, Jubilees follows the account in Gen. 17.1–23 faithfully. There is added, however, apparently from the LXX, a command missing in MT, Gen. 17.14, that one not circumcised "on the eighth day" is to be cut off from his people. Jubilees adds to the recapitulation of the account in Genesis a series of observations about circumcision: this command is eternal, and it must take place on the eighth day, and it is a commandment written on the heavenly tablets. One who is not circumcised does not belong to the children of the covenant, and has on him no sign that he is the Lord's. He is a son of destruction, destined to be destroyed from the earth. The angels of the Presence and the angels of Sanctification were created circumcised. The offspring of Ishmael and Esau (apparently even though they practiced circumcision) were not chosen by God to be His people; it was Israel whom He chose. These other peoples have over them spirits who can lead them astray, but Israel is led by God. It is known that the children of Israel will not observe this commandment, but treating their members like Gentiles, will forsake the covenant. There will be no pardon or forgiveness for these.[118] The words are unquestionably directed against the hellenizers of the period. Abraham does what is proper; the hellenizers do not.

contemporaneous Temple worship. The rabbis on the other hand, infer from the passage a variety of revelations of the future made to Abraham, *Gen. R.* XLIV.

[114] Jub. VI, 4–10.
[115] Jub. VI, 18–19.
[116] Jub. XIV, 20.
[117] Jub. XIV, 21–24.
[118] Jub. XV, 25–34.

Jubilees XVI abridges the visit of the three men of Gen.18. It passes lightly over the destruction of Sodom, pausing only long enough to denounce Lot and his daughters for their incest, the result of which is the commandment, engraven in the heavenly tablets, to root out their descendants on the day of condemnation.[119]

Of the long incident of Abimelech in Gen. 20, Jubilees retains only the bare statement of Abraham's moving to Gerar.

The birth of Isaac is compressed from the account in Gen. 21. In being circumcised, Isaac was the first for whom the commandment was properly observed.[120] Even before Isaac was born, the "angel of the Presence" appeared to Abraham to reveal to him that he would be the father of six more sons[121] but that the descendants of all these would be Gentiles, while the offspring of Isaac would be a holy seed: a kingdom, and priests and a holy nation.[122] In joy at the announcement, Abraham celebrated *sukkot*, for a period of seven days.[123] He and his household observed the festival, and there was neither a stranger nor an uncircumcised person with them. Abraham celebrated the festival, as the heavenly tablets ordained, in its due season. It is a festival eternally to be observed.[124]

The account of the banishing of Hagar and Ishmael is rather close to the biblical account.[125] When Ishmael grows up, his

---

[119] Jub. XVI, 8–9. The predominating rabbinic view is one of condemnation of the daughters. Josephus, *Ant.* I, XI, 5 and a comment in *Gen. R.*, LI, however, credit the daughters with a worthy desire, to repopulate what they consider to be an unpopulated world. See below, note 303.

[120] Jub. XVI, 12–15.

[121] Born out of Keturah, Gen. 25.40; Jub. XIX, 11.

[122] Charles so renders the citation of Ex. 19.6; *op. cit.* II, p. 38, and the footnote.

[123] Jub. XVI, 21–31. The manner of celebration departs in some details, in the number of animals sacrificed, from the rules in Num. 29.12–40.

[124] The observance is in part paraphrased from Lev. 23.33–44. Jubilees omits mention of the *shabbaton* (Lev. 23.39) on the eighth day. The biblical account mentions neither the wreaths of Jub. XVI, 30, which Charles, *op. cit.*, II, 39, says is peculiar to Jubilees, nor the morning *haqapot* of Jub. XVI, 31.

[125] Jub. XVII. There are a few minor additions and alterations. Sarah resents Abraham's joy at Ishmael's "playing," Jub. XVII, 4; the basis, Gen. 21.9–10, has a number of variants in the versions, indicating that the

mother gets him an Egyptian wife[126] who bears him a son named Nebaioth.[127]

Jubilees omits the second contact with Abimelech as found in Gen. 21.22–34.

A heavenly scene introduces the events of the binding of Isaac, Gen. 22. Mastema suggests to God that He try Abraham by commanding him to offer Isaac as a sacrifice.[128] God replies that Abraham has successfully withstood all the previous trials[129] and in everything he had been found faithful; his soul had not been impatient and he had been slow to act, for he was faithful and a lover of God.[130] The story of the Binding is quite close to

מצחק of MT was read differently, and probably was more, originally, than this one laconic word. The rabbis infer idolatry from the word, *Tar. Jon. ad loc.* Elsewhere, Ishmael's playfulness is specified as his shooting arrows at Isaac, *Tos. Sotah*, VI. The שׂיחים of Gen. 21.15 becomes an olive tree in Jub. XVII, 10.

[126] *Tar. Jon.* Gen. 21.21, names her Fatima. As Ginzberg V, 247 points out, *PRE* XXX gives the two wives of Ishmael, in rabbinic tradition, the names of Aisha and Fatima, names borne by Mohamed's wife and daughter.

[127] Gen. 25.13. It seems strange that the author of Jubilees should mention only this one son of Ishmael by name, and to do so in apparently turning from his context in Gen. 21 to Gen. 25. Perhaps the reason lies in the contemporaneous importance of the Nabateans. I am at a loss to explain the etymology which Jubilees provides for the name. See, also, below, page 71, note 320 on *Ant.* I, XII, 4.

[128] The story is paralleled in general in *Sanhedrin* 89b. Some details there differ: it is Satan rather than Mastema; it is asserted that Abraham had enjoyed everything without ever offering even a turtle-dove or pigeon. This version is unacquainted with, or else rejects, the view of Jubilees that Abraham had offered sacrifices.

[129] At this point the author enumerates six trials. The "Binding" would be a seventh. In Jub. XIX, 8, the death of Sarah is listed as Abraham's tenth trial. The rabbis speak frequently of ten trials, though the list varies from passage to passage, Abot V, 2 and elsewhere. See below, page 87 and Ginzberg, V, 218.

[130] Jub. XVII, 15–18. The epithet "lover of God," or "friend of God," Jub. XIX, 9, as applied to Abraham is not found in MT Gen. 18.17, though it is found in *Tar. Jer. ad loc.* It is absent, too, from LXX Gen. 18.17 in the versions which we now possess. Philo presents this problem, that he cites the verse twice, adding to MT in one case *Sob.* 56 the epithet "friend of God," and in the other case, *LA* III, 27 "servant of God." MT gives a basis for the epithet in II Chron. 20.7, and Isa. 41.8, but in each of these cases we encounter not φιλόθεός but the verb ἠγάπησα. φιλόθεός then, is wanting in LXX.

the account in Gen. 22. The two young men[131] are left, considerately, near a well of water.[132] Where Gen. 22.9 reads "they arrived at the place which God had told him," Jubilees XVIII, 7 reads "he drew near the mount of God."[133] The angel of the Presence and Mastema stand in the presence of God at the crucial moment; God instructs the angel to call to Abraham and to prevent the slaughter.[134] The date of the event is apparently Passover.[135]

Jubilees XIX, 1–9 compresses the narrative of the death of Sarah and the purchase of the double cave.[136] The death of Sarah is called Abraham's tenth trial.[137] Jubilees XIX, 9 records that Abraham did not claim the plot as he might have done as part of the divine promise, but begged for a place.[138]

Where then did Philo and James get the epithet? Ryle, *Philo and Holy Scripture*, 1895, 74–75, conjectures that a now lost version of the LXX contained the epithet; the phrase "servant of God" would be a deliberate substitution in the interest of avoiding undue familiarity. Ryle's explanation may be well-founded, but it does not indicate how any epithet either came into the verse, or coming in, was eliminated in the extant LXX. That both *Tar. Jer.* and Philo read a longer verse than is now found in both MT and LXX may point to a scribal omission from MT, and that the LXX was later corrected to the short version of the verse. But this is, by and large, unrewarding conjecture. MT gives adequate basis for the epithet; and while LXX lacks the exact epithet, the idea is clearly expressed. It is, accordingly, not surprising that the epithet is found in Philo and in James. Cf. Ginzberg, V, 207–208.

[131] Gen. 22.5.

[132] Jubilees XVIII, 4.

[133] Verse 13 identifies the hill as Mount Zion. This identification is biblical in basis, II Chron. 3.1. Josephus and the rabbis also make the identification; see Ant. I, XIII, 2; *Gen. R.* XLV and *Sifre Deut.* XVIII.

[134] Jub. XVIII, 10. Verse 12 mentions the ram, but says nothing about the atoning power of the horn for later generations, a motif frequent among the rabbis. Jub. XVIII, 16 inserts "Go in peace," possibly from I Sam. 1.17.

[135] Jubilees does not here mention Passover by name. Earlier, the calling of Abraham is allocated to the 12th day of the first month; three days later would make it the fourteenth or fifteenth of the month, *Nisan.* I do not find any similar view in rabbinic literature. This depiction of Abraham observing the offering of a sort of paschal sacrifice would complete the list of the festivals which Jubilees is asserting that Abraham observed. Jubilees assigns the length of the festival to the seven days occupied by Abraham's going and coming, Jub. XIX, 18–19.

[136] Ephron is not mentioned at all.

[137] Jub. XIX, 8. See above, note 129.

[138] So, too, the Rabbis, *MHG* to Gen. 23.4; *Tan. Wa-yera* II, extols

The lengthy Chapter 24 of Genesis is summarized in one verse, that Abraham took a wife for Isaac named Rebekkah.[139] The marriage of Abraham and Keturah and their six children is briefly related.[140]

Jubilees now forsakes the biblical order to insert a number of different items. The remainder of the Genesis material is found as follows: Gen. 25.5–6, the giving of gifts to the children;[141] and the death[142] of Abraham greatly elaborated.[143]

Reverting now to the material which is not a paraphrase of Genesis but free in composition, Abraham was still alive at the birth of Jacob and Esau.[144] Abraham observed the deeds of

Abraham's humility in offering to buy this land already virtually his by the divine promise.

[139] Jub. XIX, 10.

[140] Jub. XIX, 11. The verse states that Hagar had died before Sarah; Charles *op. cit.*, II, 41, interprets the statement to be an explanation of why Abraham did not take Hagar back. *Tar. Jer.* Gen. 25.1 and *PRE* XXX, however, aver that Hagar and Keturah were the same person; in marrying Keturah the rabbinic Abraham was taking Hagar back.

[141] Gen. 25.6, says only that Abraham sent these children eastward. Jub. XX, 11 tells that the sons of Ishmael and the sons of Keturah went together and dwelt "from Paran to the entrance into Babylon in the land towards the east facing the desert." These mingled with each other and their name was called Arabs and Ishmaelites.

[142] Gen. 25.7–10.

[143] Jub. XXIII, 1–8. The death of Abraham occurs immediately after he gives a blessing to Jacob, with Jacob lying asleep in his bosom. Jacob wakes, realizes Abraham is dead, and runs and tells Rebekkah. She goes to Isaac, in the night, and tells him. The three go together, Jacob bearing a lamp. Isaac falls on the face of his father and kisses him. The sound of their wailing reaches to the home of Abraham where Ishmael, hearing the sound, immediately goes to Abraham and joins in the weeping. The lamentation over Abraham lasts for forty days. The mourning is participated in by the household and the sons of Keturah. From Noah on the life-span had become shorter and men had grown old quickly because of wickedness, but Abraham had a fullness of days. I have found no rabbinic parallels to these additions, though the decrease in the span of life is mentioned in Josephus, *Ant.* I, VI, 5.

[144] Jub. XIX, 13. Rabbinic tradition preserves Abraham alive until Esau is fifteen, *B. B.* 16b. The soup of Gen. 25.29 was cooked on the day of Abraham's death as a meal of condolence for Isaac, *ibid.*, and *Tar. Jon. ad loc.* Abraham died that day, before his time, so as not to be alive when Esau raped a betrothed girl, killed a man, denied the existence of God, repudiated resurrection of the dead, and despised his primogeniture, *B. B.* 16b. Jub.

Esau, and thereby knew that his name and seed would be "called in Jacob."[145] The preference for Jacob which Scripture assigns to Rebekkah is in Jubilees only mediated by Rebekkah, but stems from Abraham.[146] Since Abraham knows that Rebekkah too prefers Jacob, he commands her to watch over Jacob more than over Esau, since Jacob is to be in Abraham's stead on the earth.[147] The blessings which Abraham inherited from Shem, Noah, Enoch, and the other ancestors are to go to Jacob.[148] Abraham summons Jacob and, in the presence of Rebekkah, blesses him in that Jacob, and then his seed, are to receive those things promised to Abraham; Mastema will not rule over Jacob and his seed; God will be a Father to Jacob, as the first-born son, and to the people forever.[149]

Abraham then summons Ishmael and his twelve sons, Isaac and his two sons, and the six sons of Keturah and their sons. He commands them to observe the way of the Lord, to work righteousness and love each his neighbor, and to do justice and righteousness in the land. They should circumcise their sons, and refrain from fornication and uncleanness, lest they meet the fate of the Sodomites.[150] He charges them not to worship idols and not to make graven images, for these are useless, but to worship God, the source of blessings.[151]

Some five years later[152] Abraham speaks to Isaac. He is aware, he tells him, of his approaching death, since he is now 175 years old. All his life he has hated idols and those who worship them. He has tried always to do the will of the true

XIX, 14 tells that Esau was fierce, that he learned war, and that he was illiterate; Jacob, however, learned to write.

[145] Jub. XIX, 16.

[146] Jub. XIX, 15; Abraham loves Jacob; but Gen. XXV, 28 says that Rebekkah loved Jacob; both agree that Isaac loved Esau. The motive of the alteration is probably the aggrandizement of Jacob by associating him with the great Patriarch instead of with a woman.

[147] Jub. XIX, 16–19.

[148] Jub. XIX, 20–25.

[149] Jub. XIX, 26–31.

[150] Jub. XX, 1–6.

[151] Jub. XX, 7–10. The blessing is a mosaic of Scriptural passages: Ex. 20.5 and 23.25, and Deut. 7.13; 28.8.

[152] Jub. XXI, 1.

God Who shows no partiality to men but Who righteously executes justice. Isaac should accordingly not turn to idols or graven images. He should eat no blood, neither of animals nor of birds.[153] On slaying a victim as a peace offering, the blood should be poured out on the altar. The details of the sacrificial procedures are enumerated.[154] These details are written in the books of the forefathers,[155] Shem and Noah. Attention should be paid to the use of the salt of the covenant[156] and only the appropriate wood [157] should be used with the sacrifices. Washing must precede and follow the offering of sacrifices.[158] The disposition of the blood must be handled punctiliously.[159] Abraham then urges Isaac to abstain from the ways of other men, lest sin cause God to turn His face away. By doing the will of God Isaac will receive a blessing from God, and neither Abraham's name nor his name will be forgotten in the earth.[160]

The same year Isaac and Ishmael come to Abraham at Beer-Sheba to observe Shabuot. Isaac had many possessions at Beer-Sheba, and he used to go there both to see these and to visit his father. Abraham rejoices to have his two sons together. Isaac offers a burnt offering and a thanks offering; Rebekkah has made new cakes of the new grain and given them to Jacob to take to his grandfather; she has sent, also, some first fruits, that Abraham might bless these before his death. Abraham eats and drinks and blesses God, thanking Him for being able to see that day. He then prays that God's mercy and peace may rest on him and on his descendants and that these may be a chosen nation. He calls Jacob and blesses him, praying that Jacob may have righteous seed whom God will sanctify. He asks that many nations may serve Jacob's seed. He wishes his

[153] This legislation is found in Lev. 7.26.

[154] These accord with Lev. 3.7–10.

[155] The notion that Abraham inherited ancestral books is found also in *PRE*, VII.

[156] Lev. 2.13.

[157] Charles, *op. cit.*, II, 44 explains this as an expansion in specific details of Ex. 25.5 and 10. Jubilees appears to be stricter than *Tamid* II, 3.

[158] Based on Ex. 30.19–21.

[159] Based on Lev. 6.20 and 17.13–14, and Num. 35.33.

[160] Jub. XXI, 24.

own blessing to pass on to Jacob, and that his own covenant be renewed with him. Jacob is enjoined not to eat with Gentiles but to separate himself from them, and not to be associated in their works which are unclean. Gentiles offer sacrifices to the dead and worship evil spirits, and they eat over graves. They have no true understanding for they worship idols. Jacob must not take a wife from among the Canaanites. Jacob is charged to perpetuate the house of Abraham.[161]

Isaac conveys to Jacob the blessing given to Abraham and to him.[162]

Another dozen or so scattered allusions to Abraham, of no special significance, are to be found in Jubilees. Two, however, might be mentioned. Joseph rejects the offer of Potiphar's wife because Abraham has prohibited fornication;[163] Judah's wish to have Tamar burnt for being a prostitute, accorded with the judgment of Abraham.[164]

The Abraham portrayed in Jubilees is greatly concerned with the encroaching Hellenism of the period in which the book was written. There is the ever-present enticement of idolatry. Gentiles are in the immediate vicinity, and it is necessary that one should not eat with them and surely not intermarry with them. The way of the Gentiles is an abomination, and the imitation of their practices can lead to sharing in the abomination. Indeed, some disloyal Jews follow the Gentiles and abstain from circumcision. The remedy for avoiding their contamination is a rigid separation from them, and the strictest kind of adherence to the ancient laws of ritual purity, which are to be found in the Mosaic Law of ritual observance. Abraham observed and enjoined the Mosaic Law. He observed the three festivals joyfully. Moreover, Abraham learned Hebrew and transcribed the ancient books. He is the model for those who would stand firm against the temptation of the Greeks.

[161] Jub. XXII, especially v. 24.
[162] Jub. XXVI, 23–24 is a paraphrase of Gen. 27.27–29. The transmission of the blessings is added by Jubilees. It reappears in Jub. XXVII, 11.
[163] Jub. XXXIX, 6.
[164] Jub. XLI, 28.

The pseudonymous work, *The Antiquities of Philo*, mentions Abraham only *passim*. It provides a series of legends centering mostly on Abraham's career before his migration from home. As Pseudo-Philo relates the story, Abraham was one of twelve who refused to obey the command of Nimrod to build the Tower of Babel. The other eleven fled to the hills. The populace, angry at Abraham, cast him into the furnace along with the bricks. An earthquake, brought on by God, caused the fire in the furnace to consume all those near-by, to the number of 83,500. Abraham was unhurt; he summoned the other eleven to return in safety.[165]

The Tower was nevertheless built. God therefore determined to scatter the people, but he chose Abraham from their midst, and led him to the land selected before the flood and not destroyed by it. The language of the people was confused and the people were scattered.[166]

The Apocalypse of Abraham, as its title indicates, presents a rather typical apocalypse centered around Abraham and developed by embellishments of Gen. 15.[167] Abraham and an angel, Joel, ride to heaven on the wings of the pigeon and the turtledove of Gen. 15.9. Abraham has revealed to him not only the various sights of the seven heavens, of Hell and the Garden of Eden, but he sees the history of the past and the unfolding of the future. His vision includes the punishment of the heathens who oppress Israel; the woes of the premessianic times; and then the Elect One who, when God sounds the trumpet, gathers Israel from among the peoples. At that time those who stood

---

[165] *Antiquities of Philo*, VI, 3–18.

[166] *Ibid.*, VII, 1–5. Pseudo-Philo then seems to lose interest in Abraham, telescoping a few other matters into a very brief account. He mentions the marriage with Hagar, the birth of Ishmael and the twelve sons of Ishmael, Lot's dwelling in Sodom; God's appearance to Abraham and the promise that his seed would inherit the land. The Abraham section concludes with the birth of Isaac. Only the legend given above is dwelled on. Cf. *Antiquities of Philo*, VI–VIII.

[167] The apocalypse is Part Two of the book. Part One is still another legend of the youth of Abraham and of his merry adventures with the idols of his father, Terah, not unlike the legend summarized above, note 86.

firm will rejoice over the downfall of those who have turned to idols.[168]

The interest in the book is in the revelation to Abraham, and not in Abraham himself. The central character could just as readily have been Moses or Isaac.

The Testament of Abraham, probably an earlier book,[169] is an expansion in the haggadic manner of the foretaste of the world to come which Abraham enjoyed before his death. Michael is despatched to gather in Abraham's soul, but Abraham declines to give it up. He is permitted to ride in the heavenly chariot and to look down on the earth beneath. The trip has to be interrupted, because Abraham commands Michael to destroy sinners. God rebukes Abraham, for God prefers that the sinner repent and live. Accordingly, Abraham is taken to the gate of Paradise to see what happens to souls at death. A narrow gate is prepared for the just, and Abraham fears that his bodily stature is too large for the entrance, but God assures him that he may enter unhindered, as may those who are like Abraham. A wide door is available for those who are not just. Recording angels scan the written accounts of a man's deeds in an enormous book, and they weigh the man in the balance. Those whose good overbalances the evil enter into Paradise; the others go into Gehenna. Abraham is confronted with the instance of a man who required only one more meritorious deed to qualify him for Paradise. Abraham intercedes for the man and he is allowed to enter Paradise.

Restored to earth, Abraham again refuses to surrender his soul. The angel of death appears to him in the guise of a young and beautiful angel, but Abraham discerns his true appearance. Indeed, a glimpse of the angel as he actually is brings death to seven thousand of Abraham's slaves; these are restored to life, however, by Abraham's prayers.

Abraham's passing takes place in a dream. Michael and a

---

[168] Cf. Box, *The Apocalypse of Abraham*, 1918, and Ginzberg in *JE*, I, 91–92, "Abraham, Apocalypse of." Ginzberg dates the book as coming from the end of the first Christian century. A number of Christian interpolations have been inserted into the book.

[169] Cf. Ginzberg in *JE* I, 96.

host of angels wrap him in linen made in heaven and anoint his body with ointments which come from Paradise. His body is laid to rest at Mamre three days later, but Abraham's soul is taken to Paradise to the abode prepared for him, for Isaac, and for Jacob. In this abode there are no traces of trouble or grief or sighing, but only peace, rejoicing, and eternal life.

Two hellenistic Jewish fragments agree that Abraham lived in Babylon. One account summarizes his early career by telling that his genealogy goes back to the giants there. All of these were destroyed by God for their impiety except Belos; he built a tower and dwelled in it, and the tower was named after him. Abraham learned astrology; first he went to Phoenicia and taught it to the Phoenicians, and then he went to Egypt.[170]

A longer account, from a writer whom Eusebius calls Eupolemos,[171] begins with the founding of the city of Babylon by the giants who are saved from the flood and who live in the well-known tower. After the tower fell through the action of God, the giants were scattered throughout the whole earth. In the tenth generation, it is said, in the city of Kamarine of Babylon, Abraham was born.[172] Others call the city Οὐρίης.[173] Abraham surpassed all men in the nobility of his birth and wisdom.

---

[170] Eusebius, *Praep. Ev.* IX, 18. Freudenthal, *Hellenistische Studien*, I, 82–89, believes that this "anonymous" fragment is in reality an excerpt from or an abbreviation of Pseudo-Eupolemos, but that it became confused in Alexander Polyhistor's hands and that he failed to recognize it for the excerpt that it is.

[171] Freudenthal, I, 82–89, shows that this author and another Eupolemos are two different people. Our present author is, as will be seen, a Samaritan; the other Eupolemos is a Jew. The present author is therefore called Pseudo-Eupolemos by Freudenthal; so, too, Stearns, *Fragments from Graeco-Jewish Writers*, 67.

[172] The text first ascribes his birth to the tenth generation, and promptly states that it was in the thirteenth. Freudenthal suggests that a phrase "or, as others say," may have been omitted through a scribal error, I, 94–95. Freudenthal notes a similarity in idea to the quotation in Josephus *Ant.* I, VII, 2 from Berosus.

[173] The biblical Ur. The account adds that the name, translated, means "city of the Chaldeans." Freudenthal conjectures that *'ur* has been confused with *'ir*, city, I, 87–88 fn.

He founded Chaldean astrology; he was well-pleasing to God because of his piety. At God's command he went to Phoenicia to settle; there he taught the Phoenicians the movements of the sun and the moon and all other things. He pleased their monarch greatly.[174]

Later the Armenians made war on the Phoenicians,[175] and in their conquest they captured his nephew. Abraham and his household came to the rescue, and there ensued a deliverance of the captives and a capture of the children and wives of the enemy. The oldest[176] (of those released) suggested that Abraham keep the property but release the people. Abraham, however, did not choose to take advantage of the unfortunate. He accepted the repayment of the food of his young men, but restored the spoils. Then he settled near Argarizin,[177] which translated means "mountain of the lofty."[178] He received gifts[179] from Melchizedek, the priest of God and king.

When a famine broke out, Abraham moved to Egypt with all his household and dwelled there. The Egyptian king married his wife, Abraham saying that she was his sister. The king was not able to consort with her because his people and his household were stricken with disease. Priests, summoned, told him that the woman was not unmarried.[180] The king restored her to Abraham when the priests revealed that she was Abraham's wife. Abraham dwelled in Heliopolis among the priests, and he taught them many things, astrology and other matters. He explained to them that the Babylonians had founded these studies, and that they went back to Enoch, who discovered them, not the Egyptians. The Babylonians say that first there

---

[174] This is unique to Pseudo-Eupolemos.

[175] Pseudo-Eupolemos relates the events of Gen. 14 as though they occurred prior to the events of Gen. 12.10–20.

[176] In Gen. 14.21, it is the king of Sodom.

[177] Mount Gerizim. This section is persuasive proof that Pseudo-Eupolemos was a Samaritan; cf. Freudenthal I, 89.

[178] The basis of the etymology is most uncertain. Cf. Freudenthal I, 87–88.

[179] An allusion to the wine and bread of Gen. 14.18. The account omits mention of the tithes which Abraham gave.

[180] Josephus likewise introduces the priests who are not found in the biblical account, *Ant.* I, VIII, 1.

was born Belus, who is Cronus. His children were Belus and Cham.[181] The latter begat Canaan, the father of the Phoenicians, and Chous[182] whom the Greeks call Asbolos, the father of the Ethiopians, and the brother of Mestraeim,[183] the father of the Egyptians. The Greeks say that Atlas discovered astrology. Atlas and Enoch are the same person. Enoch's son was Methuselah who learned everything through angels of God and who taught that to us.[184]

A third fragment, of Artapanus, derives the name "Hebrews" from Abraham.[185] Abraham went with all his household to Pharethothes the king of the Egyptians, and taught him astrology. He remained there twenty[186] years and then returned to Syria. Many of those who went with him remained in Egypt because of the prosperity of the land.[187]

A fourth fragment, by Demetrios, gives a brief summary of the events of Gen. 22. It is so abridged that it is of no significance for our study beyond the fact that it shows that Demetrios retold the incident.[188]

The fifth fragment comes from a prophet Cleodemus who is also known as Malchus.[189] Josephus cites from Cleodemus in support of the Mosaic contention that descendants of Abraham by Keturah occupied Lybia and that Africa is named after one of them. Cleodemus mentions three of the sons who gave their

---

[181] Ham, the son of Noah.

[182] Gen. 10.6.

[183] *Ibid.*

[184] Eus., *Praep. Ev.*, IX, 17.

[185] Moses is identified as Hermes, by the same writer, Eus., *Praep. Ev.*, IX, 27. Cf. Freudenthal I, 153–154.

[186] In Jub. XIII, 11, the sojourn is five years.

[187] Eusebius, *Praep. Ev.*, IX, 18. The apologetic note in attributing the antiquity of the unbroken Jewish settlement in Egypt to the time of Abraham is a mark of the lack of subtlety of Artapanus; cf. Freudenthal, I, 143–144.

[188] Eusebius, *Praep. Ev.*, IX, 19. Demetrios tells only that God commanded Abraham to sacrifice Isaac. Abraham led the lad to the mountain, built a pyre, and put Isaac on it. As he was intending to slaughter him he was prevented by an angel who provided him with a ram. Abraham took Isaac down from the pyre and offered the ram.

[189] Josephus, *Ant.* I, XV.

names to countries: Sures[190] to Assyria; Japhres[191] to Aphra, and Apheras to Africa. These latter joined Heracles[192] in his campaign against Libya and Antaeus. Heracles married the daughter of Apheras and begot a son Diodorus, who in turn begot a son Sophon; from Sophon comes the name Sophakes by which barbarians are called.[193]

The outstanding note of the mention of Abraham in the fragments of Graeco-Jewish writers is the apologetic. Abraham's native place is identified as Babylon, probably because it was a more definite allocation than Ur or Chaldea. His superiority over others is described in terms of his high birth and wisdom; it is averred that his piety pleased God.

It accords with the rabbis that Abraham knew astrology. The rabbis, however, do not, as do the Greek writers, depict Abraham as teaching astrology to the other peoples.[194] He even teaches astrology to the king of Egypt and to the Egyptian priests. Neither the Egyptians nor the Greeks discovered astrology; Enoch, whom the Greeks call Atlas, was the true discoverer. Without the mediation of Abraham, the Egyptians would not have known the science.[195] Against the implication

[190] *Ashurim*, Gen. 25.3.

[191] The identification with the particular biblical son is uncertain. Gen. 25.4, mentioned Efah and Efer.

[192] Freudenthal I, 133–135, identifies Heracles as a Phoenician God, and not as the son of Jupiter and Alcmene.

[193] It is to be recalled that in I Maccabees XII, 10 and 21, and II Maccabees V, 9, the Spartans and the Lacedaemonians are held to be of the γένος of Abraham.

[194] That two of the sources portay Abraham as teaching the Phoenicians is regarded by Freudenthal I, 96–97, as supporting evidence for the view that the author (or authors) are Samaritans, on the basis that the Phoenicians were regarded by the Samaritans as kin, *Ant.* XI, VIII, 6 and XII, V, 5. That Pseudo-Eupolemos, almost certainly and Cleodemus, probably, were Samaritans does not materially affect the conception of Abraham, though the fact colors the writings perceptibly; Samaritans shared the necessity for apologetic explanations that Jews felt, and the apologetic message took the same form of pride in the antiquity of the tradition and a claim for the true priority in publicly approved endeavors.

[195] Nor, in the view of Josephus, *Ant.* I, VIII, 2 would the Greeks, since they learned it from the Egyptians.

of the biblical account that the Egyptian sojourn was a brief one,[196] Pseudo-Eupolemos portrays Abraham as settling in Helio-polis at least long enough to teach the priests science, while Artapanus makes it twenty years, and even denies that all those who came with Abraham left with him; the Jews have dwelled continuously in Egypt since Abraham's time.

It is impossible to know, because of the scantiness of material preserved, whether certain of the Biblical episodes, such as circumcision and the covenant of Gen. 15, were deliberately omitted by the authors, or omitted circumstantially by Alex-ander, or by those who read him. It is useless to speculate on the point.

What material on Abraham is preserved, however, is almost entirely apologetic in purpose. Even the interest in the extraction of related peoples is apologetic in intent, as demonstrating the pre-eminence of Abraham both with respect to his antiquity and with respect to the achievements of his various descendants. The writers appear to be enhancing their own origin by pointing to the common extraction of other ancient and eminent peoples. Insofar as one can see, there are no specifically "Jewish" qualities to Abraham; as presented he is quite intelligible to Greeks. As the progenitor of the Jews, he is their property, but his signifi-cance extends beyond the Jews; his achievements benefit other peoples.

The mentions of Abraham are few in Fourth Maccabees. The book illustrates, through the story of Hannah and her seven sons, the power of εὐσεβὴς λογισμός, pious reason, to control the passions and to produce in the individual the four cardinal virtues, φρόνησις, δικαιοσύνη, ἀνδρεία and σωφρο-σύνη. Λογισμός[197] is defined as the mind preferring with right reason the life of wisdom.[198] Wisdom is the knowledge of things

---

[196] Three months, in the rabbinic view, *Seder Olam*, I.

[197] IV Maccabees, I, 1–6.

[198] *Ibid.* I, 15. There are some textual difficulties to the passage which seem readily to fade when the various versions are consulted; cf. Swete, *The Old Testament in Greek*, 1930, III, 730, *ad loc*. The case endings of the nouns in the versions vary, so that some ambiguity results as to what words go

divine and human, and their causes.[199] It is the instruction
(παιδία) of the Law, through which we learn divine things
reverently and human things profitably.[200]

Of the four virtues, the dominant one is φρόνησις; it controls
the πάθη, pleasure and pain and their derivatives, for reason
is the master of the passions and the guide of the virtues.[201]
Σωφροσύνη is the repression of desires; it is that which moves
a man to abstain from eating those things prohibited by the
Law.[202] Ἀνδρεία enables one to endure pain, while δικαιοσύνη
teaches one to act fairly and piously, to worship only the truly
existent God.[203]

The Law is divine and there is no more forceful necessity
than obedience to the Law.[204] Even if the Law were not divine,
Jews should obey it to maintain their reputation for piety, since
the philosophy of the Law accords with εὐλογιστία.[205] The
author's viewpoint, then, is quite clear. The Law could be
obeyed on the ground that its philosophy would show that it
accorded with reason; but the true basis for obedience to it is
that it is a divine Law. The Law is the prescription for the
conquest of the passions and for obtaining the cardinal virtues.

The primary illustration of the thesis that the Law leads to
the conquest of the passions is the narrative of the events of
the Maccabean revolt. The author, however, turns to Abraham,
Isaac, and Jacob, as proof of his contentions. He has illustrated
how the priest Eleazer, trained in the knowledge of the Law
and eminent in philosophy[206] has through pious reason conquered

together. I follow here R. B. Townshend in Charles II, 668. "Right reason"
is ὀρθὸς λόγος.

[199] The definition is attributed by Plutarch to the Stoics in *Plac. Phil.* I, 1.

[200] IV Maccabees, I, 16–17.

[201] *Ibid.*, I, 18–30.

[202] *Ibid.*, I, 31–35.

[203] *Ibid.*, V, 21 ff.

[204] *Ibid.*, V, 16. Townshend in Charles II, 672, renders πολιτεύεσθαι in
terms of the law "of our country." There is no basis in the verse for this phrase
which seems to me unnecessarily to localize the Torah as a Palestinian force;
the author seems to me to be speaking about all Jews, wherever they are, and
not about the government of Palestine. The rendering is infelicitous.

[205] *Ibid.*, V, 16–22.

[206] *Ibid.*, V, 4.

pain and abided by the Law even to the point of death.[207] It may be contended, says the author, that not all men can master their passions. Those alone who make piety their primary thought with the whole heart are able to control the passions of the flesh. Such faithful people do not die to God but live to Him, as was the case with Abraham, Isaac and Jacob. It is not a contradiction that some people, through the weakness of their reason, succumb to their passions. But if a person follows the whole rule of philosophy piously and trusts in God, through his piety he does conquer his passions.[208]

Hannah, like Abraham, was not moved from her purpose by the passion of love for her children.[209] Her choice of death for her sons called to mind the reverential courage of Abraham whose true daughter she was.[210] She urged her sons to be true to God and to endure all pain for His sake, as Abraham hastened to sacrifice Isaac, and as Isaac did not shrink when he saw the knife in his father's hand.[211] The sons, too, knew that men who die for God live to God, as do Abraham, Isaac, and Jacob.[212] The majesty of her action is the greater in that her sons were descendants of Abraham.[213]

Hannah and her sons were gathered to the place of the ancestors, having received pure and immortal souls.[214] Abraham, Isaac, and Jacob are alive to receive and praise those who die for the keeping of the Law.[215]

A true son of Abraham endures torture without flinching.[216] Children born of the seed of Abraham obey the Law.[217] Sons of Abraham cannot play counterfeit parts. They live by the truth, even to old age, and, as sons of Abraham, they must be ready to die nobly for the sake of the Law.[218]

---

[207] *Ibid.* VI, 30.
[208] *Ibid.* VII, 17–22.
[209] *Ibid.* XIV, 13–20.
[210] *Ibid.* XV, 28.
[211] *Ibid.*, XVI, 18–20.
[212] *Ibid.* XVI, 25.
[213] *Ibid.*, XVII, 6.
[214] *Ibid.*, XVIII, 20–24.
[215] *Ibid.* XIII, 17.
[217] *Ibid.* XVIII, 1.

[216] *Ibid.* IX, 21.
[218] *Ibid.* VI, 17–22.

The mentions of Abraham (and the other patriarchs) are quite incidental in IV Maccabees. He is the model after whom the protagonists of the narrative fashion their own actions. The things that they do are the things which Abraham before them did. This achievement is not directly stated as observance of the Law; the illustrations derived from Abraham are his unswerving purpose, his reverential courage, and his obedience. That pious reason in controlling the passions leads to the cardinal virtues is true of the actions of Abraham and true also of the Law; but this equation, though implicit, is our own and not explicitly that of the author.

Josephus introduces Abraham with a statement about his forebears; and he adds that Abram was the tenth generation from Noah.[219] He tells how many years after the flood the birth of Abraham takes place.[220] Terah is seventy when Abraham is born.

Abram has two brothers, Nahor and Haran. Haran left a son, Lot, and two daughters, Sarah and Milcan.[221] Abraham marries Sarah and Nahor marries Milcan. Haran has died in Ur of the Chaldees, where his sepulchre is still to be seen. Terah has come to hate Chaldea because of Haran's death there.[222] Josephus comments, about the age of Terah at his death

[219] So, too, Abot, V, 2.

[220] The mss. disagree. Most of them read 993 years, apparently the true reading; others read 292 years, apparently a correction to accord with MT; the LXX yields 1072 years. Cf. Weill, Oeuvres complètes de F. Josèphe, I, 34.

[221] Sarah is thus Abraham's niece. The rabbis similarly identify Iscah, Gen. 11.29, with Sarah, Meg. 14a: Iscah means "seer" and the name proves that Sarah was a prophet. The statements conflict with Gen. 20.12, which identifies Sarah as the half-sister of Abraham.

[222] Josephus seems to indicate that he has fuller information which he is not supplying. Perhaps Josephus knows the legends of Abraham's youth, which involve Haran, either in the form of Jubilees, in which Haran perishes in trying to save some idols from the fire, Jub. XII, 14; or in the rabbinic form of Haran's being cast into the fiery furnace from which Abraham was rescued, Tar. Jon. to Gen. 11.28. The motive ascribed here for the departure is peculiar to Josephus. For other views see Judith, V, 9 and the stories of Nimrod and Abraham as reproduced in Ginzberg, I, 185–203. Philo assumed that the call of Gen. 12 comes in Ur; he makes no allusion in De Abrahamo to the events of

in Haran in Mesopotamia[223] at 205 years, that the decrease in the ages of the patriarchs had now begun, and reached the norm of 120 as in the case of Moses.[224] Josephus adds a genealogy to show the descent of Rebekkah.[225]

Abram adopts[226] Lot since he has no legitimate son, and he takes Lot and Sarah to Canaan. Josephus ascribes his migration to a divine command, but he reproduces almost none of the contents of Gen. 12.1–3. Abraham is a man of ready intelligence in all matters, persuasive with his hearers, and infallible in his conclusions. He has begun to have conceptions of virtue loftier than those of the rest of mankind, and has determined to change and improve the ideas current concerning God. He first has dared to proclaim God one, and to declare that if any other thing[227] helped a man's welfare, this was due to God's command and not to any inherent capacity in itself. Abraham has made this inference from the irregularity in the movements of the heavenly bodies, the irregularity proving that these are subject to a higher power.[228] These opinions have roused the Chaldeans

Gen. 11.26–32. The difference seems to be that Josephus indicates a knowledge of legends about Abraham's youth; Philo gives no indication of such knowledge.

[223] Mesopotamia is not mentioned at this place in MT or LXX. I take it to be a place-name which would be known to Greeks.

[224] Cf. Gen. 6.2 and Deut. 34.7. The rabbis, too, associate the age of Moses with Gen. 6.2, *Gen. R.* XXVI. The notion that the age span had begun to diminish is found also in Jub. XXIII, 9; see above, note 143.

[225] *Ant.* I, VI, 5.

[226] Peculiar to Josephus, the term seems selected for Greek readers.

[227] I prefer to render τι by "thing" rather than Thackeray's "being," IV, 77.

[228] The notion that Abraham arrived at the knowledge of the existence of God by celestial observations is found both in Jub. XII, 17 and among the Rabbis, *Gen. R.* XXXIX. Peculiar to Josephus is the notion that this inference stemmed from the irregularity of the heavenly movements. Philo's view is significantly different from Josephus'; Philo scorns astronomical observation as a possible means of inferring the existence of God, and he portrays Abraham as abandoning this kind of foolishness in favor of learning the existence of God by an analogy: just as there exists a mind in man so must there be a mind in the universe, *Abr.* 71 ff. Josephus, the rabbis, Jubilees, and Philo, unite in portraying Abraham as diverging from the beliefs of his environment, and they unite in deriding the worship of celestial objects as deities. But the manner of Abraham's divergence seems to portray a range: The rabbis simply assert

and the other Mesopotamians against him, so that Abraham, with the will and help of God, determines to emigrate, and he settles in Canaan.[229] Josephus adds to the statement of Gen. 12.8, which depicts Abraham as only building an altar, the statement that he offered a sacrifice.[230]

Josephus then turns to two historians, Berosus and Nicolas of Damascus, for proof that Abraham is a well-known person.[231]

Next Josephus recounts the sojourn in Egypt. Josephus adds to the Biblical account that Abraham hears of the prosperity of the Egyptians.[232] He has a motive in addition to obtaining food. He wants to visit the priests and hear their discourses about the gods; he intends either to be convinced by their superior doctrine or else to convert them to his own better doctrine.[233] As Josephus tells the story, Abraham knows of the Egyptians' frenzy for women[234] and it is for this reason and in view of Sarah's beauty, that he fears for his life and pretends to be her brother. Pharaoh is not satisfied with the reports he hears about her, but he wants both to see her and to lay hands on her.[235] God thwarts this criminal passion by an outbreak of disease[236]

that Abraham saw something anterior to celestial objects; Josephus gives an attempted explanation of what it was that Abraham observed; Philo denies the assertion of both Josephus and the rabbis in favor of an entirely different process. See below, note 48.

[229] The enmity of the Chaldeans was noted above. Josephus assumes that the call to migrate came in Haran, while Philo (*Abr.* 61–67) and the rabbis take it to have come in Ur, possibly under the influence of Gen. 15.7 and Neh. 9.7.

[230] *Ant.* I, VII, 1. Jubilees XIII, 9 also records that Abraham offered a sacrifice; they interpret Gen. 12.8 "and he called in the name of God" to mean that he prayed, *Tar. Onk.* and *Tar. Jon. ad loc.*; or that he made converts, *Gen. R.* XXXIX. The rabbis portray Satan as charging Abraham with not having offered any sacrifices, and therefore he should be tested with Isaac, *San.* 89b. The verse does not appear at all in Philo in the works which have survived; it is apparently deliberately ignored as foreign to Philo's purpose in *De Abrahamo.*

[231] On these historians, cf. Weill, I, 37.

[232] So, too, *Tan. Lek*, VIII.

[233] This is peculiar to Josephus.

[234] So, too, *Tan. Lek*, VIII.

[235] Josephus makes no mention of Sarah's being taken to Pharaoh's palace. Philo portrays Pharaoh as sending for Sarah, *Abr.* 94.

[236] Gen. 12.17.

and by political disturbance.[237] Pharaoh vainly offers sacrifices; his priests inform him that the plagues are due to his wish to outrage the stranger's wife.[238] Pharaoh confirms the truth of the relationship by questioning Sarah.[239] He apologizes to Abraham and gives him abundant riches.[240] Abraham consorts with the most learned of the Egyptians, and as a result, the fame of his virtue and reputation becomes still more conspicuous.[241]

Josephus explains how Abraham gained his fame. The Egyptians have a variety of customs and opinions, and factions are always differing with others and disparaging them. Abraham confers with each party, proving that its view has nothing true in it. The Egyptians admire him not only for his intelligence but for his powers of persuasion. He introduces them to arithmetic and transmits to them the laws of astronomy,[242] of which sciences the Egyptians had been ignorant. The knowledge which Abraham had brought from Chaldea then spread to the Greeks.[243]

Josephus abridges the events of Gen. 13, omitting entirely the divine promises of the land, 14–17. The mention of Hebron (Νάβρο) leads Josephus to comment that its age is greater than that of Tanis in Egypt by seven years.[244]

---

[237] The political disturbance is peculiar to Josephus.

[238] Priests reveal the true relationship also in a fragment by Pseudo-Eupolemus, in Eusebius, *Praep. Ev.* IX, 17.

[239] This is peculiar to Josephus.

[240] The scriptural account makes the giving of gifts follow the "abduction" of Sarah and precede the plague.

[241] *Ant.* I, VIII, 1.

[242] Artapanus, in Eusebius, *Praep. Ev.* IX, 18, portrays Abraham as teaching astrology to Pharaoh. Rappaport, *Agada und Exegese bei Flavius Josephus*, believes that legends depicting Abraham disputing with Nimrod or with proselytes, lie behind this passage (pages 16–17, and notes #85 and #86 on pages 102 and 103); this seems barely possible, but hardly persuasive.

[243] *Ant.* I, VIII, 2.

[244] Jub. XIII, 12 similarly cites this information at this place, apparently from Num. 13.22. It seems to be more than coincidence that both make this somewhat unexpected citation in exactly the same context. The Syriac, Gen. 13.10 reads Tanis. Tanis is צען while the city found in our present text is MT צער, LXX Ζόγορα. In context, Gen. 13.10, the name of an Egyptian city is more to be expected as descriptive of the "garden of Egypt" than the mention of this Sodomite city. That the LXX also reads צער would tend to show that the replacement of the Egyptian city by the Sodomite one, through an

Josephus next turns to the wars of the kings of Gen. 14. He summarizes the four kings as the Assyrians,[245] but does not mention them by name. The conquest by the four kings (implied in Gen. 14.4, but not explicitly stated), as he describes it, is achieved through a siege of Sodom by the Assyrians who have divided their army into four bodies, with one general in command of each. The victorious Assyrians impose tribute on the Sodomites who pay for twelve years and then rebel. An army of the Assyrians proceeds against them. Josephus then lists as commanding generals the men mentioned as kings in Gen. 14.1. These ravage the whole of Syria[246] and they subdue the descendants of the giants.[247] The Assyrians encamp in the bitumen pits which existed before the destruction of Sodom and the conversion of the valley into the Asphalt lake. There a battle is joined; it is a stubborn contest.[248] Many are killed and others taken prisoners, among them Lot, who has come to fight as an ally of the Sodomites.[249]

When Abraham hears of the disaster, he is moved alike with fear for his kinsman, Lot, and with compassion for his friends and neighbors, the Sodomites.[250] He sets out immediately, and on the fifth night[251] he falls upon the Assyrians in the neighbor-

---

easy scribal error, is quite early. Possibly in the days of the composition of Jubilees, a still fluid text read צען. By the time of Josephus, however, the text seems to have been fixed; *Onkelos* and LXX both read צער. The mention of Tanis in Josephus rests either on a now lost version of the Bible, or on some secondary source, probably Jubilees.

[245] Again he seems to use a geographical name more easily to be identified by his Greek readers.

[246] This is derived from Gen. 14.5-8.

[247] "Descendants" is added by Josephus. "Giants" is the reading of LXX.

[248] Added by Josephus, possibly to glorify Abraham's exploits in conquering the Assyrians.

[249] *Ant.* I, IX. This last is peculiar to Josephus; Gen. 19 portrays Lot as dwelling right in Sodom. Josephus omits the fugitives to the mountains Gen. 14.10 and the refugee of 13.

[250] This evaluation of the Sodomites is peculiar to Josephus, and at wide variance with the rabbinic view of the unneighborliness of the Sodomites. Its purpose is to aggrandize Abraham.

[251] This is added by Josephus. Possibly it stems from an estimate of the time required for an army to move from Hebron to Dan in northern Palestine.

hood of Dan — the name, Josephus adds, of one of the two sources of the Jordan.[252] It is a surprise attack; some Assyrians are slain in their beds, asleep; some awake before they can arm themselves; and others, though awake, are incapable of fighting through drunkenness, but these manage to flee.[253] The victory proves that triumph does not depend on numbers but on the ardor and the mettle of the combatants.[254]

The incident of Melchizedek then follows. His name means "righteous king."[255] For this reason he was made the priest of God.[256] Salem was afterwards called Jerusalem.[257a] The wine and bread are changed into a "hospitable entertainment" in the midst of an "abundant providing."[257b] The king of Sodom encourages Abraham to keep the spoil.[258] Abraham declines for himself, but accepts portions for his servants and for his three friends, Eshkol, Aner, and Mamre.[259]

[252] The river gets its name, say the rabbis, because it descends (*yored*) from *Dan*, *Bekorot* 55a.

[253] Thackeray IV, 88, alludes to Philo's *Abr.* 233 as a striking parallel. The differences are just as striking. Philo says nothing of drunkenness and nothing of fugitives fleeing to Damascus; Josephus says nothing of Philo's insistence that Abraham's trust was not in his small force but in God. Both Josephus and Philo are giving naturalistic explanations of "divided the night" of Gen. 14.15, which the rabbis in their way interpret extravagantly. I see no signs here of dependency on Philo.

[254] While this view would probably evoke the approval of military men, the rabbis and Philo see in the episode the proof that man, when aided by God, can triumph, and they would have regarded Josephus' comment as somewhat blasphemous.

[255] So, too, *Tar. Jon.* to Gen. 14.18 and Hebrews VII, 2.

[256] Peculiar to Josephus. Rabbinic views, undoubtedly in opposition to the identification of Christ with Melchizedek as found in Hebrews, portray him as ultimately forfeiting his priesthood, *Nedarim* 32b.

[257a] So, too, the rabbis; the *Targumim* render Salem by Jerusalem. In *Apologia* VII, 67 and *B. J.* VI, 438 Josephus accepts the etymology which makes Jerusalem a combination of the Greek ἱερός and the Hebrew *Salem*. A rabbinic view gives as the etymology the Hebrew *yire'*, after Gen. 22.14 plus *Salem*; the two parts were combined for the name of Jerusalem, for to have omitted Salem would have been an injustice to Melchizedek, and to have omitted *yire'* would have offended Abraham, *Gen. R.* LVI.

[257b] Philo says that he "feasted them handsomely," *Abr.* 235.

[258] λείαν; MT *rekush*; LXX ἵππον.

[259] *Ant.* I, X, 2. Josephus lists these in the order of the LXX rather than

Josephus next turns to the events of Gen. 15. Again he indicates that a sacrifice has been offered of the various animals.[260] Before the altar could be erected[261] birds of prey[262] lusting for blood[263] come flying to the scene.[264] Josephus does not speak of an enslavement in a foreign land, but of future evil neighbors in Egypt;[265] the allusion may be to the anti-semitism of Alexandria which was pronounced at least in Josephus' earlier days. The chapter is abridged; Josephus makes no mention of the covenant of Gen. 15.18, nor of the tongue of fire and the smoke[266] which pass through the pieces.[267]

As Josephus relates the events of Gen. 16, he portrays Abraham as dwelling near the oak of Ogyges, rather than Mamre.[268] He beseeches God to grant him the birth of a male child.[269] By God's command[270] Sarah brings Hagar to his bed. This servant once pregnant, insolently abuses Sarah, assuming that the dominion will pass to her unborn son.[271] Hagar, fleeing,

MT. Philo, however, takes Mamre consistently as the name of a place, not a person, *Mig.* 164.

[260] Jub. XIV, 11 also tells that Abraham built an altar and sacrificed these.

[261] Not in Genesis; see note above.

[262] οἰωνῶν. LXX reads ὄρνεα birds, while MT reads עיט.

[263] Not in Genesis.

[264] Josephus omits the deep sleep which comes over Abraham, Gen. 15.12. Josephus puts into one sentence the coming of the birds of prey and the enslavement to Egypt. It may be conjectured that behind this juxtaposition may lie the interpretation of the 'ayit (*Tar. Jon.* and *Tar. Jer. ad loc.*) as the four kingdoms destined to subject Israel. The conjecture rests only on what Josephus assembles for one sentence; there is no clear allusion, however.

[265] Egypt is not mentioned in Gen. 15.13, which speaks only of "a land not theirs."

[266] Gen. 15.17.

[267] *Ant.* I, X, 3.

[268] Josephus uses both names, Thackeray IV, 92–93, suggests that he is using a name, familiar to his Greek readers, of a very ancient personage.

[269] This request is implied in Gen. 15.2. Josephus seems to use a few verses from the beginning of Gen. 15 as the prelude to his present account.

[270] Not in Genesis. The rabbis, however, interpret Gen. 16.2, "he hearkened to the voice of Sarah" to mean that he obeyed the holy spirit in her. *Gen. R.* XLV.

[271] The motive for the insolence is added by Josephus. Some similar, though far from identical, statements are found in *Gen. R.* XLV and *Tar. Jer.* and *Tar. Jon.* to Gen. 16.5.

meets the angel of God who bids her return to her master and mistress. He assures her that she will obtain a better state of affairs through prudence.[272] Her present plight was due to her arrogance and presumptuousness.[273] If she disobeys God and pursues her way, she will perish;[274] but if she returns home she will become the mother of a son destined to rule over the country.[275] Josephus adds to the biblical account not only that Hagar returns home, but that she is forgiven.[276]

Josephus omits in his recapitulation of Gen. 17 the change in name from Abram to Abraham and from Sarai to Sarah.[277] The promise of the land, omitted in his account above of Gen. 15.18 appears now, though it is paraphrased as extending from Sidon to Egypt rather than from Egypt to the great river Euphrates.[278] He gives a motive for circumcision, that Abraham's posterity may be kept from mixing with others.[279] Josephus remarks that he will expound the reason for circumcision elsewhere.[280] Josephus does not mention the covenant notion of circumcision of Gen. 17.9–10.[281]

---

[272] Gen. 16.9 simply tells her to "be afflicted"; the *Targumim* render this by "be enslaved" (*Onk.*), or by "be submissive," (*Jon.*).

[273] Peculiar to Josephus.

[274] Peculiar to Josephus.

[275] The last phrase, alluding to the wilderness, is peculiar to Josephus; it probably stems from his contemporaneous observation of Ishmaelites in the desert.

[276] *Ant.* I, X, 4. The forgiveness is peculiar to Josephus.

[277] Philo's great efforts to defend the addition of an alpha to Abraham's name suggest that Josephus deliberately suppressed the change so as not to be bothered with justifying it. See *Mut.* 66 ff.

[278] Perhaps the alteration is influenced by the circumstance that the Jewish territory had not reached to the Euphrates, and Josephus is making the prediction accord to the geographical facts of his day.

[279] This motive, as thus expressly stated, is lacking in the rabbinic writings. A rabbinic comment portrays Abraham as fearing that his circumcision may estrange prospective proselytes, *Gen. R.* XLVI; this is hardly a true parallel, for it expresses Abraham's fear that circumcision would be a barrier to conversion rather than an intention to exclude.

[280] Weill I, 45, appropriately comments that Josephus seems to distinguish between the purpose of circumcision and the rational or symbolic meaning of it.

[281] *Ant.* I, X, 5.

The material in Gen. 18 and 19 is somewhat rearranged. Josephus begins with the transgression of the Sodomites, Gen. 18.20, and then introduces the contents of Gen. 18.1 ff. The Sodomites become overweeningly proud of their numbers and their wealth.[282] They show themselves insolent to men and impious to God.[283] They forget the benefits they have received from God.[284] They hate strangers and decline all intercourse with them.[285] God determines to punish the Sodomites; he will not only uproot the city, but blast the land so completely that neither plant nor fruit will grow from that time forth.[286]

After God has decreed the doom of the Sodomites, Abraham, seated before the door of his courtyard,[287] sees three angels whom he takes for strangers.[288] Abraham offers them hospitality; they lead him to believe that they eat his food.[289] The angels promise that they will return in the future[290] and that they will find Sarah then already a mother. Sarah smiles[291] and says that her advanced age and that of her husband preclude their having

---

[282] Their rebelliousness stemmed from their abundant possessions, *San.* 109a.

[283] So, too, *Tar. Jon.* to Gen. 13.13.

[284] They rebelled against God, *ibid.*

[285] So, too, *PRE* XXV. Cf. also *ARN* XII, 7 and *Gen. R.* XLI.

[286] *Ant.* I, XI, 1. So, too, Philo, *Abr.* 140.

[287] The tent has become a Greek courtyard.

[288] For the usual rabbinic views on Gen. 18.1 see below, page 84; for Philo's view, see pages 119 ff. There may be added to this material the fact that one rabbinic comment implies that Abraham has two distinct visits; God appears to him, and the appearance is interrupted by the appearance of the three angels, *Gen. R.* XLVIII, but the usual view, *ibid.*, and the *Targumim ad loc.*, explain the vision of God as the vision of the three. That the men were "strangers" is emphasized by the rabbis; Abraham thought they were Arabs, *Sifre Deut. 'Ekeb*, LVIII. It is to be noted that Josephus omits the words, "God appeared to him."

[289] So too *Tar. Jon.* to Gen. 18.8 and *B. M.* 86b; see also *Abr.* 116, and below, chapter III, note 82.

[290] εἰς τὸ μέλλον. LXX reads εἰς (κατὰ) τὸν καιρὸν τοῦτον εἰς ὥρας. Josephus seems here to be in accord with *Tar. Jon.* to Gen. 18.10, in softening the miraculous; the rabbis elsewhere heighten it by portraying an angel drawing a line on the wall; the birth of Isaac is to take place when the sun comes around again to the line, *Tan. Wa-yera* XIII.

[291] μειδιάζω "smile," LXX γελάζω "laugh."

a child. The angels thereupon reveal their true nature[292] as angels of God, one of whom had been sent to announce the news of the child and the other two to destroy the Sodomites.[293]

The account of the bargaining with God is greatly abbreviated, with only its conclusions summarized, that there are less than ten righteous men in Sodom. The angels come to Sodom where Lot invites them to be his guests, because he has learned hospitality from Abraham.[294] The Sodomites see the angels as young men of very fair appearance,[295] and they want to do violence and outrage to them. Lot offers them his daughters, but even this will not content them.[296]

God blinds the criminals[297] so that they cannot find the door. He condemns the Sodomites to destruction. Lot, however, has been forewarned, so that he departs[298] with his wife and two daughters, who are still virgins; their suitors[299] scorn the notion

[292] Scripture portrays God, not the men, as hearing the laughter, Gen. 18.13–14.

[293] *Ant.* I, XI, 2. The rabbis treat the passage similarly. The identification is not only the same, but the rabbis go even further and give the name and precise missions of each of the three: Michael is to announce the tidings to Sarah; Raphael, to heal Abraham from his circumcision of three days before; and Gabriel to overturn Sodom, *B. M.* 86b. This last comment is in conflict with *Tar. Jon.* and *Tar. Jer.* to Gen. 18.2, both of which insist that an angel can have but a single mission; it would therefore be impossible for Raphael to go on to Sodom; these passages do not name the three. The problem is "solved" in *Gen. R. L.* by substituting for the healing of Abraham the mission of Raphael to save Lot from Sodom. Josephus apparently bases the revelation of their nature to Abraham on Gen. 18.17, "Shall I conceal from Abraham what I am about to do?" I find no rabbinic parallel to Josephus' portrayal of the angels' identifying themselves. I doubt that any haggadah lies behind this added touch.

[294] So, too, *Tan. Wa-yera* XI. The Rabbis draw a contrast, however, between Lot's stature and Abraham's. The angels promptly accept Abraham's offer, but Lot has to persuade them, *Gen. R. L.*

[295] These additions probably stem from the portrayal, explicit in Scripture, of the Sodomites as homosexuals.

[296] *Ant.* I, XI, 3.

[297] Gen. 19.11 makes it the "men," not God, who blind the Sodomites.

[298] Gen. 19.16 portrays the men as taking hold of the tarrying Lot and his family and bringing them out of the city.

[299] Gen. 19.14 portrays Lot trying to persuade his "sons-in-law," LXX γαμβρούς who have "taken" his daughters. But above, verse seven, Lot has

of departure and they ridicule what Lot tells them. Josephus does not repeat the details of the destruction of Sodom, but refers the reader to his earlier account in the Jewish War.[300] He remarks that he himself has seen the pillar of salt into which Lot's wife was changed.[301] Lot flees to Ṣo'ar, where, isolated from mankind and in lack of food, he passes a miserable existence.[302]

Josephus ascribes the incest of the daughters of Lot to their desire to prevent the extinction of the race.[303] The Ammonites and Moabites are still extant in Josephus' day.[304]

---

offered to the Sodomites his daughters who "have not known a man." Josephus escapes from this contradiction by altering the sons-in-law to suitors μνησ-τῆρες; the daughters are, accordingly, still virgins. One rabbinic comment, *Gen. R.* L, by forced exegesis which interprets MT לְקֹחֵי as a future, rather than לָקְחֵי as a past, accords with this view of Josephus. The prevailing rabbinic solution, however, escapes from the contradiction by equipping Lot not with two daughters but with four, two of whom are married and two virgins. See *Gen. R.* XLIX: Abraham believes that there might be ten righteous in Sodom: Lot, his wife, *four* daughters and *four* sons-in-law; *Gen. R.* L, which states expressly that Lot had four daughters; and *PRE* XXV, which ascribes to Lot's wife her turning to look at Sodom out of solicitude for two of her daughters married to two Sodomites.

[300] *B. J.* IV, 483–485; Josephus seemingly rejects the view that the Salt Sea covers Sodom. So, too, Philo, *Abr.* 141.

[301] There is frequent mention in rabbinics that the pillar of salt still stands, *PRE* XXV; cf. Rappaport, 105–106. Wisdom of Solomon X, 7 speaks of the pillar of salt as a memorial of a soul devoid of faith.

[302] *Ant.* I, XI, 4. These latter comments are in anticipation of a notion to be argued in the next pericope, that the isolation and a worthy desire to repopulate a supposedly empty world motivated the incest, rather than lust. The Bible (Gen. 19.30) portrays Lot as dwelling on a mountain in a cave, since he feared to enter Ṣo'ar, and I find no parallel to the lack of food and miserable existence; it seems, however, readily derivable from the Bible.

[303] This view is paralleled in many rabbinic passages: *Gen. R.* LI; and *PsR* XLII. Other views regard the action as pure incest, *Tan. Balaq,* XXVI. So, too, Jub. XVI, 8. Josephus' view is readily deducible from Scripture. Aptowitzer in *Parteipolitik der Hasmonäerzeit,* cited in Rappaport, 106–107, argues that the view exculpating Lot's daughters, stems from the Davidic partisans who were anti-Hasmonean; it is recalled that David was a descendant of Ruth the Moabite; the severe condemnation of the daughters would represent the Hasmonean parties.

[304] *Ant.* I, XI, 5.

The incident of Abimelech[305] is related with some fidelity to Scripture. Josephus adds that a grievous disease was inflicted by God on Abimelech, and the physicians despaired of his life.[306] Josephus omits the mention of Abraham as a prophet.[307] Sarah, as before, is Abraham's niece, not his sister. He portrays Abimelech as assuring Abraham that Sarah had remained untouched, as God and Sarah could testify. He offers Abraham the choice of remaining in the land, in full abundance; or, should Abraham wish to depart, he will be given an escort, but only after he will have obtained what he has come to the land to get. They settle matters amicably and swear an oath at Beer-Sheba.[308]

Josephus next relates the birth of Isaac. He gives the etymology of the name as "laughter," though he repeats that Sarah had "smiled." The child is born a year later.[309] Josephus adds to the bare account of the circumcision that from that time on the Jewish practice has been to circumcise after eight days.[310] The Arabs defer the ceremony, Josephus adds, until the thirteenth year because Ishmael was circumcised at that age. Josephus again mentions his intention to discuss circumcision at length.[311]

At first Sarah loves Ishmael as if he were her own son, since he has been trained for rulership.[312] After the birth of Isaac, she holds it wrong for him to be brought up with Ishmael, since she

[305] Gen. 20.

[306] Amplified from Gen. 20.7, "let him (Abraham) pray for you, that you may live," etc.; and from 17–18, which describe the disease as sterility. Josephus may have paraphrased this chapter quickly and somewhat carelessly.

[307] Gen. 20.7.

[308] *Ant.* I, XII, 1.

[309] τῷ ὑστάτῳ ἔτει. The allusion is, of course, to the prediction in Gen. 18. There is this difficulty that ὕστατος does not seem usually to mean "next," but "last." Weill, I, 50, follows Bekker in reading ὑστέρῳ. Josephus does not follow the rabbinic view by which miraculously the birth of Isaac takes place precisely one year after the visit of the three travelers.

[310] Gen. 17.12. The rabbis infer it exegetically from the word מול in 21.4, *Kiddushin* 29a.

[311] *Ant.* I, XII, 2.

[312] ἡγεμονία. I find no parallels.

fears that Ishmael might do Isaac harm after Abraham's death.[313] She therefore urges Abraham to send Ishmael and his mother to some other settlement.[314] Abraham at first refuses, since he thinks nothing is more brutal than to send away an infant[315] with a woman destitute of the necessities of life.[316] Abraham yields, however, when he learns that Sarah's behest is sanctioned by God. The water and food give out, and Hagar, not wishing to see the little boy expire, puts him under a fir tree.[317] The angel of God meets her and gives her the promise of Ishmael's future greatness. She meets some shepherds[318] and through their help escapes from her miseries.[319] When Ishmael is grown, Hagar obtains a wife from among the Egyptians for him.[320]

[313] A somewhat similar fear of difficulties after Abraham's death is found in *Tos. Sotah* VI. Josephus writes the account in such a way as to justify the harshness of Sarah; the rabbis, who are faced with no such apologetic need, tell tales of attempts by Ishmael to kill Isaac or of Ishmael's idolatry.

[314] The Bible says merely "drive out this maid servant and her son." Again Josephus is softening the harshness.

[315] Νήπιος. It seems to be forgotten that in the biblical account Ishmael is at least an adolescent. Josephus is influenced by Gen. 21.14, which seems to say that Ishmael was put on his mother's shoulder. The rabbis, *Gen. R.* LIII, ask how a lad of twenty-seven could be so carried; it is replied that Sarah has put an evil eye on Ishmael so that he is smitten by a fever, cannot walk, and therefore must be borne. Because of the fever Ishmael drinks a great deal, and that is why the container of water is soon emptied. In *PRE* XXX substantially the same story is told; Ishmael's age is there given as twenty-four. See below, note 286 in Chapter III.

[316] Similarly, this is regarded by the rabbis as Abraham's severest trial up to this point, *PRE* XXX.

[317] Josephus seems to have written this passage on the model of Euripides, *Hercules Furens* 323–324. He has omitted the statement in the Bible that Hagar lost her way, Gen. 21.14, which *Tar. Jon.* emphasizes even more than does MT.

[318] This is peculiar to Josephus.

[319] *Ant.* I, XII, 3.

[320] *Ant.* I, XII, 4. As in Jubilees XVII, at precisely this point Josephus turns from the contents of Gen. 21 to Gen. 25, to enumerate the sons of Ishmael. Jubilees mentioned only Nebaioth; Josephus lists all twelve of them. Josephus mentions Nabatea by name; I suggested above, page 44, that the sole mention of Nebaioth in Jubilees might have been due to the importance of the Nabateans at the time of Jubilees (and Josephus).

Josephus now turns to the Binding of Isaac[321] of Gen. 22. Abraham loves Isaac because he is an only son and was born on the threshold of Abraham's old age. Isaac evokes the affection of his parents even more by his practice of every virtue and by showing obedience to his parents and zeal for the worship of God.[322] Abraham rests all his own happiness on the hope of leaving his son unscathed when he will depart from this life.[323] God appears to Abraham to test him.[324] First he enumerates all the benefits that He has bestowed upon Abraham, such as his conquest of his enemies and his present felicity, and his possession of Isaac.[325] He commands Abraham to offer his son by his own hand.[326] He bids Abraham to take the child to the mount of Moriah[327] and to make a burnt offering of him. Thereby he would show his piety in putting God's pleasure above the safety of the child.[328]

Abraham believes that he must obey, because everything that befalls God's favored one is ordained by divine providence.[329] He conceals from Sarah the divine commandment and his own

[321] Josephus like Jubilees goes directly from the marriage of Ishmael to the Binding of Isaac, omitting the second incident of Abimelech, Gen. 21.22–34.

[322] This is peculiar to Josephus. Philo has a description somewhat similar to this passage, *Abr.* 168. The differences, however, are sufficient to preclude a necessary dependency of Josephus on Philo here, since the similarity consists only in depicting Isaac in terms of endowments of his own. Josephus is here describing Isaac in terms intelligible to Greek readers, in this lies the only similarity to Philo.

[323] Peculiar to Josephus.

[324] Gen. 22.1. Philo makes no mention of the "test."

[325] Peculiar to Josephus. There is no specific mention in Josephus of Abraham's ten trials, a motif which appeared in Jubilees XVII, 15–18 in a heavenly prologue to the Binding.

[326] This last is peculiar to Josephus.

[327] Identified presently as the Temple Mount. The basis is II Chron. 3.1. Jubilees XVIII, 13 and the rabbis also make the identification; see above note 133. Josephus, like Jubilees, first mentions the mount without making the identification, but does so when Abraham arrives there.

[328] *Ant.* I, XIII, 1.

[329] For Josephus' view of providence, see Lewinski, *Beiträge zur Kenntnis der religionsphilosophischen Anschauungen des Flavius Josephus*, 36–46 and Moore "Fate and Free Will in Josephus," *HTR*, XXII, 371–389.

intention to obey it; he tells it to none of his household.[330] Josephus is rather faithful to the account in Genesis of the saddling of the ass[331] and the journey to the mountain. He portrays the servants as left on the plain while Abraham and Isaac proceed to the mountain.[332] It is the mountain on which David afterwards erects the Temple.[333] Isaac, now twenty-five,[334] asks what will be sacrificed, and Abraham replies that God will provide for them in everything, and that He will send a sacrifice.[335]

The altar is now all prepared. Abraham then tells Isaac of his prayers for Isaac's birth, the birth itself, his care for Isaac's upbringing, and of his hope to bequeath his dominion to him.[336]

Isaac replies in kind, and rushes to the altar.[337] God intervenes to stop the slaughter. He reveals that it is all only a test which Abraham has passed creditably. Isaac, accordingly, will be blessed with offspring who will inherit the land of Canaan. God then brings a ram into their view.[338] They offer the ram

[330] Scripture makes no mention of Sarah in the context, so that this silence is readily to be inferred. Philo also portrays Abraham as telling no one of the divine oracle, *Abr.* 170. The rabbis, however, portray Abraham as telling Sarah that he is taking Isaac, now thirty-seven, to school, *PRE* XXXI and *MHG* to Gen. 22.2.

[331] Philo omits this, *Abr.* 170–171.

[332] The mention of the plain is peculiar to Josephus, but deducible from Gen. 22.4; Abraham raises his eyes to see the mountain. He must, therefore, have been on a lower level. Jubilees XVIII, 4 provides a well for the servants. Philo identifies these as the oldest and most faithful of the numerous servants, while Josephus does not identify them. The rabbis identify them as Ishmael and Eliezer, *Lev. R.* XXVI and elsewhere.

[333] See above, note 327.

[334] The rabbis consider him thirty-seven, *PRE* XXXI.

[335] *Ant.* I, XIII, 2.

[336] *Ant.* I, XIII, 3. Such speeches are found in the many rabbinic embellishments, *Gen. R.* LVI and *Tan. Wa-yera* and elsewhere. So, too, Isaac's reply. The rabbinic stories, like Jubilees, introduce Satan in a prologue and have him reappear throughout the episode. Josephus seems familiar with such narratives; if they are known to him it is likely that it is his naturalism which leads him to suppress the appearances of Satan.

[337] Josephus, like Philo, *Abr.* 176, omits the mention of the actual binding. Philo, however, portrays Abraham as putting Isaac on the altar.

[338] Josephus transposes the blessing of Isaac to precede the divine promises. He omits God's oath, Gen. 22.16.

and, in joy, return to Sarah.[339] They live in bliss, with God
helping them in all they desire.[340]

Not long afterwards, Sarah dies.[341] The Canaanites offer her
burial-ground at public expense[342] but Abraham buys the spot.
He and his descendants build their tombs at this place.[343]

Next Josephus mentions Abraham's marriage to Keturah,
and their offspring. Abraham sends out all these to found colonies.
They take possession of Troglodytis and the part of Arabia
Felix which extends to the Red Sea.[344] Africa is named after
Eophron (either Eyfa or Efer of Gen. 25.4) who led an expe-
dition against Libya and occupied it; his grandsons settled there
and named the land after him. This is attested to by Alexander
Polyhistor who cites from Cleodemus the prophet, also called
Malchus, that of the several sons of Abraham three gave their
names to a land: Sures (Ashurim) to Assyria, Japhras (?) to
Apheras, and Aphra (Efar) to the country of Africa. These latter
joined Heracles in his campaign against Libya and Antaeus.[345]
Heracles married the daughter of Aphra, begot Didorus,
who begot Sophron after whom the "Barbarians" are called
Sophakes.[346]

Josephus next turns back to Abraham's sending Eliezer to
Aram.[347] Eliezer brings Rebekkah back with him; Isaac, now

---

[339] Genesis records only that Abraham returned. The rabbis infer that
Isaac went on to Shem's school; Satan tells Sarah, meanwhile, that Isaac has
been sacrificed, and Sarah dies from shock, *Tar. Jon.* to Gen. 22.19–20.

[340] *Ant.* I, XIII, 4. Peculiar to Josephus.

[341] Josephus omits Gen. 22.20–24, the genealogy of Rebekkah and her
family.

[342] Perhaps Josephus alludes to burial at public expense as a form of
public honor among the Greeks.

[343] *Ant.* I, XIV. Josephus makes no mention of the double cave, which the
rabbis regard as the tomb of Abraham and Sarah, and even of Adam and Eve,
PRE XX; cf. *Erubin* 53a.

[344] Peculiar to Josephus. Gen. 25.6 says only that Abraham sent them
eastward into the east country.

[345] The legends of Heracles are found in Plutarch, *Sertor.* 9.

[346] *Ant.* I, XV. I discuss this citation in the section on hellenistic Jewish
writers. See page 55.

[347] *Ant.* I, XVI, 1–3. The marriage of Keturah is found in Gen. 25; the
sending of Eliezer in Gen. 24. There is little to our purpose in pursuing the
narrative of Eliezer.

the master of his father's estate[348] marries her.[349] Not long afterwards Abraham dies, a man supreme in every virtue and honored by God for his zeal. He is buried at Hebron, beside Sarah, by Isaac and Ishmael.[350]

It is difficult, in a positive way, to state the significance of Abraham to Josephus. The truth is that Josephus does not exhibit any striking, unified, coherent conception of the Patriarch. He gives little more than a pedestrian recapitulation of Scripture, omitting some minor details, naturalizing others, and supplying some traditional embellishments, but his Abraham is written without betraying any meditation, insight, or assessment.

The traditional material which Josephus preserves provides him with some details, but these details are never shaped into a body of discerning material. Josephus writes as the kind of historian who records incidents and dates, but who shows little interest in the significance of what he is writing about.

The Abraham who roams about his pages is dressed in the garb of a Greek philosopher, but Josephus gives no true insight into what kind of a philosopher he is; he makes the assertion, but he follows the assertion with only a pitifully weak demonstration.

The abundant use of haggadic material would seem to point to the possibility of Josephus' knowledge of traditions of Abraham as an observer of the Law, especially since this viewpoint is found in Jubilees. Josephus says not one thing about Abraham's relationship to the Law of Moses or to the Greek notions of law. Josephus' assertion[351] that much of his book, which professes to treat of laws and historical fact, is devoted to "physiology" is hardly borne out by the rest of his book. In fact, he defers to another time the writing of "Customs and Causes"[352] in a spirit

[348] Gen. 25.5: Abraham gave all that was his to Isaac. Josephus retains the idea but shapes it somewhat differently.
[349] *Ant.* I, XVI, 3.
[350] *Ant.* I, XVII.
[351] *Ant.* Proem, 4.
[352] *Ant.* VI, VII, 4.

of "profound and highly philosophical inquiry."[353] Josephus'
Abraham is not a crucial figure to Josephus. He is simply one
of many biblical characters. Josephus makes no mention of
Abraham as a source of merit to his descendants; he says not
one word about Abraham as an exemplar of any kind. He omits
the mention of the covenant. Abraham is simply the philosopher
who left the land of Canaan to his descendants. Abraham is the
first to declare the unity of God. He goes to Egypt to learn if
Egyptian doctrine is superior to his own; he teaches the Egyptians mathematics and astronomy, and is the medium by which
this knowledge comes ultimately to the Greeks. Abraham is able
to refute all the Egyptians. The picture, a most superficial one,
simply casts the patriarch into an ill-fitting mold of a philosopher,
and apologetically credits him with matters honorable in the
Greek scene.

To put it another way, Josephus omits in his presentation of
Abraham those very distinctive qualities which exalted Abraham
in Jubilees and in the later rabbinic literature; by a touch here
and there (the tent becomes a house, the war of the kings becomes
a military expedition, Sarah could have been buried at public
expense, Abraham possesses "virtues") Josephus gives Abraham
something of a hellenistic color, but only a faint one. He deprives
Abraham of the striking hues in which the rabbis paint him;[354]
he fails to give Abraham any deeply true characteristics in the
Greek tradition.

In rabbinic literature, in conformity with the elaborate exegetical method developed by the rabbis, the relevant Scriptural
passages served as means of inferring extended and magnified
conclusions explicit from the text, as well as new conclusions
which are bound to Scripture only by the tenuous thread of the
exegetical method. Gen. 18 tells an incident of Abraham's hospitality, and the rabbis deduce from almost any conceivable
passage that Abraham was hospitable. The view that Abraham

---

[353] *Ant.* Proem, 4.

[354] If Josephus used Jubilees, he must have known the legend of Abraham
smashing idols. His failure to use this material may be the fear that it would
be offensive to his Greek readers, and weaken the effectiveness of his apologetics.

was a great missionary, a matter not expressed at all in Scripture, takes on in rabbinic exegesis a rigidity and formality almost equal to the biblical view that Abraham was hospitable.

The rabbinic exegesis, like the Philonic, pays little regard to the context. The verse itself, lifted completely out of its setting, serves the *darshan* for whatever purpose he might wish. The point of departure is the *darshan*'s immediate need or his immediate interest, and, accordingly, the rabbinic Abraham is a character associated with the problems and speculations not of patriarchal days but of rabbinic times. One could construct an almost complete picture of rabbinic theology and rabbinic attitudes from only the Abraham material.

a. *The Recognition of the Existence of God*

The rabbis agree that Abraham was the first man who recognized the existence of God; they disagree at what age he came to that praiseworthy conclusion. By one view he was still a babe, only a year old;[355] by another he was three;[356] by a third, ten; the usual view, repeated most frequently, was that Abraham was forty-eight.[357] The recognition came to him as a result of an inference; he saw a lighted house, and he conjectured that the house must have a master. Similarly, the existence of the world meant that it had a Guide.[358]

b. *God's Elect*

Abraham had come to the recognition of God in an impure land, for idolatry prevailed there.[359] God enjoined upon him to depart not only from the province and, not only from the immediate vicinity, but also from his father's house.[360] God, in fact, appeared to Abraham in the guise of a friend who pushes and says, "Go."[361]

[355] *Gen. R.* XCV.
[356] *Ibid.*; *Mid. Esther* VI.   [357] *Gen. R.* XXX.
[358] *Gen. R.* XXXIX.
[359] *MHG.* to Gen. 12.1
[360] *Gen. R.* XXXIX.   [361] *MHG.* to Gen. 12.1.

The vagueness of the proposed destination was deliberate; it was a device whereby the obedience of Abraham would be all the more rewarded in that he departed without knowing where he was going.[362] The call came out of God's eagerness for the clean to depart out of unclean surroundings.[363] Abraham was like a precious stone sifted from a pile of rubbish, or, like a vial of fragrant perfume uselessly lying unknown and unobserved in a corner of the house; at the divine call the vial, being moved, shed its fragrant aroma all over.[364]

Abraham was blessed by God as the father of nations; it is true that the (seventy) nations of the world derive from Noah, but the choice nation stemmed from Abraham.[365] The blessing made a new creation out of Abraham.[366] He was "inserted" into the *Shemoneh Esre*, even preceding God.[367]

The blessing extended to his associates. No one priced a cow in a transaction with Abraham without being blessed; ships at sea were saved on his behalf; even where "profane" wine was expensive, "*kosher*" wine was inexpensive; sick people whom Abraham visited immediately improved.[368] That Gen. 12.2–3 uses the root *gdl* three times and *brk* four times is a clear indication that the blessing pointed to the existence of three patriarchs and four matriarchs.[369] These seven mentions accord with the seven occurrences in Gen. 1 of *ki tob*.[370]

Abraham's fame was such that coins depicting him and Sarah on one side, and Isaac and Rebekkah on the other, were widespread throughout the world.[371] Abraham was not only a blessing (*berakah*), he was a spring (*berekah*) which purifies the impure.[372]

---

[362] *Gen. R.* XXXIX.
[363] *Num. R.* XIX.
[364] *Gen. R.* XXXIX.
[365] *Gen. R.* XXXIX.
[366] *Ibid.*
[367] *Ibid.* The benediction מגן אברהם precedes מחיה המתים.
[368] *Gen. R.* XXXIX.
[369] *Gen. R.* XXXIX.
[370] *Num. R.* XI.
[371] *Gen. R.* XXXIX.
[372] *Gen. R.* XXXIX.

God transferred to Abraham His own prerogative to deliver blessings;[373] from Abraham stemmed the priests whose function it was to bless.

The blessing of Abraham was a clear indication of the requirement that one use the wine cup of blessing.[374] Priests who bless others derive their own blessings from that which was given to Abraham;[375] indeed, a priest who fails to bless others loses his share in the blessing of Abraham.[376] God's promise to curse those who cursed Abraham indicates God's greater solicitude for the righteous than for Himself, for those who curse God are not cursed but only despised by fellowmen.[377] One who curses the descendants of Abraham discovers that the curse reverts to him;[378] this was the experience of Balaam.

The blessings acquired through Abraham by the nations of the world are an allusion to Ruth the Moabite and Naamah the Ammonite.[379] The dew and the rain were the blessings given to the world through Abraham.[380] The blessings of the nations are not those of wealth, for in this they exceed Israel; it is that when trouble overtakes them, they can turn to Israel for relief.[381] The entire world was blessed through Abraham and Sarah.[382]

The world derived its blessing from Abraham, but Abraham's blessing came directly from God.[383] The full blessing of Abraham ensued after he had withstood ten severe trials.[384] Scripture declares that God blessed Abraham[385] ba-kol (in everything). This means that his lack of a daughter was made good through the birth of a baby girl, named Ba-kol. His knowledge of astrology

---

[373] *Tan. Lek.* V.   [374] *Berakot* 55a.

[375] *Hullin* 49a.

[376] *Sotah* 38b.

[377] *Gen. R.* XXXIX. Derived from I Sam. 2.30.

[378] *Tan. Balaq* XII.

[379] *Yebamot* 63a. The exegesis relies on a play of words, equating *brk*, to engraft, with *brk* to bless.

[380] *Gen. R.* XXXIX.

[381] *Ibid.*

[382] *Yal. Shim.* I, 169.

[383] *Gen. R.* LIX.

[384] *Tan. Be-ha'aloteka.* XIII (Buber's edition).

[385] Gen. 24.1

prompted all the nations of the world to come to his tent to await his words. Another view is that a precious stone suspended from Abraham's neck brought immediate cure to any sick person who beheld it; after Abraham's death the stone was suspended from a wheel of the sun's chariot.[386] Other views interpret *ba-kol* to mean that Ishmael repented during Abraham's lifetime, or that Esau's rebellion was deferred until after Abraham's death.[387] Still other views regard *ba-kol* as indicating that Abraham in this world received a foretaste of the world to come; or, that the evil inclination did not rule over him; or, that after death, worms did not consume his flesh.[388]

The blessing promised numerous offspring, and it was fulfilled when Israel came out of Egypt.[389] The land of Canaan was promised, and the promise was kept.[390]

In another sense, Abraham was a blessing in that he taught his guests the blessing of Grace after the Meal.[391] God made him a partner in the possession of the earth.[392] This partnership gave Abraham authority, however, both over heavenly creations as well as earthly ones.[393] It was such authority, transmitted, which enabled Joshua to make the sun stand still.[394] The possession of the heaven was fulfilled in the descendants' inheritance of the Torah which came from heaven, while the heritage of the earth was their great number; and both of these heritages derived from Abraham's piety.[395]

There was, in fact, no blessing which God omitted to confer upon Abraham: wisdom, understanding, knowledge, and intelligence; wealth and possessions; heaven and earth.[396]

---

[386] *B. B.* 16b.
[387] *Ibid.*
[388] *Ibid.*, 17a.
[389] *Num. R.*, XI.
[390] *Mekilta, Bo*, XVII.
[391] *Gen. R.* XLIII.
[392] The view regards *qoneh shamayim wa-areṣ* of Gen. 14.19 as alluding to Abraham as well as to God.
[393] *Num. R.* XIV.
[394] *Tan. Aḥare Mot.* XIV.
[395] *Mid. Prov.* XIX.
[396] *SER.*, VI.

c. *His Virtues*

Abraham showed his obedience by departing from Haran immediately after the divine command, and, in taking Lot with him,
obeyed beyond what was commanded.[397] This, despite the fact
that Lot was a hindrance.[398] Abraham consumed no time in
questions about his destination, or where he should lodge on the
way, or in any such delaying questions.[399] That famine overtook
him as soon as he arrived in Canaan did not elicit rebellious
complaints from him.[400] On being commanded to circumcise, he
obeyed on the very same day.[401] He obeyed promptly the command to sacrifice Isaac.[402] He arose early to take Isaac to the
binding, because he obeyed with gladness.[403] He saddled the ass
joyously.[404] The frame of mind of affection erases the aspect of
burden, and though Abraham had plenty of servants, he himself
saddled the ass.[405]

The obedience conformed with his righteousness. He was
the righteous man[406] summoned from the east.[407] The fact that
he was tested proves his righteousness, for only the righteous are
tried.[408] The foremost among righteous men,[409] he was the progenitor of the righteous.[410] He offered the strangers bread,[411] but
actually gave them a banquet, for it is the custom of the righteous
to promise little but do much. The verse,[412] "God is righteous
with the righteous," applies to Abraham.[413] That God prepares

[397] *Gen. R.* XLI.
[398] *Gen. R.* XLI.
[399] *Mid. Psalms*, CXIX, 3 (Buber's edition, p. 489).
[400] *Gen. R.* XL.
[401] *Mid. Psalms* CXII.
[402] *Gen. R.* LV.
[403] *Mekilta, Beshalaḥ*, II, 1.
[404] *Gen. R.* LV.
[405] *Gen. R.* LV.
[406] Isa. 41.2.   [407] *Gen. R.* II.
[408] *Gen. R.* LV.
[409] *Cant. R.* VIII.
[410] *Ibid.*
[411] Gen. 18.2 ff.
[412] Ps. 18.26.
[413] *Mid. Psalms* XVIII.

rewards for the righteous, taking them from the wicked to bestow them, is proved by the wars of the kings, as a result of which Abraham took their possessions.[414] As Abraham was righteous so would his descendants[415] never lack thirty righteous men.[416] It is proved from Abraham that righteousness is a greater thing than repentance. Indeed, the greatness of righteousness lies in this, that it was in righteousness that Abraham was exalted.[417]

Abraham's faith was great, and it was the merit of that faith that enabled him to inherit both this world and the world to come.[418] The faith of Abraham was great enough to induce God to split the Red Sea.[419] Because of Abraham, Israel is spoken of as "the faithful, sons of the faithful."[420] The Song of the Sea, sung in the faith, was sung through the merit of Abraham who had faith.[421] The phrase, "pure in heart,"[422] is a description of Abraham's faith.[423] The faith which Israel lacked and for which Jeremiah chided them[424] was Abraham's faith.[425]

Humbly he described himself[426] as a servant.[427] It was this humility which prompted the angels to pause and visit him.[428] Even in the hour in which God condescended to converse with him,[429] Abraham retained his humility, for though God was aggrandizing him, he termed himself dust and ashes.[430] Indeed, humility is a sign that one is a disciple of Abraham.[431] Although he had been promised the entire land by God, nevertheless when

---

[414] *Tan. Lek*, VII.
[415] Gen. 15.5.
[416] *Mid. Psalms* V. Derived from the *gematria* of יהיה.
[417] *Mid. Prov.* VI.
[418] *Mid. Prov.* XIV.
[419] *Mekilta, Beshalaḥ*, III.
[420] *Shab.* 97a.
[421] *Ex. R.* XXIII.   [422] Ps. 24.4.
[423] *Mid. Psalms*, XXIV.
[424] Jer. 5.3.
[425] *Mid. Psalms* CXIX.
[426] Gen. 18.3.
[427] *Sifre, Wa-etḥanan*, XXVII.
[428] *Lev. R.* XI.
[429] Gen. 18.23–27.
[430] *Hullin* 89a.
[431] *ARN* XLII.

he wanted a burial ground he bought it.[432] The verse, "I have exalted a lowly tree,"[433] is an allusion to Abraham who was exalted through his humility.[434] He rejected the efforts of people to deify him.[435]

Doubts occasionally troubled Abraham; his question, "How shall I know that I shall inherit?"[436] showed such doubt, and it was the cause of the punishment of Israel by the sojourn in Egypt.[437] God's reassurance,[438] "do not be afraid—" was occasioned by Abrahams's fear that in the war of Gen. 14 he might have unwittingly slain a righteous man; or else he might have feared that the descendants of the slaughtered kings would attack him; God, however, was Abraham's shield.[439] Yet in every matter about which Abraham doubted, God made good the divine reassurances.[440]

Abraham was a model of courtesy and propriety. He pitched Sarah's tent before his own.[441] On his return from Egypt he stopped at the inns he had lodged in on the way to Egypt to pay his bills.[442] He kept his cattle muzzled so they would not graze on property not his own.[443] While Lot, careless of pollution, first invited the strangers to spend the night and then to wash, Abraham carefully invited them first to wash and then to lodge.[444] To avoid the gossip about Lot and his daughters he moved to Gerar.[445] He waited until he had married off Isaac before he wed Keturah.[446]

[432] *MHG* to Gen. 23.4.
[433] Ezek. 17.24.   [434] *MHG* to Gen. 21.1.
[435] Gen. R. LVIII.
[436] Gen. 15.8.
[437] *Ned.* 32a. This view is in conflict with a statement in *Gen. R.* XLIV which denies that Abraham doubted; therefore Moses protests against the punishment, *Ex. R.* VI.
[438] Gen. 15.1.
[439] *Tan. Lek* XIX.
[440] *Tan. Qedoshim,* XIII.
[441] *Gen. R.* XXXIX.
[442] *Gen. R.* XLI.
[443] *Ibid.*
[444] *Gen. R.* L.
[445] *Gen. R.* LII.
[446] *Gen. R.* LX.

There is much that can be learned about proper conduct from his life and experience. It is right, if famine comes, for man to move.[447] Travel lowers standards.[448] A man who lowers himself becomes lowered in the eyes of the world.[449] A man should have regard for the honor of his wife, since only on her account does blessing rest on his household.[450] Sexual irregularities bring plagues.[451] It is advantageous to associate with the rich.[452] One who chases after adultery ends up by feasting on his own flesh.[453] Quarrels lead to mortal dangers for the quarrelers.[454] It is better to have no descendants than to have evil ones.[455] An inclination to sleepiness is the beginning of a man's downfall.[456] If one departs from a city, he should do so in the daytime.[457] A joker is never believed, even when he is telling the truth.[458]

Abraham's hospitality was greater than Job's, for while Job passively welcomed strangers, Abraham, though just recently circumcised, sat before his tent seeking them.[459] He opened a "good door" to passers-by.[460] His tent was open on all sides, so that he could run in any direction to greet passers-by.[461] The reception of guests is a greater thing than receiving the Shekinah.[462] Actually it was nine, not three measures of fine meal which he bade Sarah use, and three calves, not just one.[463] When the destruction of Sodom brought an end to wayfarers, Abraham moved southward.[464] The 'eshel which Abraham planted at Beer-

---

447 *B. K.* 60b.
448 *Gen. R.* XXXIX.
449 *Ibid.*
450 *B. M.* 59a.
451 *Arakin* 16a.
452 *B. K.* 93a.
453 *Gen. R.* LI.
454 *MHG.* to Gen. 13.11.
455 *Gen. R.* XLIV.
456 *Ibid.*
457 *Mekilta, Bo.* XI.
458 *San.* 89b.
459 *ARN* XIII.
460 *Gen. R.* XLVIII.
461 *Ibid.*
462 *Shebuot* 35b.
463 *ARN* XIII.   464 *Gen. R.* LII.

sheba[465] was a garden, according to one authority, designed to produce food for passers-by, but another authority insists that it was the storehouse for the food for wayfarers.[466] Still another view regards the 'eshel as the abbreviation for okel (food), shetiyah (drink), and lewayyah (company).[467] What generosity Lot showed was learned from Abraham.[468]

But Abraham did more than bring strangers into his home, he brought them under the wings of the Shekinah.[469] The phrase used of Abraham, "he called in the name Yahwe,"[470] means that Abraham made converts.[471] Abraham converted the children of the people rescued from the four kings.[472] Abraham's descendants were punished for Abraham's failure to convert the parents of these.[473] His circumcision came late in life so that circumcision should not be an obstacle to discourage proselytes.[474] Abraham began his missionary work in Haran.[475] The children whose mothers brought them reverently to be nursed by Sarah became proselytes.[476] Abraham is regarded as the father of all proselytes, who are more precious than Israel which stood at Mount Sinai.[477] That Israel had a covenant does not make them more precious than proselytes, for the "homeborn"[478] of Abraham also had a covenant.[479]

Abraham at first wondered about circumcising himself, since some of his associates advised him against it, but his friend Mamre rebuked him for delaying.[480] The circumcision removed

[465] Gen. 21.33.
[466] Sotah 10a.
[467] Mid. Psalms CX.
[468] Gen. R. L.
[469] Ibid.
[470] Gen. 12.8.
[471] Gen. R. XXXIX.
[472] Gen. R. XLIII.
[473] Ned. 32a.
[474] Gen. R. XLVI.
[475] Tar. Jon. to Gen. 12.5; San. 99b.
[476] Gen. R. LIII.
[477] Tan. Lek VI; cf. Pal. Bikkurim I, 4.
[478] Gen. 17.13.
[479] Mekilta, Mishpatim, XVIII.
[480] Gen. R. XLII.

Abraham's only blemish, and thereafter he was perfect.[481] He was circumcised before Isaac was born so that Isaac could issue from a holy source.[482] Circumcision preserved his virility.[483] Before Abraham was circumcised his visitors were human; after his circumcision it was God who visited him.[484] This visit[485] was God's visit to the sick Abraham, suffering the after-effects of his circumcision.[486] The father, if available, and no other, must circumcise the son.[487] Abraham's circumcision took place on Yom Kippur.[488]

Abraham was a scrupulous observer of the commandments, and therefore God commanded him to depart from among the idolaters.[489] Abraham observed all the commandments, including the law of the 'erub of dishes.[490] That he left his father behind in Haran was not an oversight, since God had freed him from the law of respect for one's parents.[491] He observed Passover.[492] He heeded the rules of ritual purity, refusing to eat the cakes defiled by Sarah's becoming menstruous.[493] He practiced the giving of *terumah*.[494] He knew and observed all the sacrifices.[495] He was the first to tithe.[496] He instituted the period of morning prayer.[497] The law of the fringe and of the phylactery derives from him.[498] When he was commanded to offer Isaac as a burnt sacrifice, Abraham protested that the offering required a priest; God

[481] *Gen. R.* XLVI.
[482] *Ibid.*
[483] *Ibid.*
[484] *Gen. R.* XLVII.
[485] Gen. 18.1.
[486] *Tar. Jon.* to Gen. 18.1.
[487] *Tar. Jon.* to Gen. 17.10; *Kiddushin* 29a.
[488] *PRE* XXIX.
[489] *Tan. Lek*, I.
[490] *Yoma* 28b.
[491] *Gen. R.* XXXIX.
[492] *Gen. R.* XLII.
[493] *B. M.* 87a.
[494] *Gen. R.* XLIII.
[495] *Gen. R.* XLIV.
[496] *Num. R.* XII.
[497] *Num. R.* II.
[498] *MHG* to Gen. 14.23.

reminded him that he was a priest.[499] The law that a mourner is
exempt from reciting the sh'ma' is derived from Abraham.[500]
Abraham's circumcision was only the crowning observance of an
already full observance of the commandments.[501] Abraham's
observance of the law of 'omer merited his inheriting the land of
Canaan.[502] The law that a man should divorce his childless wife
after ten years is hinted at in Gen. 15.3.[503] Abraham observed
all the commandments cheerfully.[504] Because Abraham "did" all
the Torah before it was actually come into the world he was
rewarded with possessions in his youth and hope in his old age.[505]

d. The Testing of Abraham

Abraham was tested ten times.[506] In none of these was he found
wanting. The tests prove Abraham's righteousness, for God tests
only the righteous.[507] The binding of Isaac was equal to all the
other tests.[508] The manner of the enjoining of this last test, with
uncertainty as to whether Ishmael or Isaac was meant, was for
the purpose of increasing the trial and of increasing Abraham's
reward.[509] Abraham did not want an eleventh test.[510]

[499] Gen. R. LV. The basis is the interpretation of Ps. 110.4.

[500] Gen. R. LVIII.

[501] Mekilta, Jethro I.

[502] Lev. R. XXVIII.

[503] Tosefta Yebamot VIII, 4.

[504] Mid. Psalms CXII.

[505] Pal. Kiddushin IV, 12; Kiddushin 82a.

[506] Abot V, 2. The sources, while agreeing that Abraham underwent ten
trials, do not agree as to what the trials were; a composite of the incidents
regarded as trials would total at least fifteen. For lists of ten, cf. ARN XXXIII
and PRE XXVI. The notion that the tests were more than the single one
mentioned in Gen. 22.1, is at least as old as Jub. XIX, 8. A usual list, ARN
XXXIII, is this: the departure from Ur; the famine in Egypt; the abduction
of Sarah; the banishment of Ishmael; the banishment of Hagar; the covenant
of Gen. 15; the fiery furnace of Ur; the war of the kings; circumcision; the
binding of Isaac. By withstanding these tests, a miracle came to Israel in
return for each of the ten successes. ARN XXXIII, there is a play on the word
nissah and nes.

[507] Gen. R. LV.

[508] Gen. R. LVI.

[509] Gen. R. LV.   [510] Gen. R. LVI.

e. *The Rewards to Abraham*

God rewarded Abraham for each footstep.[511] Abraham inherited both this world and the future world.[512] While God rewarded Abraham with material things in this world, his true reward awaited him in the world to come.[513] Abraham despised rewards from men,[514] and it was for that reason that rewards from God were prepared for him.[515] His rewards surpassed even those of the angels.[516]

f. *The Rewards to Israel*

Great and numerous as were the rewards to Abraham himself, they are exceeded by the rewards made to Israel on behalf of Abraham. Each of the ten trials which he withstood resulted in some miracle for his descendants.[517] The ten plagues of Egypt were a reward for the ten trials, and Abraham's descendants escaped these ten plagues.[518]

Because Abraham bowed to the three visitors, kings bowed to his descendants.[519] Because Abraham served the visitors well, God served Israel in the same measure.[520] When Abraham ran towards the visitors, blood dripped from him, since he had been circumcised but three days before; therefore God gave his descendants two means of evoking divine mercy: the blood of the Passover and the blood of circumcision.[521] The water which Abraham gave to the visitors became the water[522] given to his descendants in the wilderness.[523] The meal prepared by Abraham

---

[511] *Gen. R.* XXXIX.
[512] *MHG* to Gen. 12.
[513] *Gen. R.* XLIV; *PRE* XXVIII.
[514] Based on Gen. 14.23.
[515] *Tan. Lek*, XVII.
[516] *ARN* XXXIII.
[517] *ARN* XXXIII.
[518] *Ibid.*
[519] *Tos. Sotah* IV.   [520] *Ibid.*
[521] *Tan. Wa-Yera* IV.
[522] Num. 21.4 ff. and 16 ff.
[523] *Tos. Sotah* IV.

was greater than the banquet of Solomon.[524] Everything that Abraham did for the visitors was done in reward to Israel; what Abraham himself did, God himself rewarded, and what Abraham did through an accessory, God did through an emissary. Abraham ran to the cattle[525] so that God sent the quail.[526] The curd and milk[527] became the manna rained from heaven.[528] As Abraham stood by the visitors under the tree,[529] so God stood over the rock at Horeb.[530] As Abraham accompanied the angels,[531] God accompanied Israel out of Egypt.[532]

Because Abraham left Ur at 75, Israel was saved by Esther when she was 75.[533] Haman was hanged on a high tree because Abraham stood under a tree.[534]

Because Abraham described himself as dust and ashes[535] Israel was rewarded with the commandments of the red heifer and the law of *Sotah*.[536]

As God visited Abraham while he was sitting,[537] so God goes from house of learning to house of learning to bless Abraham's infant descendants who are sitting (and studying the Torah).[538]

Because Abraham fought the kings at night,[539] God redeemed his children on the same night, Passover.[540] As God spoke to Abraham, "I" (am thy shield), so, in the ten commandments, He began "I" (am the Lord thy God).[541]

---

[524] I Kings 5.
[525] Gen. 18.7.
[526] Num. 11.31.
[527] Gen. 18.8.
[528] Ex. 16.4.   [529] Gen. 18.8.
[530] Ex. 17.6.
[531] Gen. 18.16.
[532] Ex. 13.21; *B. M.* 86b.
[533] *Yal. Shim.* I, 66.
[534] *Ibid.*, 256.
[535] Gen. 18.27.
[536] *Sotah* 17a.
[537] Gen. 18.1.
[538] *Tan. Wa-yera*, IV.
[539] Gen. 14.15.
[540] *Gen. R.* XLIII.
[541] *PR.* XXI.

g. *The Merit of Abraham*

The visitors who went to Sodom did so in merit of Abraham, and not in the merit of Lot.[542] Lot himself was saved through Abraham's merit.[543] It was the merit of Abraham which permitted the daughters of Lot to conceive.[544]

The pitcher of water which Abraham gave Hagar remained full no matter how much was drunk, through the merit of Abraham, until the time that Hagar began to worship an idol in the desert.[545] Hagar's prayer was heard through the merit of Abraham.[546] The merit which provided a well for Hagar abided to provide a well for Abraham's descendants.[547]

In Abraham's merit, the children of Israel were given the laws of the fringe and the phylacteries, the tabernacle, and the animal sacrifices.[548] Indeed, Yom Kippur and the three festivals were a reward on his behalf.[549]

Abraham's cleaving of the wood[550] cleaved the Red Sea for his descendants.[551] That he used a knife (from the root *'akl*) is the merit through which food (from the same root) is provided for his descendants.[552]

The merit of Abraham made Aaron eligible to enter the Holy of Holies.[553]

Abraham's merit made his intercessory prayers effective. The cure of Abimelech was effected in this way.[554] He is the first who prayed on behalf of another.[555] Worship brings its reward; it

---

[542] *Gen. R. L.*
[543] *MHG* to Gen. 19.15.
[544] *Gen. R. LI.*
[545] *PRE* XXX.
[546] *Gen. R. LIII.*
[547] *Yal. Shim.* I, 764.
[548] *Gen. R. XLIII.*
[549] *MHG* to Gen. 14.23.
[550] Gen. 22.3.
[551] *Gen. R. LV.*
[552] *Gen. R. LVI.*
[553] *Ex. R. XXXVIII.*
[554] *Gen. R. LII.*
[555] *Gen. R. LVI.*

saved Isaac at the time of the Binding.[556] Abraham instituted
the morning prayers.[557] Abraham's reward for praying on behalf
of Abimelech's sterility was that Abraham's barrenness ceased
even before Abimelech's.[558] Abraham "prayed" between Bethel
and Ai,[559] and it is therefore well for a man to pray before trouble
overtakes him, for Abraham's prayers saved his descendants
there.[560] He accomplished his conquest of the kings not by means
of weapons but by prayers and supplications.[561] Abraham's
"raising of his hand"[562] was an act of prayer.[563]

Abraham's merit was used by Joseph.[564] Daniel's prayer[565]
was answered through the merit of Abraham.[566] Through Abraham's merit, Isaac was blessed with five things: beauty, strength,
wealth, wisdom, and years.[567] His merit led to the Exodus,[568]
and to the singing of the Song of the Sea.[569] Through his merit
the Shekinah comes to the Temple.[570] Through Abraham, Israel
merited the Priestly Benediction.[571]

Just as the Binding of Isaac was Abraham's greatest test, so
was it the source of the greatest merit to Abraham's descendants.
The recollection of it would evoke God's mercy for Abraham's
descendants.[572] The sounding of the ram's horn on Rosh Hashanah would bring release to his descendants from the clutches of
sin, and they would be redeemed ultimately from subjection to
other nations through the horn.[573] When God sent an angel to de-

---

[556] Gen. R. LVI.

[557] The three periods of prayer, morning, afternoon and evening, were
established, respectively, by Abraham, Isaac, and Jacob, Berakot 26b.

[558] B. K. 92a.

[559] Gen. 12.8.

[560] Josh. 7.4; Mekilta Beshalaḥ, II.

[561] Lev. R. XXVIII.

[562] Gen. 14.22.

[563] Tar. Onk. ad loc.

[564] Gen. R. VI.

[565] Dan. 9.4–19.

[566] Berakot 7b.

[567] Tan. Toledot, VII.

[568] Ex. R. XV.

[569] Ex. R. XXIII.

[570] Lev. R. XXXI.

[571] Gen. R. XLIII.

[572] Gen. R. LVI.

[573] Gen. R. LVI.

stroy Jerusalem,[574] He saw the "blood of the Binding of Isaac" and repented.[575] In a period of fast, there is added to the *Shemoneh 'Esre,* among six additional benedictions, this blessing: "May He Who answered Abraham on Mount Moriah answer you."[576] Abraham reminded God of the *'Akedah* at the time of the destruction of the Temple.[577] Abraham prayed to God that the merit of the Binding be valid for future generations.[578]

h. *The Prophet*

God made many revelations to Abraham. He conversed with him both in speech and in visions, whereas with other prophets God conversed in either one or the other, but not in both.[579] Abraham inferred from astrological devices that he would be childless; God rebuked him for this, commanding him to be a prophet and not an astrologer.[580] God lifted Abraham up to heaven, and showed him the streets there.[581]

God revealed to Abraham the conquests by the Babylonians, the Persians, the Greeks, and the Romans. He revealed to him the princes both of Israel and of the nations; he showed him the hostility of nations to each other. He showed him the place where the great Sanhedrin would sit.[582] He showed him Gehenna, the Revelation on Sinai, and the Temple.[583] He revealed to him the Crossing of the Red Sea.[584] While one authority believes that Abraham was shown only this world, another insists that he was shown the world to come.[585] Similarly, the view is expressed that he was shown only those matters which were to

---

[574] I Chron. 21.15.
[575] *Mekilta Bo,* XI.
[576] *Ta'anit* 15a.
[577] *Lam. R. Proem* XXIV.
[578] *Tar. Jon.* to Gen. 12.14. Cf. Ginzberg, V, 252–253 for various views on the atoning power of the *'Akedah.*
[579] *Gen. R.* XLIV.
[580] *Shab.* 156a.
[581] *Gen. R.* XLIV.
[582] *Gen. R.* XLIV.
[583] *Ibid.*
[584] *Ibid.*   [585] *Ibid.*

take place up to the time of the Exodus from Egypt, but it is averred, to the contrary, that he was shown the future even beyond the Exodus.[586]

A prophet, he knew that Abimelech would not harm Sarah.[587] He knew that Rebekkah would be born,[588] and he knew what would occur to Eliezer at Laban's.[589] He journeyed to the site of the Temple.[590] God revealed to Abraham not only the Temple but the order of sacrifices to be offered there.[591]

i. The Sage

Abraham is the man whom wisdom makes stronger than seven rulers;[592] Abraham was the wisest man in the generations from Noah to Abraham.[593] It is he who is alluded to as the sage;[594] the sage whose wisdom endures[595] is Abraham.[596]

j. Abraham's Seed

In conformity with the biblical promise, the seed of Abraham was numerous. The offspring of Abraham and Keturah replaced those swept away in the flood.[597] Despite the efforts of Pharaoh, his descendants numbered at the time of the Exodus six hundred thousand.[598] The true seed of Abraham is that which arose through Isaac, and not through Ishmael.[599] More specifically, part of Isaac's descendants (that is, excluding the offspring of Esau) are the true descendants of Abraham.[600] The true seed

---

[586] Ibid.   [587] Gen. R. LII.
[588] Gen. R. LVIII.
[589] Gen. R. LX.
[590] Gen. R. XXXIX.
[591] Mekilta, Jethro, IX.
[592] Eccl. R. VII, 19.
[593] Gen. R. XXXIX.
[594] Eccl. R. II, 14.
[595] Eccl. 2.26.
[596] Eccl. R. II, 26.
[597] Gen. R. XXXVII.
[598] Ex. R. I and III.
[599] Tar. Jon. to Gen. 21.12.   [600] Gen. R. LIII.

are only those who believe in the existence of two worlds, this world and the future world.[601] The true seed of Abraham are only those, who like Abraham, beget offspring.[602] The true seed of Israel are only the circumcised.[603]

k. *Abraham's Old Age*

Abraham was greatly blessed in his old age. Because Abraham had advanced the cause of God, he merited this old age which is an imitation of God's eternity.[604] The crown of glory[605] which is the mark of the hoary head is derived from the experience of Abraham.[606] The marks of old age did not exist until Abraham's time; they were the result of a request Abraham made so that people could distinguish between him and Isaac.[607] He evoked the praise of his fellowmen, being known in the gates.[608] He sat in the Academy (of elders) which existed from the earliest days.[609] His old age was proof that he acquired wisdom.[610] The marks of old age and the respect these elicited were the rewards, transcending gold and silver, which Abraham's righteousness won for him.[611] While some acquire the characteristics of old age without the actual count of days, and some acquire the total of days without the marks of old age, Abraham acquired both.[612] In his old age he received a foretaste of the world to come.[613] His virility did not forsake him in his old age.[614] As a reward Ishmael repented in Abraham's old age.[615]

[601] *Ibid.*
[602] *Yebamot* 64a.
[603] Gen. 17.9 as interpreted in *Yal. Shim.* 82.
[604] *Gen. R.* LVIII.
[605] Prov. 16.31.
[606] *Gen. R.* LIX.
[607] *B. M.* 87a.
[608] *Tan. Ḥayye Sarah* III, based on Prov. 31.23.
[609] *Yoma* 28b.
[610] *Sifra, Qedoshim,* VII.
[611] *Tan. Ḥayye Sarah* IV.
[612] *Gen. R.* LIX.
[613] *SER* V.
[614] *Kiddushin* 82a; *Tan. Ḥayye Sara* 7.
[615] *Tar. Jon.* to Gen. 25.8.

1. *The Death of Abraham*

At Abraham's death the great among the nations of the world declared that the world had lost its guide and helmsman.[616] He went into the future world, a glimpse of which had previously been given to him.[617] He was joined there by Isaac and Jacob and by their righteous descendants.[618] He continues his activity in the future world; he sits at the gate of Hell and permits no circumcised Jew to enter. Those, however, who have sinned very much have their "foreskins" restored by Abraham, by grafting on foreskins taken from babes who died before their eighth day; thereby the sinners enter Hell, and Abraham saves the babes.[619] His capacity as an intercessor endures for many generations.[620]

The rabbinic literature reads back into the career of the patriarch its own interests and concerns. Abraham observes the written Torah and the Oral Torah. He sits in an Academy learning *halakot*. He gives tithes; he prays. He travels to the site of the Temple; he teaches the Grace after the Meal. The originator of faith in the true God, he abides in that faith against persecuting idolators.

His sagacity is great; he is a source of gnomic wisdom, and he conducts himself in accord with the amenities and with high standards of courtesy. He is not without imperfections, and he makes errors; he rises to greatness without losing his humanity.

Abraham is depicted in such terms that were one to be a perfect imitator of Abraham, he would thereby be conforming to the highest of rabbinic standards and be an executor of rabbinic laws. To the rabbis, one might say, Abraham is a rabbi.

---

[616] *B. B.* 91.
[617] *Gen. R.* LXII.
[618] *SER VI.*
[619] *Gen. R.* XLVIII.
[620] *Gen. R.* XXXV.

CHAPTER THREE

ABRAHAM IN PHILO'S WRITINGS

I

Troublesome problems in methodology inhere in any effort to give an exposition of Philonic thought.[1] These are occasioned by the character of Philo's treatises, with their rapid shifts of figures and even of subject matter, and with their frequent apparently inconsistent and occasionally contradictory terms or even notions. In the present instance, an immediate problem stems from what might be described as Philo's double approach to Scripture, namely his use of what he terms the literal and the allegorical.

The difficulty is that Philo himself gives us such a division, but he is by no means rigid about the division, and the commentator who would separate these strands too sharply can find himself doing inadvertent injustice to Philo's thought. To anticipate a distinction discussed in detail below, there is a literal Abraham in Philo and there is an allegorical Abraham. The literal Abraham is the historical character of the simple biblical account, though by no means a character of such simplicity in Philo; it is the Abraham who migrated from Chaldea, to Haran, and then to Palestine, who was the husband of Sarah; who rescued Lot; who begot Ishmael and Isaac; and who ultimately passed away in good old age. The allegorical Abraham is the historical character who abandoned pantheistic materialism and went on to the cognition of the true God by a process of freeing his soul from domination by the body. Philo inherited both of these Abrahams and he propagated them both. Yet, while he

[1] Cf. scholarly expressions of methodological dismay assembled in Völker, *op. cit.*, 5 ff.

himself distinguishes between them, he cannot present his literal Abraham in a treatise such as *De Abrahamo* without the intrusion of allegorical overtones which are in some instances merely nuances while in others they are direct statements. We shall see that Philo begins one passage in this treatise as "allegory," but terminates it as though it had been "literal," and he then proceeds to allegorize an already allegorized incident. Accordingly, the literal Abraham is in several ways more than only a recasting of biblical narratives.

Next, the allegorical Abraham is also a number of related and associated matters: It is the "figure for the good mind," a peg on which Philo suspends his quasi-philosophical inferences from the Scriptural text. Again, the allegorical Abraham is the figure for any good mind, for Philo's own mind, or for the mind of the historical patriarch. This "figure" varies from being a type to being an individual. Where it is a type, the specific "Abraham" can be de-emphasized to the point of disappearance, as when Philo discussed with some philosophical objectivity the *logos tomeus*, or the value of the encyclia, or the nature of *ecstasis*. But these discussions obtain their relevance for Philo by their association, however tenuous it may be in context, with the allegorical Abraham.

A large portion of Philo's writings are given over to objective explanations of the "type." But Philo goes considerably beyond the objectivity of explanation; he portrays the historical Abraham as the individual who experienced these explained abstractions vividly and intimately. That is to say, Philo not only tells us what, for example, *ecstasis* was, he also tells us that Abraham underwent it. The literal Abraham can be described as the record of Abraham's "body"; the allegorical Abraham is Philo's account of the progress and destiny of Abraham's soul.

The methodological problem involved in the allegorical Abraham is that some passages both explain philosophical ideas and utilize these in a "spiritual biography" of Abraham; but some passages state only one aspect explicitly, leaving the other aspect to be inferred. Initially I set out to arrange the philosophical explanations in some reasonable order, and I proposed thereafter to fit the individual into that series of explanations.

I found myself presenting a series of vignettes from Philo's thought in a manner that has ultimately seemed as unnecessary as it was pedestrian. These philosophical explanations fit in with the entire body of Philonic explanations; indeed, they coincide with and overlap them. Philo explains the body, the senses, the mind, the encyclia, and other matters in contexts unrelated to Abraham. The exodus of Israel from Egypt, for example, requires Philo to parallel and duplicate in that "spiritual" journey many of the matters he touches upon in the history of Abraham. Since my task is not primarily to reproduce the totality of Philonic thought,[2] but Philo's conception of Abraham, I have determined to present the allegorical Abraham as the experience of the individual, and to present in annotation the relevant explanations associated with the type. I am not satisfied that I have eliminated all repetitiousness. Philo's manner precludes success, no matter how zealously the commentator tries.

Still another problem in methodology has been that of arranging the allegorical material. A verse by verse sequence of the germane passages in *Genesis* does not yield a cumulative picture. For while Philo does utilize a number of verses in a series for individual treatises such as *Heres* or *Migratio*, or in some portions of *Quaestiones in Genesin*, he by no means binds himself to the biblical sequence. For Philo the culmination of the religious experience is the "vision of God"; this culmination ensues for a sage who goes beyond the encyclia into true philosophy and virtue. Philo interprets passages in Gen. 12 and Gen. 15 to prove that Abraham had this culminating experience; but he utilizes Gen. 16 (Hagar as the encyclia) as a preparatory and preliminary matter. Similarly, Keturah (the sense of smell) appears virtually at the end of the biblical portion on Abraham, Gen. 25, and Philo interprets Keturah, as we shall see, as an early stage which Abraham passed beyond.

Philo plucks his verses, individually or in a series, from whatever chapter these chance to occur in, and he brings them, regardless of the biblical position or context, into congruency with

---

[2] The Abraham material alone touches on virtually every problem in Philo. I have no intention here of recapitulating what Wolfson, Drummond, and Bréhier have done.

his predetermined purpose. Therefore, there was little to gain from presenting the allegorical Abraham in the biblical sequence.

I present the allegorical material, instead, as a range of matters in what seems to me to be true to Philo's use and intent. I have found a Philonic device, his interpretation of Gen. 15.9, helpful in arranging the allegorical material, in that it has enabled me to use subdivisions of Philo's rather than some arbitrary arrangement of my own.

One final item, an understanding of which may perhaps give cohesiveness and clarity to the inevitable reflection in my own exposition of Philo's discursiveness, tergiversations, and crotchets. To begin with an example, I have frequent occasion in the footnotes to comment that Lot is at times Abraham at a stage in his development, yet at other times a figure in contrast with Abraham. Such a disparity in treatment does not result from any genuine inconsistency in Philo but rather, it seems to me, from his over-all conception of Scripture. While it has been frequently noted that Philo tells us over and over again that the allegory of Scripture is the record of the progress of the Soul,[3] and commentators have noted this facet in strands or sections of Philo's writings, I have seen nowhere any effort to depict the significance of Scripture *as a totality* to Philo.[4]

---

[3] See Bréhier, 45 ff. for the relevant passages.

[4] Virtually all the commentators, Drummond, Kennedy, Wolfson, etc., content themselves with noting that Philo reads "Greek philosophy" into OT. Ergo, most commentators search and research the philosophical problems raised by Philo's exegesis. The by-product is that all too often the commentators, as for example Wolfson, give us what was latent in Philo's mind, but abstain from recreating and interpreting Philo's direct and avowed intent. All too little attention has been paid to the essentially Philonic in Philo's writings, namely, his religious experience and orientation and his exhortation to his readers to practice religion! Bréhier, it would seem to me, is the nearest of the general commentators to state the quintessence of Philo; but there is a margin of difference between, on the one hand, what Philo sees *in* Scripture, and, on the other hand, what Philo sees Scripture *as*. Goodenough says many perceptive and enlightening things that touch on the matter, but these are found in various sections of his *By Light, Light*, with the result that they are not quickly seen as a totality. My effort to portray the forest rather than the various trees owes a debt primarily to Goodenough. But the forest remains undepicted as far as I know in the scholarly writings.

Goodenough has written on Abraham in his *By Light, Light*, Chapter 5, "Enos, Enoch, Noah, and Abraham," and in *An Introduction to Philo Judaeus*,

I have treated this matter in an as yet unpublished paper[5] and I shall here give only a brief resumé.

Philo sees in Scripture the experience of every man. In its literal sense it dealt with ancient times, events and personalities; allegory, however, makes Scripture the record of the unfolding experience of the reader.[6]

The original Adam (of Gen. 1.27) was a heavenly creation, and unmixed with material things. He is the rational, pre-existent soul. This soul becomes mixed with clay from the earth when God "fashions" the earthy Adam of Gen. 2.7. There is joined to him Eve, sense-perception; but the serpent, pleasure, intrudes to divert man from lofty obligations into harmful ones. Man (mind) thereupon is quite different in his individual earthy state from what pure, generic mind was before it became mixed with body (in birth), and the mind intent on salvation must therefore free itself of the encumbrance of the body so as to regain its pristine immaterial purity. Every man spends his babyhood in pursuing the vices of the body, Egypt; later he encounters the vices of adolescence, Canaan. It is then that he has to make his choice whether to remain in body, as did the king of Egypt; or whether to be foolish, as was Abimelech the king of the Philistines; or to depart from senses and passions, as the good man does. At this stage of choice every man faces the contradictory tendencies and therefore he wavers like Lot, inclining partly to what is good and partly to what is evil.

especially pp. 187–189. Professor Goodenough is my mentor in Philonic studies, and I owe him many debts. The figure of Abraham is not central in his studies as it is in the present manuscript of mine, and consequently my exposition, however derivative, is fuller and also diverges at points.

[5] "The Authority of the Bible for Philo" read at the Week of Work of the National Council on Religion in Higher Education, Meadville, Pa., August, 1952. See *Judaism* IV (1955), I, pp. 47–57.

[6] I recognize the proximity of these words to the "religious existentialist" interpretation, made somewhat fashionable by the wide interest in Kirkegaard. I have not yet seen G. Kuhlmann's *Theologia naturalis bei Philon und bei Paulus* (*Neutestamentliche Forschungen*, Heft 7, 1930), which Völker, 43, sneers at, in that it appears to make Philo the outstanding representative of modern existentialism, "der mit scharfem Blicke bereits alle Probleme des Jahres 1930 kannte." It is, of course, essential for a case not to be overstated; I ascribe to Philo a kind of "existentialism," but that is far removed from making him a disciple of modern Protestant theologians.

The soul, or mind, which is to progress, goes through three stages on its march to perfection. Initially he must have hope, Enos. Next, he must have repentance, Enoch, the abandonment of his previous ways. Thereupon he has arrived at the stage of rest or tranquility, which is Noah. At this stage his mind is righteous, if weighed by a standard which is less than truly exalted.

To press on towards perfection, each mind has natural endowments, which number three, and which are present in every perfectible mind, though in varying degrees. They are, respectively, the ability to be taught (Abraham), natural virtue (Isaac) and perfection attained through practice (Jacob).

The perfection through being taught involves the departure from error and from adolescent vice for a sojourn in the university education, the "encyclical studies," Hagar. At that stage the mind being less than perfect can produce only sophistry (Ishmael). Progressing beyond factual knowledge the mind comes upon Sarah, "wisdom" or "virtue." But man does not achieve his own happiness; it is a gift to man from God, born out of man's virtue; hence God sows seeds in Sarah who bears the offspring, joy (Isaac), to man.

Isaac, natural perfection, mates with Rebekkah, constancy. Jacob, the practicer, marries Leah, "virtue attained through toil" (out of whom God produces offspring, individual virtues). Laban, "brightness," the way of thinking governed by the senses, has no real understanding of the proper sequence in the attainment of virtue, and insists that Jacob must marry Leah even before Jacob has gone beyond Rachel, "superficiality." Jacob bears Dan, "distinguishing," out of Bilhah, "swallowing," sustaining life. Zilpah ("walking mouth") is the power of proper and correct expression of thoughts. Man must migrate with all his capacities from the area of the "senses," Haran, as Jacob fled from Laban, to become metamorphosed from the "practicer" into Israel, "seer of God."

Every perceptive man can see in the experiences of the patriarchs reflections in himself of the use and development of his innate capacities. By following their example, he can come to perfection, that is, he can live on the level of pure mind, unencumbered by the body. Indeed he can live on the level of the divine mind, the Logos.

It is the experience of some men who, having attained to such perfection, abandon the concern with heavenly matters and turn to the lowly human affairs, as did Joseph. Insofar as Joseph had attained perfection, he had the qualities of the statesman, but his concern with mundane matters made him from time to time the objectionable "politician." Each of us who deals with human affairs descends from heavenly matters to earthly ones.

The man who is able to marshall his gifts of teaching, nature, and practice is able to live on the level of "right reason." Such a level is that of Moses, who is the symbol of pure thought. Related to Moses, though lower, is his brother Aaron, "uttered thought." The cult practices of Judaism are the level of Aaron, a lower mystery, attained through the observance and execution of the literal laws of Scripture. But for the perfect soul, these laws are not as much requirements as they are exhortations. They are copies of the law of nature and are in conformity with that law. Hence, the literalist who observes the requirements of Judaism is automatically acting in conformity with nature. But if a man penetrates to the level of Moses, then he knows the deeper significance of the enacted laws, and, accordingly, he is living not by laws but by "nature" itself.

The patriarchs and Moses are the exemplars of living by nature. The enacted, specific laws are the tool through which man can either consciously or unconsciously live by the higher law. That is, the Bible is the vehicle by which man, a mixture of body and soul, can gain salvation; he can escape the domination of the body, for which the enacted laws provide the formula, and ultimately live by divine reason itself. Indeed, through God's grace he may from time to time receive the vision of God.[7]

---

[7] I think it has not been noted that there is a clear intimation of all the above in Philo's Exposition. *Opificio* deals with Creation and with the two Adams; *De Abrahamo* presents the triad, Enos, Enoch, and Noah as preparatory to the patriarchs, before concentrating on Abraham. The treatises on Isaac and Jacob are lost. The next treatise, *Joseph*, deals with the problems of

From the standpoint that the biblical materials are the experience, actual or potential, items otherwise enigmatic become intelligible. Thus, Philo mentions his own desire to be mated with Sarah (wisdom). He exhorts those of us who read him (and he writes with exhortatory imperatives) to abandon Chaldea and migrate to the wilderness.

In our context, the methodological problem is that such exhortations to us or attestations of his personal experience become intermingled with his exegetical exposition of the biblical personalities. At every opportunity Philo may not state that it was his allegorical Abraham who married Hagar, the "encyclical studies"; he may do no more than tell what transpires when he, or one of us who reads him, "marries" her. In assembling my material on Abraham I have attempted to abstain from going beyond Philo's own utterances; but very often there are passages in which the "Abraham-type" is so vividly implicit in Philo that it has not seemed to me straining too much to make it explicit.

Moreover, the point of departure for such material in Philo is some verse or sequence of verses in the chapters in which the Bible portrays Abraham. Accordingly, even where Philo does not always specifically mention Abraham, such Philonic passages have a relevance for us in that they can illuminate what Philo saw in the verses which in the Bible deal with Abraham.

After I present the literal and the allegorical Abraham as separate aspects, I discuss the relationship between them. I find this necessary not only as a logical procedure, but as a corrective of whatever inadvertent distortion can result from a too-rigid separation of the two.

Thereafter I discuss the religious import of Abraham to Philo. I show that Abraham is an exemplar of the religious mystic who rises above sense and body into communion with God. Abraham is one of Philo's proofs that the Philonic formula for true religious living, by metaphysical reality, is not only feasible, but that it was accomplished in history.

human affairs. Next come the treatises on *Moses*, ensued by the *Decalogue* and the four treatises on *The Special Laws*.

Finally, I conclude that the Philonic Abraham owes few debts, if any, to the rabbinic Abraham, or to the various Abrahams of the extra-canonical writings. I conclude, also, that the connection between Philo's Abraham and the Abraham of the earlier hellenistic Jews is very tenuous, and distinguished more by differences than by sporadic and superficial similarity.[8]

II

The primary source for the literal Abraham is the treatise *De Abrahamo*. (This treatise is part of the Exposition and is often confused by students with *De Migratione Abrahami*, which is part of the Allegory.)

There is a little material in *Quaestiones in Genesin*, but Philo's typical treatment there is to state that the literal meaning is obvious, and he therefore proceeds immediately to the Allegorical. This section of our study deals primarily with *De Abrahamo*, and we will presently revert to it as our main interest.

A summary passage in *Virt.* gives us Philo's view of Abraham succinctly. Though Abraham's ancestors were men of guilt, Abraham's own life is worthy of emulation[9] and full of good report. Though the son of an astrologer, whose creed is that there is no originating cause outside what we perceive by the

[8] The literature most frequently cited in this section is as follows: Goodenough, *By Light, Light*; Wolfson, *Philo*, two vols.; Bréhier, *Les idées philosophiques et religieuses de Philon*; Drummond, *Philo Judaeus*; *or, the Jewish Alexandrian Philosophy in its Development and Completion*; Colson and Whitaker, *Philo* (Loeb Classical Series) I–IX (Colson alone for VI–IX); and Ginzberg, *Legends of the Jews*. I cite these only by the author.

[9] A clear expression of an item frequently hinted at is Knox's notice that in Philo Abraham is an exemplar of the proselyte who voluntarily abandoned astrology in favor of the truth. See "Abraham and the Quest for God," *HTR* XXVIII (1939) 55–60. A note of my own, "Abraham's Knowledge of the Existence of God," *HTR* (XLIV) (1951) 137–139 suggests only a slight modification of Knox's thesis which I hold to be sound. The motif, frequent in rabbinic literature, that Abraham was the great missionary, is lacking in Philo. Disparities in time and the danger of comparing the one Philo with the many rabbis inhibit a facile generalization; one might tentatively suggest that, with respect to proselytism, for the rabbis Abraham is the missionary *par excellence*, while for Philo he is the significant "convert."

senses, Abraham perceives that there is nothing more grievous to the nobility of the soul than that knowledge of secondary things should lead to the ignoring of the One, the Primal. This perception, along with divine inspiration, induces Abraham to leave his native country, his race, and his paternal home. He knows that if he stays, the delusions of the polytheistic creed will stay within him and render it impossible for him to discover the One God. But if he moves, the delusion will move out of his mind, and the false creed will be replaced by truth. At the same time he yearns to know God, and this yearning is fanned up by divine injunctions. With these to guide his steps, he goes forth, never faltering in his ardor to seek for the One, nor does he pause until he receives clearer visions.[10] Abraham is properly spoken of as the first to believe in God,[11] for he first grasped a firm and unswerving conception that there is one Cause above all.[12]

There are two classes of men, some earth-born, and some heaven-born. Men of God are those who refuse to accept membership in the commonwealth of the cosmos. Abraham is such a man of heaven, who rises from the world to a better state, to the commonwealth of ideas which are imperishable and incorporeal. He is himself a man of God.[13]

Respecting *De Abrahamo,* its form was recognized by Priessnig[13a] as hellenistic. Priessnig terms the treatise an edifying theological biography, and he finds it in accord with the literary conventions of the period.[14] Philo uses a topical arrangement;

[10] *Virt.* 211–215. The passage is a good example of Philo's merging of the literal and the allegorical. Abraham leaves Chaldea; Abraham leaves astrology; departure from the literal Chaldea ensures departure from astrology.

[11] Based on Gen. 15.6.

[12] *Virt.,* 216.

[13] *Gig.* 58–61.

[13a] "Die literarische Form der Patriarchenbiographien des Philon von Alexandrien," *MGWJ,* LXXIII (1929), 143 ff.

[14] Wendland had antecedently shown that Philo's literary form was similar to the Cynic and Stoic writings, "Philo und die kynisch-stoische Diatribe," in Wendland, Paul und Kern, Otto, *Beiträge zur Geschichte der Griechischen Philosophie und Religion,* 1895. Wolfson, recognizing this hellenistic influence, would nevertheless assert the "native Jewish midrashic" character of Philo's writing; I, 95–96. Wolfson's remarks may be appropriate

he departs from the biblical order and presents his Abraham in a series of episodes at variance with the biblical sequence.[14a]

The topics, as Philo presents them (after a lengthy introduction ##1–59) are Abraham's piety, ##62–80; his perfection in wisdom, ##81–88; the reward of his piety, ##89–98; his hospitality, a by-product of his piety, ##114–132; his greatest act of piety, the sacrifice of Isaac, ##167–207. So far Philo has been discussing Abraham's relation to God. His topics now turn to relations with men: his justice, ##208–216; his courage in war, ##217–244; his cultivation of moderation, ##245–261; and finally, his faith ##262–273. The human qualities are discussed, as Goodenough puts it,[15] in terms of the Greek four great cardinal virtues, justice, courage, self-control, and wisdom.

These, however, are matters of form, and not of content. It would not be impossible that the form of a treatise be hellenistic and the content Pharisaic Jewish. Such, however, is by no means the case. The content of *De Abrahamo*, and indeed, the Abraham explicit literally or implicit allegorically, throughout Philo's writings is thoroughly hellenized. Apologetic motifs,[16]

---

to the *Allegory* and to *QG* and *QE. Abr.* and the other treatises of the *Exposition*, however, are not in form midrashic homilies based on verses of the Bible, but rather topical treatises dissociated from a single verse or group of verses. The hellenistic form of *De Abrahamo* does not seem to me to be open to question.

[14a] Philo hearkens back to the Biblical passages in this order: Gen. 12.1–9; Gen.11.26–32; Gen. 18; Gen. 12.10–20; Gen. 18; Gen. 19; Gen. 22; Gen. 13; Gen. 14; Gen. 16; Gen. 23; Gen. 15; Gen. 24; and Gen. 26.

[15] *By Light, Light,* 142. Philo seems, however, to replace "prudence" with "faith" in this tractate. On Abraham's prudence, see *QG* IV,3, based on Gen. 18.2.

[16] This is pointed out adequately in the standard works on apologetics by Güdemann, Krieger and Friedlander. The recent denial by Tscherikover (in ספר יוחנן לוי, 139–160) is not only too sweeping, but also rests on some confusion. Were it as Tscherikover believes, that Hellenistic-Jewish writers were writing only for Jews, that would still leave untouched the issue of the presence of apologetic motifs. Granted that the captious critics to whom Philo replies in *De Abrahamo* about the *Binding of Isaac* are from within the Jewish community, as I myself believe, the only difference this makes is in our awareness of towards whom the apologetics is directed. I see very little substance derivable from the supposedly radical revision which Tscherikover proposes.

as nuances and overtones, are by no means unknown in Philo's works, but Abraham is not a different character in De Abrahamo (possibly written for non-Jews) from the Abraham of the Allegory (written, probably, for Jews). The conception of Abraham is so consistent and so integral in Philo's view of the Bible that it is impossible to regard his Abraham as having, in De Abrahamo, a hellenistic garb for a judiciously selected apologetic occasion. Philo's Abraham is consistently clothed in the hellenistic wardrobe which Philo here provides, and these clothes are everywhere tailored to Philo's essential views, and not to a special presentation for Gentiles.

For Philo, as for Paul and for the rabbis, a fundamental problem regarding Abraham is the relationship between Abraham, the ancestor, and the descendant, Moses, and his Law. If Moses' Law was the divine law, how could Abraham (and the other patriarchs) have flourished without it? The rabbis solve the problem in their way by asserting that Abraham observed the Mosaic Law; in fact, Abraham observed the "Oral" Law also. Paul is caught in the dilemma of a repudiation of the Mosaic Law and some defense of it; his solution is to regard the Law as having only temporal validity, beginning long after Abraham, who did not observe it, and enduring until Jesus, at which time it was abrogated. Philo gives his own answer, an answer possible only in Greek and not rabbinic thinking: Abraham observed the law of nature, and Abraham was himself a law; the Law of Moses is the copy of the law of nature, and the Law of Moses derives its specifications from those specific things which Abraham (and other patriarchs) did.

Philo, accordingly, adds a subtitle to his treatise, De Abrahamo: "The Life of the Sage Made Perfect Through Instruction, or the First Book on Unwritten Laws." This treatise, Philo tells us, carries on an earlier one (Opificio) and both are part of an examination of "law" in an orderly sequence. He is not ready, however, to discuss the particular laws; those are only copies. First he will discuss those laws which are general (καθολικώτεροι) and which can be considered as the archetypes of the copies.[17] These original laws are men; these men lived

[17] Abr. 3.

good and blameless lives. Scripture records their virtues for a
purpose beyond sounding their praises: to instruct the reader
and to induce him to emulate these men. These men are "laws
incarnate and vocal."

What Philo is saying in effect is that the biographies of
Abraham and others in Genesis, and of Moses in Exodus are
legal documents; that the Mosaic Law is the specific and the
copy of the archetypal law found in Genesis. The rabbinic view
is completely foreign to Philo. The rabbis take as their norm
the Mosaic (and Oral) Law, and they bring Abraham up to
the norm by portraying him as an observer. Philo, however,
takes Abraham (and the Patriarchs) as the norm, and shows
in what way the Law of Moses fits in with the norm. The
rabbis say that Abraham observed the Law; Philo says that
the Law sets forth as legislation those things which Abraham
did.[18]

Philo is saying two different, though supplementary, things
about Abraham and Law. First, he is telling us that Abraham's
deeds become recorded law; second, he tells us that there is a
law which Abraham observed, the law of nature, the most
venerable of statutes.[19] Insofar as he was a lawful man, it was
the law of nature which Abraham followed. Since the particular
laws, that is, the Mosaic code, are the copy of deeds of men who
followed nature, the Mosaic Law is consistent with nature.[20]
It is no difficult task, Philo tells us, to follow the particular

[18] Despite differences, Philo is near to Paul. Unlike Paul, he has no wish
to abrogate the Law; indeed, he insists that it must be preserved. But like
Paul (and against Jubilees and the rabbis) Philo concedes a temporal factor
in the Law; this pertains to its institution in Moses' time. Paul and Philo
coincide in conceiving of the Patriarchs as not living under the Law. Eusebius
gives us what is almost a blending of Philo's views on Abraham with those of
Paul in Romans; cf. *Praep. Evang.* VII, 8.

[19] For pre-Stoic and Stoic views on "law of nature," see Drummond I,
76–94; Wolfson II, 170–183. Wolfson's effort to base Philo's presentation of
natural law on Jewish tradition, *ibid.*, 183 ff., seems singularly one-sided and to
me not at all persuasive. For other material on the law of nature see Goodenough, "The Political Philosophy of Hellenistic Kingship," *Yale Classical
Studies*, I, (1928), 53–102. Additional literature is listed in Goodenough, *The
Politics of Philo Judaeus*, 44, footnote 7.

[20] *Abr.* 5.

laws, since the patriarchs followed the unwritten law[21] with ease.[22] Philo makes this double aspect even clearer in the closing words of the treatise: Abraham was the first "who obeyed the law, some will say, but rather, as our discourse has shown, himself a law and an unwritten statute."

What we deal with, then, in Abraham as a "legal" figure in Philo is a conception of natural law and specific laws which is as inherently Greek as it is alien to normative Judaism. Greek philosophers, who dealt with "natural law" and "laws incarnate and made vocal" would have understood Philo with no difficulty, since he writes and thinks in their realm. These words would, however, have been virtually unintelligible (and objectionable!) to the rabbis.

Philo has in this treatise only passing concern for the Mosaic Law; where in other treatises he expresses concern for it, he always relegates it, as a copy, to a secondary position. It is, however, more than a random copy of the law of nature; it is the best possible copy and in conformity with it.[23]

We embark in our treatise, then, immediately into matters which are in content Greek and not "native" Jewish.

Enos, Enoch, and Noah are examples of men who yearned for virtue, contrasted with Abraham, Isaac, and Jacob who attained it.[24] Philo tells us that the patriarchs, though differing from each other, must be regarded as a unit as well as individually.

---

[21] As mentioned above, Wolfson, I, 188 f., holds that "unwritten law" is occasionally an allusion to *Torah she-b-'al pe*, against Heinemann, "Die Lehre vom Ungeschriebenen Gesetz im Jüdischen Schrifttum," *HUCA*, IV, 149 ff., whose case for the view that the "unwritten law" in Philo is never the rabbinic oral law seems impregnable to Wolfson's assault.

[22] *Abr.* 5.

[23] Philo likens the outward observances of the Law to the body, and the inner meaning to the soul, *Mig.* 89–93. The pattern of his Exposition is that he discusses in this treatise, in the lost treatises on Isaac and Jacob and in Moses the "general laws"; thereafter he proceeds in *Decal.* and *Spec.* to discuss the "copies."

[24] Philo's figure of speech contrasts the first three as children, against the second three as athletes preparing for games which are really sacred. The figure is, of course, derived from the environment, and Philo does not hesitate to use such figures. I would guess that a Palestinian rabbi would have considered equating the patriarchs with athletes offensive.

Philo tells us that allegorically Isaac is the symbol of natural perfection, while Jacob and Abraham are symbols of perfection attained, in the former by practice, in the latter by being taught. These three "methods," natural endowment, practice, and teaching were by Philo's time a commonplace in Greek philosophical thought. The patriarchs, accordingly, are allegorically illustrations of the three types of perfection; that is to say, Philo sets forth his views on the Greek problem of attaining perfection through the medium of the patriarchs.[25]

The literal patriarchs are of one house and one family, father, son and grandson. They have it in common that they are God-lovers and God-beloved. In recognition of their virtues God makes these partners in a title, God of Abraham, Isaac and Jacob.[26]

The outstanding quality of Abraham is his piety ($\varepsilon\dot{v}\sigma\acute{\varepsilon}\beta\varepsilon\iota\alpha$). He is zealous to follow God; he wants to obey the divine commands. These commands, Philo insists, are not only such as are conveyed in speech and writing;[27] these commands are also such as are made manifest by nature, and apprehended by the sense which is superior to hearing: sight or contemplation. Any one who contemplates the order in nature and the constitution of the cosmos needs no teacher.[28] Abraham, then, is one who "con-

---

[25] See Wolfson, II, 196 ff. on the background. I discuss this more fully below, page 142.

[26] *Abr.* 49–51. Philo uses Ex. 3.15, as a proof text. In the passage he goes on to assert, briefly, that this is a "relative" title, not an "absolute" one. Elsewhere (*Mut.* 12 f.) Philo gives a longer explanation, that God is in actuality nameless; titles such as *Theos* and *Kyrios* describe aspects of deity, not actual deity. Here he compresses the comment, adding only that the relative name is one suited to men so that they can have a name to which to address their prayers. See also *QG*, III, 39. Philo next proceeds to foreshadow the allegorical interpretations of the patriarchs, *Abr.* 56–59.

[27] Above, *Abr.* 5, Philo has told us that as yet particular laws had not been set in writing; later, *Abr.* 275, Philo repeats that Abraham knew no written laws. Philo is not here saying that Abraham observed written laws; he is saying that commands are not only written laws, they are also unwritten commands. The passage, thus viewed, is not in contradiction with 5 and 275.

[28] *Abr.* 60–61. The implied contradiction, that is, the lack of need of a teacher, and Abraham as the symbol of perfection through being taught, is Philo's. The contradiction is more apparent than real, for to Philo the true wisdom, beyond mere knowledge, is revealed, not taught.

templates," and thereby, he leads a life which carries out the laws of nature. The divine commands which Abraham obeys are the natural law abiding with the peaceful life; it tends towards the assimilation of the beauties of nature.

Philo will now illustrate from Scripture Abraham's piety (in observing the law of nature). Philo paraphrases Gen. 12, making some significant substitutions and adding some significant features. He turns Gen. 12.1, "God said to Abraham" into "under the force of an oracle."[29] The motive behind this alteration is probably Philo's unwillingness to portray God as talking to a man; this would imply "hearing," whereas God, insofar as He is knowable, is known through sight (of the soul). The paraphrase permits Philo to avoid the anthropomorphism implied in Scripture, and yet to retain God as the motivator of Abraham's departure.

Philo says laconically that Abraham is to seek a new home; he makes no mention of the biblical words "to the land which I shall show thee." This, we shall see, is no oversight, but a deliberate, indeed a necessary omission. Abraham, he tells us, is like someone going home from a strange land and not like someone going to a strange land from home.[30] The divine oracle, then, is having the effect of bringing Abraham not to a strange land but "home."[31] The emigration, Philo adds, is one of soul rather than of body; heavenly love overpowers Abraham's desire for mortal things.[32] The Scriptural patriarch who moved with family and flocks is replaced by the Sage who makes a journey of soul not to a new land, but home. Scripture relates that Abraham takes Sarah and Lot with him; such company would be natural for a bodily trip. But in this trip of the soul, Philo appropriately reduces Abraham's companions to an equivocal "few" and then

---

[29] λογίῳ πληχθείς.

[30] Abr. 62.

[31] Philo hints here at a notion he often states specifically elsewhere; God does not permit the virtue-lover to dwell in the body, as in his own native land, but only to sojourn in it as in a foreign country, Heres 267 ff.; QG III, 10, interpreting Gen. 15.13; and QG III, 45, on Gen. 17.8. This is a common Stoic sentiment.

[32] Abr. 66.

further reduces it promptly to a lonely departure.[33] The mystic journey is necessarily lonely; this tiny item, unparalleled in the rabbis, is a key to Philo's unique view of Abraham.

Philo tells us that Abraham hastens to obey, since he considers quickness in executing the command to be as much to be honored as full accomplishment.[34]

Philo has preceded his statement that Abraham's migration was one of soul rather than one of body by a digression on leaving home. The effect of this digression is to build up a contrast of other migrators with Abraham. Others leave home as a result of banishment, or for business, but their ties to home are so strong that when possible they return. Abraham, however, leaves for good. These others are examples of those who emigrate in body; Abraham, however, migrated in soul. "Home," in the sense of "his father's house," seems by implication to be equal in Philo's mind with bodily matters; he makes no such direct statement in this passage, but the words seem to me to be quite pointed in that direction.[35] By his digression, Philo has built a clear picture of other migrants,[36a] with the result that his reverting to Abraham in contrast is all the more striking.[36b]

But, having stated that it is a migration of soul, Philo proceeds to give a list of "bodily" things which Abraham leaves. The Bible mentioned only "thy land, thy birth-place, and thy father's house."[37] Philo expands the list to include fellow-tribes-men, wards-men, schoolmates, comrades, blood-relatives, ancient

[33] μετ' ὀλίγων . . . ἢ καὶ μόνος.

[34] *Abr.* 66. The rabbis too extol Abraham for departing immediately *Mid. Ps.* CXIX, 3 and frequently. The words of Scripture "Abraham went, as God commanded him" (Gen. 12.4) suggest an immediate departure; it is unnecessary to suppose a dependence here of Philo on the rabbis or the rabbis on Philo. The inference of an immediate departure is a natural one. I find no rabbinic parallel to "quickness in executing to be as much to be honored as full accomplishment."

[35] So especially *Abr.* 63. A fuller discussion is found in *Mig.* 2 ff. There "house" is "speech," that is, "uttered thought" which is inferior to unuttered thought. See below, notes 281 and 285.

[36a] *Abr.* 63–66.

[36b] *Abr.* 66 ff.

[37] Gen. 12.1.

customs, society, and social intercourse.[38] These terms suggest that Philo is describing what a man in his own day would leave behind in migrating. The references to wards-men, schoolmates, and social intercourse suggest that Philo conceives of Abraham as a compatriot of Philo leaving his native Alexandria. We shall see in other passages that Philo tends to make an Alexandrian of Abraham.

The divine oracle of Gen. 12 seems to have come, according to Philo, in Ur of the Chaldees, rather than in Haran, as Gen. 11 implies. Rabbinic tradition assigns the call to Haran.[39] Some now lost oral tradition may lie behind the assignment of the call to Chaldea; but it is possible that the notion rests on Neh. 9.7[40] and not on oral tradition. The verse states that God brought Abraham out of Chaldea; it conflicts with Gen. 11.31, which tells us that Terah brought Abraham out.

Once he has mentioned Chaldea and Haran[41] with their physical properties which would make Abraham's migration one of body, Philo promptly turns to allegory. Abraham is allegorically the virtue-loving soul seeking the true God.[42] The Chaldeans glorify visible existence and they take no notice of invisible and intelligible existence. They conclude that the universe itself is God.[43] Philo has already told us that Abraham is a believer in God; he has already told us of Abraham's apprehension by the highest of the senses.[44] The Abraham we have hitherto met is poles apart from the Chaldean creed,[45] but, now, when we encounter Abraham, he has been, as yet, in Chaldea, in materialistic pantheism. He has long been reared in this creed,[46] but recognizing its falsity he abandons it. As a result, he discerns that

[38] *Abr.* 67.

[39] Cf. Ginzberg, V, 219.

[40] A possible objection to this explanation is that we do not have any quotation by Philo of Neh. 9.7.

[41] *Abr.* 67.

[42] *Abr.* 68.

[43] *Abr.* 69.

[44] *Abr.* 60.

[45] See below, note 261. This creed is often assumed to be Stoicism but it is more likely that it is astral determination.

[46] *Abr.* 69.

there is a God in the universe. He has begun to abandon Chaldea, pantheism, in favor of an incipient theism; as Philo puts it, he has opened his soul's eye and begun to see the pure beam instead of the deep darkness; following the ray, he discerns what he had not beheld before, a charioteer and pilot presiding over the world.[47]

Philo now tells us precisely how Abraham proceeds to recognize the existence of God. He has abandoned a preoccupation with the material universe. Instead he turns to study himself as a microcosm,[48] and as a result he will learn about the macro-

[47] *Abr.* 70. The passage contains an aspect which is of interest beyond its content. Philo begins it by an explicit statement that he is turning to allegory. In the allegory Abraham is the virtue-loving soul. But promptly, as though he had forgotten that he was in allegory, Philo reverts from the soul to Abraham. If we were to limit Philo to a rigid distinction between the literal and the allegorical, we should conclude that here Philo has broken his allegorical figure. But such a comment, though justifiable, is superficial. It is true that Abraham is allegorized as the soul (or, elsewhere, as the mind). Philo, however, deals with the person, Abraham, in two supplementary ways. There was the Abraham who migrated from Ur to Haran; there was also the Abraham who departed from materialistic pantheism. When pressed to it, we might explain that it is the mind rather than the person which abandons such a thing as pantheism. There are other passages in which the distinction between the mind of a person like Abraham and the person himself is rigidly drawn by Philo. For example, he tells us in several places that the allegorical Isaac is not a man; he tells us at the end of *Congress.* that neither Sarah nor Hagar is a woman. In some passages, then, the content is such that Philo feels impelled to go beyond only saying that he deals in allegory, but clearly he insists that he is not dealing with people. In other passages, those labeled literal ones, he gives clear over-tones of allegorical connotations, but the humanity of his protagonists is tenaciously held on to. But there are not infrequent passages like the present one where there emerges what seems to me to be the tendency most peculiar to Philo: to keep a double interpretation in as neat a conjunction as possible whenever he can.

[48] Philo is here far removed from the rabbis who ascribe to Abraham a knowledge of the existence of God from viewing the material world, and the deduction that a power lies behind it. Such a view is present in Philo, but attributed to the lesser Bezalel, who knows of the existence of God from created things by a process of reasoning, contrasted with Moses who receives the clear vision of God directly from the first cause, *LA* III, 102; cf. Wolfson, II, 83–84. I touch on this difference in "Abraham's Knowledge of the Existence of God," *HTR*, XLIV, 1951, 137–139. On Josephus, see above, note 228 in Chapter II.

cosm. Philo argues that since there is a mind in man appointed as ruler, which all the community of the body obeys and each of the senses follows, the world, which is the most beautiful, the greatest, and most perfect of all, must also have a ruler; and just as the mind in man is invisible, so is the ruler of the world. One who reflects on these things need not concern himself with distant things (such as sun, moon, and stars) but only with himself. Accordingly, Abraham turns to examine himself.[49] Haran, "sense perception," is the process or point at which Abraham examines his own nature, instead of examining the material world. The proof that Abraham migrated from "astrology," Philo tells us, is that "God was seen by Abraham."[50] This is a proof text, he avers, that God was not manifest to him before, while he was still in Chaldean pantheism.[51]

Our Abraham, then, has been summarized succinctly as a sage who turned from materialistic pantheism to the recognition of God, and as a result received the vision of God. This turning, Philo goes on to say, is attested by the alteration of Abraham's name; Abram is the meteorologist; Abraham is the Sage.[52]

The meteorologist sees nothing greater than the universe; the sage sees, through his mind, the ruler and governor.[53]

But Haran was only the first migration. A second takes place, Philo tells us, into the *wilderness*.[54] Abraham wanders about without complaining of the wandering and the insecurity. He has not

[49] *Abr.* 73–75.

[50] Philo says this takes place εὐθύς, *Abr.* 77. Colson seems troubled that apparently the vision of God takes place "in Haran," whereas the text allocates the vision to Canaan, Gen. 12.7. I show, in my section on the allegorical Abraham, that there are actually many stages between Haran, "sense perception," and the vision of God. Philo leaps over these stages here, but elsewhere makes clear that the vision is the result of a quite lengthy process.

[51] The force of λογίῳ πληχθείς above, *Abr.* 62, now becomes more apparent; the words "God said to Abraham," which Philo avoids, do not mean to him a manifestation of God to Abraham while he is still Abram.

[52] I discuss the change of names in the allegorical Abraham, below, notes 278–279.

[53] *Abr.* 82–84.

[54] LXX Gen. 12.9. As in several other places, Philo gives here an interpretation crucial for him which rests on the LXX and which would not be readily derivable from MT. MT reads "south," LXX "wilderness," ἐρήμῳ.

only left his own country, but he has left city life,[55] and gone into the pathless areas. While others might have been tempted to retrace their steps, Abraham alone is content; he thinks no life is as pleasant as one lived without association with the multitude. Philo's intent is perfectly clear here, though his statement is shorter than the same motif in other passages.[56] Solitude is the setting in which union with God takes place; as God is alone, solitude is precious to God, so that he who seeks God must make himself like God, a dweller in solitude.[57]

It cannot be over-emphasized that Philo has little or no concern for Palestine. As we shall see, the Land of Canaan is "adolescence" and its vices. In our context he seems deliberately to avoid the biblical verses which enjoin Abraham to migrate to Canaan, and he selects as the goal of the second migration of Abraham not the land flowing in milk and honey but, as we see, an entirely different place, mentioned in a relatively minor verse in the LXX text. The focus on this verse by Philo is no accident. It is a deliberate and judicious selection. Abraham, he is telling us, abandons pantheism, begins to examine himself and comes to theism, and promptly seeks out solitude as a means of seeing God. This verse, then, is a crucial one in Philo's Abraham, for it is one of the striking statements in this treatise of Abraham's mysticism.

Abraham, the man, Philo tells us in a summary,[58] draws away from his old associations; his mind does not remain in falsity (Chaldean pantheism) or in the world of the senses (Haran), but it speeds upwards by means of reason ($\lambda o \gamma \iota \sigma \mu \tilde{\omega}$) to the nature which is superior to the visible world, and to God, the maker and ruler of both the visible and the intelligible world.

Philo has depicted Abraham in general outlines. He turns now to recount, within that framework, specific deeds which, he says, call for anything but contempt. First he tells of the incident of

---

[55] Philo here again seems to conceive of Abraham as an Alexandrian, now far from the city, wandering in the wilderness.

[56] The motif of separation from the hub-bub of the city and its somewhat contemptible multitudes is frequent in Philo.

[57] *Abr.* 87.

[58] *Abr.* 88.

Abraham's sojourn in Egypt and of the incident of Pharaoh and of Sarah. Philo alludes to Abraham as the friend of God (φιλό-θεος).[59]

Philo feels it necessary to supply an explanatory preface. From the Genesis account, one might possibly infer that the great patriarch was something of a prevaricator, and that Pharaoh acted innocently. Philo's telling of the story, however, makes Abraham clearly the hero and Pharaoh clearly the villain. As though conceding that the story is susceptible of a wrong interpretation, Philo tells us prefatorily that Abraham's greatness in the incident is not clear to everyone, but only to those who have tasted virtue and who scorn what the multitudes prefer.[60] Philo, we shall see, does two things with the incident: he recasts it in tone and import, and then he allegorizes it.

Abraham's marriage is threatened, Philo tells us, but as a reward for the deeds related above, God keeps the marriage safe and unharmed.[61]

As Philo recounts the incident, he adds certain details of a naturalistic character which are not present in the Bible. There has been a considerable period of crop failure. The crop failure extends, it would seem, over periods of both excessive rainfall and periods of drought. Philo adds also that Abraham is not the only resident of Syria who leaves there to seek food.[62] On the other hand, Philo is careful to point out that the supply of corn in Egypt, for materialistic reasons, was plentiful.[63]

Philo tells the story without mentioning by name either Sarah or the king of Egypt.[64] Abraham's wife is distinguished in beauty, both of body and of soul. The chief people of Egypt[65] see her,

[59] *Abr.* 89. On the epithet and problems attendant, see above, Chapter II, note 130, and below, note 347.

[60] *Abr.* 89.

[61] *Abr.* 88–90.

[62] *Abr.* 91. Philo's motive in these additions is to justify Abraham's going to Egypt.

[63] *Abr.* 91–92.

[64] Throughout the treatise Philo refrains from naming names such as Lot and Melchizedek. The names might have been meaningless to a Gentile audience.

[65] ἄρχοντες in LXX, οἱ ἐν τέλει in Philo.

admire her beauty, and tell the king.[66] Philo inserts a contemporaneous touch, undoubtedly reflecting some personal acquaintance with such affairs, that the highly placed leave nothing unobserved.

As the Bible tells the story, the chiefs send Sarah to Pharaoh; in Philo's account Pharaoh sends for Sarah. The king's action, Philo avers, paid little regard to decency, or to the laws enacted to show respect to strangers. The allusion seems unmistakably contemporaneous and apologetic, reflecting the status of Jews, or the popular regard of them, in Alexandrian law and Egyptian sentiment.[67] Pharaoh determines to take Sarah in marriage only nominally; his real motive is to give rein to his license and to bring her to shame. The contemporaneous note is retained by Philo as he continues the narrative; Sarah, in a foreign country and at the mercy of a despot, joins with her helpless husband in fleeing to God. God has pity on the strangers and he punishes the king, in both body and soul, with plagues. The household, undoubtedly an allusion to Gentile Alexandrians, fail to show indignation at the outrage, and by consenting, are almost accomplices; therefore they, too, feel the plague.

The sanctity of Abraham's marriage is preserved, and from it there is born the nation dearest to God which has received the gift of priesthood and prophecy on behalf of all mankind.[68]

Philo has omitted from his account Abraham's request of Sarah that she call herself Abraham's sister; he makes no mention of the gifts given by Pharaoh; and, significantly, he omits Pharaoh's sending Abraham out of Egypt. As Philo has told the story, a consummately evil Egyptian king has violated all laws of decency toward a stranger, the progenitor of the Jews.

---

[66] Rabbinic legends tell of Sarah's being put in a box by Abraham; she is discovered by tax collectors. Stein, *Philo u. der Midrasch*, 27, note 2, believes that τέλει of Philo is an allusion to tax collectors, and thereby an allusion to the legend which Stein says comes from "der älteren, hellenistischen Agada." This seems to me to be a quite ingenious and implausible explanation. Yonge renders the phrase "Egyptian magistrates," while Colson renders it "chief people of Egypt."

[67] Cf. *Flaccum* 29 and 53–54, and elsewhere.

[68] *Abr.* 93–98.

Philo now allegorizes the incident. The allegory, he tells us, is not original with him; he has heard it from "natural philosophers." The allegory retains Abraham as the good mind and makes Sarah into generic virtue, and the king, the body-loving mind. The literal interpretation contrasted men, the decent Abraham, and the inhospitable Pharaoh; the allegory is a contrast between the character of genuine virtue and the pretense. Abraham's virtue is genuine.

Philo proceeds with his contrast; he turns now to show Abraham's hospitality,[69] in sharp antithesis to that of the Egyptian. The basis is the narrative in Gen. 18 of the three strangers. Abraham sees three travelers, whose divine nature is not apparent to him. He runs to them and offers his hospitality. The travelers promptly accept because they recognize by Abraham's warmth even more than by his words that they are welcome. They enter his tent.[70] Abraham's soul is filled with joy. He bids Sarah to bake three measures of cakes in the ashes.[71] He himself hurries to the stalls to select a tender calf for a servant to kill and dress.[72] Philo pauses to tell that all this is done with speed, for in a wise man's home no one is slow in showing kindness, but women and men, freemen and slaves are full of zeal to serve guests.[73]

[69] *QG* IV, 10 infers from Gen. 18.8 that despite his 318 slaves (Gen. 14.4) Abraham himself waited on the guests; somewhat similarly, though without mention of these slaves, *BM* 86b.

[70] LXX speaks of a tent. Later in this passage Philo will allude to the dwelling as οἶκος. Perhaps it is not alone the biblical context but also the suggestion of wilderness implicit in the word "tent"; the passage is to be used allegorically for a mystic experience. Josephus portrays Abraham at the portal of his "court"; see Chapter II, note 287.

[71] This is based on LXX Gen. 18.6, which adds "in the ashes." Elsewhere, *Sac.* 59–60, Philo infers an allegory from the cakes, which, buried in the ashes, are like the true mysteries, buried, and not revealed. The allegory requires the LXX reading and is impossible on the MT. See below, note 364.

[72] Philo omits mentioning the dairy dishes of Gen. 18.8; possibly Philo himself observed the prohibition developed in rabbinic law regarding meat and dairy dishes. Possibly, however, the omission is not deliberate, but a result of Philo's compressing the story, in writing from memory.

[73] The "slave and free" give the passage a contemporaneous touch; it seems to be an Alexandrian allusion, possibly to the ideal of Philo's own household.

The guests feed on the good will of the host rather than on viands.[74] The guests promise him a son born in wedlock. The promise is spoken through one of the guests, the highest.[75] Abraham and Sarah consider the promise incredible. Philo excuses Sarah's denial of her laughter by attributing to Sarah the gist of verse 14 that nothing is impossible to God; in the Bible the verse is spoken by God.[76] Sarah, Philo adds, had known this truth from the cradle. As Philo ends the incident, it is rounded off by this exculpation of Sarah. In the Bible, it ends abruptly without any exculpation of Sarah. Philo adds that Sarah sees in the strangers a different and grander aspect, that of prophets or angels, transformed from their spiritual and soul-like nature into human shape.[77]

So far Philo has told the story as a contrast to the king of Egypt. But his main thesis at the moment is Abraham's piety, and he now asserts that the hospitality is a by-product of that greater virtue. The piety is clearly seen, says Philo, even if we think of the strangers as men. It is a happy and blessed house if wise men halt there. How much happier and more blessed it is if the travelers are angels of God sent to announce God's predictions to men.[78]

With overtones of allegory, Philo asks the rhetorical question,

---

[74] Philo below denies more specifically than the hint here, that the travelers ate.

[75] The text varies from the singular to the plural. Modern scholarship explains the changes as due to different sources. The text states (Gen. 18.1) that Yahweh appears to Abraham; Abraham sees three men; he runs to them. He addresses "them" in the singular in 18.3, but in the plural in 18.4–5. They are plural again in 8–9, but abruptly singular in 10. In 13 the text reverts to Yahweh. The problem of pre-modern interpreters was to harmonize the passage so as to equate, in some way, Yahweh and the three men. Both Philo and the rabbis arrive at such equations. It is not necessary to suppose dependency on anything beyond the difficulties of the text. The rabbis equate the men with three specific angels. Philo equates them with "powers" of God. The similarity is that both Philo and the rabbis resolve the difficulty; the dissimilarity is the manner in which they resolve it.

[76] See *QG* IV, 17, on Gen. 18.13–14, where Philo conforms to the biblical account, but interprets quite congruently with the present passage.

[77] *Abr.* 107–113. The material appears also in *QG* IV, 16–17.

[78] *Abr.* 114–115.

how could the angels have entered the house if they had not
known that all the household, like a well-ordered crew, were
obedient to the pilot?[79] Abraham is a kinsman and fellow servant
of the angels;[80] all of them are servants who seek refuge with the
master.[81] Since they are angels, they neither eat nor drink, though
they give the appearance of it.[82] Yet even this is secondary to
the greater miracle that, though immaterial, they assume human
form as an act of grace to the man of worth. The miracle occurs
to cause the sage to perceive that God recognizes what kind of
man he is.[83]

By turning the foregoing into allegory, Philo is enabled to assess the incident in terms of Abraham's spiritual development. It
is the vision of God achieved by the mind. The mind uninitiated
into sacred mysteries is able to apprehend God only through
God's creative or ruling aspects, whereas the initiated mind,
when purified, sees God as one.[84] The variations between the
singular and the plural in Gen. 18 are proof that the three and

[79] The figure recalls the passage in *Abr.* 73–74, the mind is the ruler (or
pilot) of the members of the body, the senses and the passions. The thought
implicit is that as wise men will enter a household well conducted by its ruler,
so will the divine appearances come into the mind controlling the household
of the body.

[80] This comes close to suggesting that Abraham is not a man. Philo does
not, however, ever get quite that far. The passage occasions some difficulty
when it is later allegorized, *Abr.* 143, in that Philo declares one of the angels to
be *To On*; how, then, could *To On* be a fellow-servant of Abraham? See
Wolfson, I, 379–380. The true difficulty is, I believe, the assumption on the
part of Gfrörer and Wolfson that Philo is rigidly consistent; Philo is not. He
can, therefore, in *Abr.* 115, call the visitors angels, and kinsmen of Abraham
and fellow-servants with him; and he can allegorize them in 143 as *To On* and
the Two Powers.

[81] *Abr.* 116.

[82] Similarly, see *QG* IV, 9, on Gen. 18.8. There Philo adds that the pious
and worthy life of a virtuous man is figuratively the food of God. With Colson,
VI, p. 598, I believe that the "Docetic" question of angels' eating is a matter
of the larger framework of angelological speculations; there is no need to
believe that Josephus, *Ant.* I, XI, 2, is dependent on this passage in Philo; see
page 67. The rabbis, too, declare that the angels only appeared to eat, though
a late midrash denounces those who deny the eating; cf. Ginzberg, V, 236.

[83] *Abr.* 107–118.

[84] *Abr.* 119–130. Compare the "second best journey," *Abr.* 123, with *QG*
IV, 48–49 on Gen. 19.21–22. See also *Somn.* I, 44.

the one are the same.[85] Abraham saw God in a single vision while others see God in a triple vision. Abraham belongs to the best class of temperaments.[86] The incident of the three travelers, then, is not only an instance of Abraham's achieving the mystic goal, it is a demonstration that Abraham belongs to the best class of those who receive the mystic vision.[87]

Abraham's distinction in belonging to the best class is made clearer, Philo tells us, in the story of Sodom.[88] We shall see that the long story eventually returns to this main point and its inclusion in the treatise rests on the contrast it supplies between the grades of mystic vision, the sight of God as one or as three. First Philo summarizes the story. Sodom was full of innumerable indignities, particularly such as arise from gluttony[89] and lewdness. The license stemmed from the great wealth of Sodom;[90] excess prosperity, Philo says in quoting from Menander, is the principal beginning of evils. The Sodomites threw off the law of nature; they drank strong liquor, fed on delicacies, and practiced forbidden forms of intercourse. Homosexuality led to effeminacy not only in body but also in soul. Had these practices spread to Greeks and barbarians, depopulation would have turned cities into deserts.[91] Divine punishment in the form of the rain of fire consumed all that was above ground and even penetrated into the earth itself. The fire[92] was still burning in his own time, Philo tells us; it continues to burn or at least to smoulder.

---

[85] *Abr.* 131–132.   [86] *Abr.* 124–125.

[87] I discuss this allegory of Gen. 18 below, page 181. Here, I try to point out no more than the significance of the section as a whole.

[88] *Abr.* 133.

[89] The rabbinic indictment of Sodom includes murder, lack of pity, and homosexuality, *San.* 109a and *Tar. Jon.* to Gen. 13.13, but lacks gluttony. I have found no passages in Philo specifically abjuring eating for sensual pleasure. Philo, who countenanced sexual intercourse for purposes of procreation but not for pleasure (below *Abr.* 137 and *Abr.* 253), countenanced eating to sustain life, but not eating for pleasure. A fuller description and denunciation of "Sodomites" is found in *Somn.* II, 61–64. See also *V. C.* 48 and notes 154 and 403.

[90] This is probably based on Gen. 13.10.

[91] *Abr.* 133–136.

[92] *Abr.* 137–140. The burning, and not the "over-turning," LXX Gen. 19.25, claims Philo's attention.

The details thus compressed,[93] Philo is ready to demonstrate how the narrative proved Abraham's eminence in mystic capacities. While three men appeared to Abraham in Gen. 18, only two of them, according to Scripture, Gen. 19, went on to Sodom. Of the five cities of Sodom, Gen. 14.2, four were destroyed, but one was preserved.[94] The two men represent the two potencies[95] of God, the beneficial and the punitive. The virtue of the preserved city,[96] was not complete and perfect; it received benefits through a potency of God, but it was not worthy of the direct vision of Him.[97] The contrast, then, is between the progressing mind which saw only an aspect of God, and Abraham who saw God Himself.

But Philo has not yet finished with his point. He now goes into a deeper explanation. The five cities of Sodom are the five senses in us: sight, hearing, taste, smell, and touch. The last three are animal senses; hearing is above these, but is feminine,

[93] Philo omits here the bargaining of Abraham and all mention of Lot and his family.

[94] See below, notes 104 and 265.

[95] In rabbinic legends, the three angels of Gen. 18 had these tasks, one task for each: Michael, to give good tidings to Sarah; Raphael to heal Abraham who has just been circumcised (Gen. 17); and Gabriel to overturn Sodom. The rabbis elsewhere identify one of Lot's two visitors as Michael; there is some squirming at the necessity of giving Michael, against all the rules of angels, an additional mission of saving Lot, B. M. 86b and Tan. Wa-yera XX. There is some accord between Philo and the rabbis in the notion that God Himself is not the immediate source of evil; cf. Ginzberg V, 5 and 241. Ginzberg accounts for this similarity of motif by suggesting that Philo has here given a philosophical turn to a popular motif, while Freudenthal, op. cit., I, 70, believes that the rabbis are dependent on Philo. However similar the motif, there are differences in the mode of expressing it; further, there is this minor difference that the rabbis regard Lot as the object of Michael's saving, while Philo regards the city Ṣoʻar as the object of the saving by the beneficial potency. My own judgment would be that both midrashim are readily deducible from the Bible, which equates God and the three angels in Gen. 18.1, and sends two of the "men" on to Sodom in Gen. 19. Philo and the rabbis are related here only through the coincidence of a scriptural opportunity for exegesis; the saving angels of the rabbis and the beneficial potencies are independently developed midrashim.

[96] Or, possibly of Lot who fled there!

[97] Abr. 142–146.

and lower than sight, the supreme sense.[98] Philo dwells on the importance of sight as the best of the senses,[99] and the benefits it provides. But the vital part of sight is that on it alone of the senses God made light shine, and light is the best of existing things. Light has a double nature. First, in common use, it is the effulgence of fire and disappears when the fire is quenched. Second, light which comes from the heavens, as the light of stars, is unquenchable and imperishable.[100] The eyes, using light, contemplate the earth and its contents, and even heaven itself.[101] The eyes leave earth and in an instant reach heaven; they draw the understanding to the observation of what they have seen.[102] The understanding takes sight as its starting point, and proceeds to the fundamental questions of the existence of a creator, of His essence and quality of His purpose.[103] The preserved city is sight,[104] which was preserved because it avoided the slavery to flesh and the senses to which the other four succumbed. Sight yearns to survey the entire heaven and the universe.[105]

Philo now turns to what he regards as Abraham's greatest action, the story of the offering of Isaac, based on Gen. 22. Isaac is a child of great bodily beauty and excellence of virtue. His perfection of virtues is beyond his years,[106] so that Abraham loves him not only with the usual love of a father for a son, but

[98] *Abr.* 147–150.
[99] *Abr.* 151–154.
[100] *Abr.* 155–158.
[101] *Abr.* 159.   [102] *Abr.* 161.
[103] Note must be made again of the difficulties which Philo provides his interpreters in his allegorical pursuits. In his recounting of Gen. 18, he states that the three men were *allegorically To On* and the Powers: here he alludes to an exactly similar explanation, carrying further the explanation already begun, as the natural and obvious rendering for the multitude. Now that this is over, he will expound a hidden and inward meaning.
[104] Colson, VI, 82–3 points out the dependency of this passage, and a parallel *Opif.* 54, on *Timaeus* 47A. Philo argues that the city is described as both small and not small; hence it must be "sight." Philo, as Colson points out VI, p. 84, does a little violence to the verse, Gen. 19.20. See note 2.
[105] *Abr.* 162–166.
[106] Allegorically, Isaac represents elsewhere natural perfection, as distinct from perfection through learning (Abraham) or through practice (Jacob); cf. *Abr.* 52.

also as one who admires worthy qualities of character. Suddenly and to his surprise[107] there comes to Abraham the divine message that he should sacrifice Isaac on a certain lofty hill[108] which, Philo tells us, was as much as a three days' journey from the city.[109] Despite his love for his son, Abraham shows at this command neither a change of color nor a weakening of soul, but remains steadfast as ever, and does not waver.[110] Mastered by his love for God, he overcomes family affection.[111] He tells no one in his household of the divine call,[112] but sets out.[113] He takes with him only two servants[114] of his numerous following. When Abraham sees the appointed place[115] from afar off, he bids his

[107] There is no biblical basis for "suddenly and surprisingly." Gen. 22.1, begins "It came to pass after these things." The rabbis speculated on what the antecedent of "these" was, and found the answer to be the quarrels which they say arose between Ishmael and Isaac; or Satan's complaint to God that Abraham has offered no sacrifices; *San.* 89b and *Gen. R.* LV.

[108] Philo makes no mention of Moriah. The rabbis and Josephus identify Moriah as the mount on which the Temple was to stand, on the basis of II Chron. 3.1.

[109] Again Philo reveals that he regards Abraham as a city dweller like himself.

[110] This seems clearly a reminiscence of Gen. 22.1, in which God tested Abraham. Philo omits the explicit word "test." The notion may have been repugnant to him. Jubilees and the rabbis, on the other hand, increase the tests from this single biblical mention to lists of ten tests.

[111] So, too, *IV Macc.* XIV, 20.

[112] The rabbis portray him as telling Sarah that he is taking Isaac to school, *Tar. Jon. to* Gen. 22.3.

[113] Scripture specifies that Abraham arose early in the morning, but Philo omits this, and also the saddling of the ass.

[114] LXX renders נעריו by παῖδας. Philo paraphrases the idea, but uses the word θεραπείας. No great violence is done to MT when the rabbis infer that the "boys" are Ishmael and Eliezer, *Tar. Jon. ad loc.* But Ishmael would hardly qualify as a "servant." One would infer that Philo did not know this widely appearing *midrash.* The Greek word παῖς can mean either boy or servant; Philo clearly understands the passage to mean servants, while the rabbis took it as boys.

[115] Philo initially speaks of the appointed area as χῶρον, *Abr.* 171, but promptly alludes to it, like LXX, as τόπος. This latter is in Philo a euphemism for God, like the rabbinic המקום. A mystic background is passingly alluded to in the words "They walked with equal speed of mind rather than body . . ." Philo develops this with some fullness in *Mig.* 166 f. I treat this below, p. 173.

servants to stay where they are,[116] while he and Isaac proceed.[117] He gives Isaac the fire[118] and the wood to carry; since these are a burden of piety, it is a light burden.

They walk, Philo tells us, with equal speed of mind, rather than of body,[119] along the road *which is holiness*, and they arrive at the appointed place.[120] By these little touches, Philo has indicated that there is something more to the story than only the obedience of a Sage. The story is an example again of Abraham's mystical experience. But Philo in this context does no more than give tantalizing allusions.

Philo continues his narrative with the building of the altar. He reports Isaac's question regarding the victim, and he tells us that Abraham does not swerve, in visage or thought, though someone else might have been moved by emotion to tears or to silence. Abraham avoids both pitfalls, and replies that God will supply the victim. This will take place even though they are in the wide wilderness;[121] God will

---

[116] Jubilees XVIII, 4 supplies a well for the servants.

[117] Another touch to set the stage for *Abr.* 190.

[118] Isaac does not carry the fire in Genesis. This appears to be one of several lapses of memory which justify the conclusion that Philo does not have Genesis open before him in writing the treatise.

[119] Gen. 22.8, states that they journeyed together. In the allegory, in which Abraham is the mind perfected through learning and Isaac the mind naturally perfect, Philo uses the verse to show that ultimately the perfection of Abraham, though an acquired one, equalled the natural perfection of Isaac, *Mig.* 166 f.; see below, page 173. The entire thought of *Abr.* 172 is dependent on the allegory which Philo does not here reproduce, but which is clearly hinted at.

[120] As pointed out above, allegory underlies the pericope. The "place" is God in the allegory, and hence the road is a holy one. Philo apparently sees three things in the events of Gen. 22. First, the literal story. Second, the mystic road to God traversed together by the naturally perfect and the one perfected by teaching. Third, as in *Abr.* 200–204, the willingness of the Sage to sacrifice his joy to God. It is not unusual in Philo, that a biblical character is allegorized in related but somewhat different ways; Isaac represents both Abraham's "joy" and also the soul which is perfect by nature.

[121] There is nothing in Genesis to justify Philo's calling the "place" an ἐρημία. We saw above, page 115, that Abraham's second migration, a mystic one, was to the wilderness. Philo's mysticism seems to be the basis for the intrusion of this rather surprising word.

even here do what is called for, for all things are possible to Him.[122]

Abraham puts Isaac on the altar.[123] He has the drawn knife in his right[124] hand, prepared to deal the death blow. God the Savior stops the deed halfway, with a voice from the air.[125] He orders Abraham not to touch the lad. In this way the slaughter is prevented[126] and Isaac is saved. God repays Abraham's piety by returning the offering which piety intended. While the action does not come to the intended ending, it is complete and perfect.[127] So Philo terminates the account, without as much as a mention of the ram of Gen. 22.13.[128]

The narrative as presented has accorded with Philo's treatment noted in the earlier episodes. The subject Philo is discussing is still Abraham's piety. As in the case of the call to migrate, Philo has turned the biblical phrase "God said" into a divine message (λόγιον). As before, Abraham obeys promptly. As before, though considerably less explicitly, the literal journey enjoined is conceived of again, in its own way, as a journey to a

---

[122] *Abr.* 175.

[123] Philo omits mentioning here that Isaac is bound. The rabbis use the term "binding," עקדה as the prime word in alluding to Gen. 22. The rabbis embellish the story with many details, especially after Isaac is bound. Philo passes over the item as though this aspect was of little importance to him.

[124] Philo adds this.

[125] Genesis says the voice comes from heaven.

[126] *Abr.* 176.

[127] *Abr.* 177.

[128] The rabbis, as noted above, page 72, identified Moriah as the place of the Temple. For them there was, accordingly, no difficulty in the thought that Abraham offered a sacrifice, so, impliedly, it was offered at the proper place. Philo makes no such identification; he fails to mention the ram. It may be conjectured that the omission stems from the fact that Alexandrian Jews did not offer animal sacrifices in Alexandria, but only when they came to Jerusalem. With such worship unusual for them, Philo may have felt no great and pressing need for it, and therefore he is disposed to pass over the incident of the ram. In here omitting the ram, Philo omits also the motif of the ram's horn, the atoning power of which is of frequent mention in rabbinic writings, and which is regarded as basic to the use of the ram's horn on *Rosh Hashanah.* Cf. *R. H.* 15a; *Pal. Ta'an.* II, 4–5, *Tan. Wa-yera* XLVI. In *Fuga* 132 ff. the ram of Gen. 22.13, held in a Σαβέκ shrub (so LXX handles סבך), is reason "keeping quiet" in suspense of judgment on matters lacking proof.

mystic goal. Philo has again dealt freely (perhaps even capriciously) with the biblical narrative, omitting certain details which could not or would not fit into his theme. The allegory of the episode tells how a Sage, in obedience to a divine command, leaves his city, unobtrusively and unnoticed, to go into the wilderness alone, to commune with God.

We can only guess at the motives which impelled Philo so to abridge the biblical account. Elsewhere[129] he utilizes some of the portions here omitted and these could easily be fitted into his scheme. It is to be noted that the abridged ending is followed by a high polemical defense of Abraham against detractors.[130] The impression can be gotten that Philo's eagerness for the attack is what had led him to abbreviate the narrative.

The attack is directed against those whom Philo describes as φιλαπεχθήμονες who misconstrue everything. He alludes to the βασκονία and πικρία of these critics.[131] He urges them to "set bolt and bar to their unbridled evil-speaking mouths, control their envy and hatred, and not mar the virtues of men who have lived a good life."[132] These are not the calm words of a detached and remote mystic, but the angry words of a man provoked by some real situation.

It is difficult to identify unmistakably these opponents who find Abraham less than unique.[133] It is usually assumed that we have here a reminiscence of some topic about which was focused some polemical and apologetic interchange between anti-Semites and Jews.[134] My own thought is that Philo's targets are fellow-Jews of an "assimilationist" character.

Philo's opponents contend that other people have sacrificed their children, to save the country in war or in drouth; Philo concedes this to be true, but he denies that such deeds actually

---

[129] *Quod Deus* 4, *Fuga* 132 and *LA* III, 203.
[130] *Abr.* 178 ff.
[131] *Abr.* 184.
[132] *Abr.* 191.
[133] *Abr.* 179 ff.
[134] For the apologetic motif in hellenistic Jewish writers, see Schürer, *A History of the Jewish People in the Time of Jesus Christ*, II, III, 262–270; Bergmann, *Jüdische Apologetik im neutestamentlichen Zeitalter*; and Kruger, *Philo u. Josephus als Apologeten des Judentums.*

represent piety. The opponents mention that child sacrifice is a usual practice among barbarians. Philo again concedes that this is so, but he declares that Moses was aware of the practice and considered it an abomination.[135] Similarly, continue the opponents whom Philo quotes, the gymnosophists burn themselves on a funeral pile; and widows have been known to share the pyre of their deceased husbands.[136]

Philo's rebuttal consists in showing that Abraham's action is in no way like these. The child sacrificers have as a motive the desire to save their cities or country, and they give their children partly under compulsion and partly to gain glory and honor; as for such as the gymnosophists, since these are following an established custom, their deeds are diminished in significance.[137] Abraham, however, was not raised where it was customary for such sacrifices to take place. He is not coerced into his deed, since no one knows of it. There is no public calamity to avert. The solitude where the deed is done, especially with the servants left behind, eliminates any suspicion that glory was Abraham's motive.[138]

The truth is that Abraham has always been obedient to God. He has not previously neglected divine commands, nor received them with any sense of complaints. He lives where it is not customary for child sacrifice to take place (Philo here repeats himself). Added to this, Isaac is his only true-born son, born in Abraham's old age, and thereby the more precious. Abraham does not turn his son over to others to slaughter, as is the case among the child sacrificers, but he himself is going to to the deed. "Thus we see that he did not partly incline to the boy and partly to piety, but devoted his whole soul through and through to holiness, and disregarded the claims of their common blood." Now Philo asks the significant rhetorical question, "Which of all the points mentioned is shared by others?"[139]

[135] Deut. 12.31.
[136] *Abr.* 179–184.
[137] *Abr.* 184–187.
[138] *Abr.* 188–191.
[139] *Abr.* 192–199.

There is, moreover, an allegorical explanation. Isaac represents joy, the εὐπάθεια and χαρά of the understanding. The Sage is said to sacrifice his joy to God. Rejoicing, says Philo, is most closely associated with God alone, for men are subject to grief and fear. Only the divine nature is wholly free from grief or fear or passion, and it alone partakes of perfect happiness. God, however, returns joy to the mind which offers it as a sacrifice to Him.[140] When joy comes to earth, Philo adds, it is never pure and free from mixture; grief is always joined to it. He illustrates this by allegorizing Sarah's fear and laughter of Gen. 18.12 and 15.[141] It is God's way not to allow the human race to undergo unrelieved grief and pain; He mixes with these something of the better nature so that the soul can at times dwell in sunshine and calm. The soul of the wise spends the chief part of its life in glad-hearted contemplation.[142]

The incident, whether allegorically or literally interpreted, is an example of Abraham's piety. Other examples might be given in addition, Philo tells us, and these exist in great plenty, but it is time now to turn from Abraham's relation with God to his relations with men. There is this connection: the observer of piety is also kindly; the person who observes holiness to God observes justice (δικαιοσύνη) to men. Of the many actions he could tell about, Philo will select only two or three.[143]

Abraham's justice is the first quality to be illustrated. Abraham is exceedingly rich. Philo seems to be speaking of his own contemporaries, and possibly of his own situation: Abraham's wealth rivals that of the wealthy natives, and he is richer than is expected of an immigrant (μέτοικος), but he incurs no censure from those who received him into their midst.[144] He is praised by all who have experience with him.[145] He smooths over and

---

[140] *Abr.* 200–204.

[141] *Abr.* 205–206.

[142] *Abr.* 207.

[143] *Abr.* 208. He next relates the incident of the separation from Lot, Gen. 13; the war with the kings, Gen. 14; the marriage with Hagar, Gen. 16; the death of Sarah, Gen. 23; and he discusses Abraham's faith, based on a number of selected verses.

[144] An environmental touch.

[145] *Abr.* 209.

eliminates the quarrels between his servants and the neighbors. He does this not only with strangers who might be stronger than he, but even with those weaker, such as relatives, related by blood but not in morals.[146]

A nephew — Philo does not mention Lot by name — is such a relative. Lot sometimes fawns on Abraham, and sometimes is rebellious. He cannot control his servants, especially the shepherds stationed at a distance.[147] The shepherds constantly quarrel with Abraham's herdsmen, who usually give way because of Abraham's gentleness. Ultimately Lot's shepherds go too far; Abraham's men begin to defend themselves, and a serious fight is under way.[148] The news reaches Abraham that his men are triumphing. He does not wish, however, to see his nephew distressed through defeat. He reconciles the disputing shepherds, but he knows that some plan must be followed to avoid future altercations. He gives his nephew the choice of a better district to move to, agreeing to take what is left. In doing this Abraham knows he will get peace, the greatest of gains. But, asks Philo, who else would give way in a single point to someone weaker, and who else, able to conquer, would be willing to be defeated? Abraham, Philo tells us, takes for his ideal a life of freedom from strife and of tranquility.[149]

Philo turns the story into allegory. Abraham is the better type of soul which honors things primary and dominant in nature, while Lot is the lower type which honors things subject and low.[150] Philo alters his figure shortly; he ceases to discuss two types of soul and discusses instead the better and lower side

---

[146] *Abr.* 210–211.

[147] Lot means "inclining." He is the wavering person, midway between the sage and the wicked man, *QG* IV, 47. Not being wicked, he is sometimes treated favorably, and not being wise, sometimes unfavorably. In addition, as a "progressing soul" he is sometimes allegorically the mind of the sage before it attains sagacity. See below, notes 218, 265, and 298. Philo seems to make of Lot what he had already made of Abraham, a city dweller.

[148] *Abr.* 212–213.

[149] *Abr.* 214–216. See also *QG* III, 8, based on the LXX to Gen. 15.11, in which the MT וַיַּשֵּׁב אֹתָם seems to have been read as וַיֵּשֶׁב אִתָּם, for further on "tranquility."

[150] *Abr.* 217–218.

within the same soul.[151] Philo sees in the incident Abraham's rising above the lower (or material) part of the soul.

Next, Philo illustrates Abraham's courage.[152] Though Abraham is peaceable and a lover of justice, he can become, to secure the peace, courageous and warlike. Philo uses as illustration Abraham's role in the war between the four kings of the east and the five kings of Sodom of Gen. 14. As Philo recounts the episode, the eastern part of the inhabited world is in the hand of four great kings, who hold in subjection the eastern nations on both sides of the Euphrates. (This geographical precision is an addition by Philo to the biblical account.) Other nations maintain a happy obedience to the four kings, but the Sodomites begin to undermine the peace by a long-planned-for revolt. Sodom, Philo tells us, is rich in corn, well-wooded and teeming with fruits; although it is small in size, it is, through its fertility, exceedingly prosperous. Therefore it has several rulers who love it and are fascinated by its charm.[153]

In conformity with his scorn of material things, Philo, through the above additions, motivates the rebellion by the Sodomites: Sodom has a superabundance of material things which leads to a love of them, and this love is the ultimate cause of the catastrophe to come.

As Philo continues, the Sodomites are surfeited with good things, and therefore their satiety begets insolence.[154] They grow ambitious beyond their powers. First they shake off the yoke; next they even attack their masters. Philo's disapproval of the Sodomites is clearly discernible; they are people who occupy themselves with material goods; they throw off a yoke which is tolerated, apparently with equanimity, by other nations.

---

[151] *Abr.* 223–224. I discuss this below, page 159.

[152] *Abr.* 225 ff.

[153] *Abr.* 225–228.

[154] *Abr.* 228. See *QG* IV, 23, on Gen. 18.20, the outcry of the Sodomites and Gomorrahites. Sodom means "blind" or "sterile"; Gomorrah means "measure." Folly is blind and barren, and "measures" by the human mind rather than God. So too *Somn.* II, 192; in *Ebr.* 222 ff. Philo, after denouncing wine-bibbing gluttony, and the basest pleasures, comments that no true gladness grows in the soul of the wicked, since it has no healthy roots, but such as were burnt to ashes.

The four kings are mindful of their high birth. They arm themselves more powerfully, and then advance to the attack with great disdain. Their onslaught is easily successful. Some of the enemy they mow down in wholesale massacre, while others are taken prisoner; among these is the nephew of the Sage.[155] As Philo recounts the incident, most of the pericope is Philonic and not biblical; Philo omits Gen. 14.5, with the account of the conquest of Nephilim, Zuzim and Emim. The allusion to higher birth is, I believe, more a reflection of Philo's scorn of the body-loving Sodomites than of his actual admiration for the victorious kings.

When the news reaches Abraham, the shock is severe. It is worse than if he had heard of his nephew's death, Philo tells us, for death is the end of everything in life, including its ills, while for the living the troubles which lie in wait are numberless.[156] Again, Philo's hellenistic "rejection of this world" shows through.

Abraham is eager to pursue the enemy to rescue his nephew. He is, however, a stranger and an immigrant — still another contemporaneous touch, added to the biblical account — so that he is at a loss to find allies, especially in view of the recent victories and great numbers of the enemy.[157] But he finds allies, Philo tells us, in a new source — as does anyone set on deeds of justice and kindness. He collects his servants and divides them into two groups, the home-bred and those acquired by purchase. The latter Abraham tells to remain at home, for he fears they might revolt.[158] He makes a roll-call,[159] distributes them into centuries, and advances with three battalions. Philo is influenced here by some military knowledge. Scripture reports no more than that Abraham took 318 slaves; Philo turns this number into

---

[155] *Abr.* 229.   [156] *Abr.* 230.

[157] *Abr.* 231.

[158] This addition by Philo seems based on an inference of this kind, that Gen. 14.14, mentions the home-born specifically; ergo, Abraham must not have taken along those acquired by purchase; ergo, there must have been a reason for it. Philo undoubtedly has had experience with servants, and had a greater measure of trust in the home-bred.

[159] This notion, based on LXX Gen. 14.14, could not rest on MT; *wayareq* is a difficult word for the rabbis, and it leads them into endless fanciful explanations, all different from Philo's naturalistic explanation.

three battalions of a hundred men. Significantly, Philo adds that Abraham's reliance was not really in these, but in God, the companion and defender of the just;[160] and Philo has previously told us that Abraham's piety underlay his other virtues.[161]

Abraham makes the attack by night, after the enemy have supper and when they are preparing to go to bed.[162] Some fall in their beds, while others, resisting, are annihilated. This victory, Philo assures us, is much more one of Abraham's courage of soul than of resources at hand.[163] Abraham slaughters the enemy completely, including their kings, and he leaves them lying in front of the camp.[164] Abraham brings his nephew back in triumph, bringing along with him the horses of the cavalry,[165] other beasts, and spoil in plenty.[166]

The high priest of God — Philo does not mention Melchizedek by name — considers the victory to have been won "not without God's directing care" ($\epsilon\pi\iota\varphi\rho\sigma\sigma\acute{\nu}\eta$) and help in arms. The priest stretches forth his hands in prayer, and offers sacrifices of thanksgiving for the victory.[167] As above,[168] Philo ascribes by implication Abraham's success, as exemplified in his courage, to Abraham's piety.[169]

---

[160] *Abr.* 232. A similar explanation is found in *Gen. R.* XLIII. There is no compelling reason to attribute the similarity to interdependence of the rabbis and Philo, for it is a natural inference that the patriarch, in embarking with a small force, trusted in God.

[161] *Abr.* 192 ff.

[162] *Abr.* 233. No wider divergence, in my opinion, between Philo and the rabbis, is to be found than in the interpretations of Gen. 14.15. Philo gives a naturalistic explanation in military terms; the rabbis tell us, in one passage (*San.* 96a) that an angel named Night attacked the enemy; in other passages, that the night of Passover was divided, half for the present event and half for the Passover night, *Tar. Jon. ad loc.*; cf. *Gen. R.* XLIII; *PRE* XXVII.

[163] *Abr.* 233.

[164] Philo again gives evidence of writing from memory, and not from an open text. He overlooks the pursuit towards Damascus, Gen. 14.15.

[165] LXX renders the MT רכוש by ἵππος; this expansion by Philo follows naturally from the LXX, but would represent a wide divergence from MT.

[166] *Abr.* 234. In this contemporaneous touch Philo seems to be describing a triumphal procession of the kind he probably himself witnessed in Alexandria.

[167] *Abr.* 235.

[168] *Abr.* 232.

[169] Philo does not here mention the bread and wine of Gen. 14, which

Philo has completed his demonstration of Abraham's courage. He next turns the incident into allegory, as illustrative of the spiritual development of Abraham.[170]

Philo is now ready to demonstrate Abraham's cultivation of moderation. His proof rests on Abraham's conduct at the death of Sarah. Like a good dramatist, Philo enhances the worth of Abraham by a rather elaborate presentation of what Abraham lost in losing his wife. (Philo does not mention Sarah by name in this section.)

The wife, Philo tells us, was gifted with every excellence. She shared Abraham's departure from homeland, the unceasing wanderings, the privations in famine, and the military campaigns.[171] She partook of both the ill and the good which befell him and did not, like some other women, run away from mishaps.[172] While Philo could tell many stories in praise of Sarah, he selects only one, the incident of Hagar.[173] Sarah magnanimously suggests to Abraham that she would not be jealous of his taking another woman, not for lust but for procreation, in fulfillment of nature's inevitable law. Sarah herself will lend to him a bride to supply the lack. If offspring results, she will adopt the child as her very own.[174] The woman is her own handmaiden — Philo does not mention Hagar by name — who is outwardly ($\sigma\hat{\omega}\mu\alpha$) a slave, but inwardly ($\delta\iota\acute{\alpha}\nu\omega\alpha\nu$) free and well-born, proved and tested by Sarah for many years. The slave is an Egyptian by birth, but a Hebrew by rule of life.[175] That Hagar was an Egyptian must have been a source of discomfort to Philo, who makes it abundantly clear in treating of the Pharaoh of Gen. 12 and the Pharaoh of Moses' day, that Egyptians are despicable lovers

elsewhere provide him with allegorical material. He speaks of a handsome feast. Philo adds that the priest shares Abraham's joy, a spirit of sharing appropriate to the good men who aim to be well-pleasing to God, *Abr.* 235.

[170] I discuss this in detail in the section on the allegorical Abraham, pages 147–151.

[171] Philo is not paralleled by the rabbis in this bit of extravagance of Sarah's accompanying Abraham on his campaigns. There is no scriptural basis.

[172] *Abr.* 245–246.

[173] Gen. 16.1–6.

[174] *Abr.* 247–250.

[175] *Abr.* 251.

of bodily things. The clear note of contempt for Egyptians probably represents Philo's own attitude towards the Egyptians of
Alexandria for whom he has a feeling of loathing.[176]

Sarah reminds Abraham that they are wealthy, indeed, they
are wealthier beyond the usual scale of immigrants, even out-
shining those of the native inhabitants who are noted for prosperity.[177] Again, the allusion seems to be comtemporaneous. It
may be indicative of Philo's own wealth.

Abraham's admiration for Sarah increases. He takes Hagar
as a mate, until she has borne a child, or, indeed, until she
becomes pregnant. Thereafter, he abstains from her through his
natural continence and the honor he pays his lawful wife.[178] A
son is born to the hand-maiden; long afterwards[179] Abraham and
Sarah have a son of their own, a reward for their high excellence,
a gift from God the bountiful.[180] Philo abstains here from
alluding to an intricately developed allegory of the incident of
Hagar.[181]

Philo now reverts to Abraham. Sarah has died. Abraham now
wrestles with sorrow like a grappler in the arena. He is determined
to obey reason ($\lambda o \gamma \iota \sigma \mu o s$), the natural antagonist of passion;
accordingly, he does not grieve as at an utterly new and unheard
of misfortune, nor does he, on the other hand, assume an indifference as though nothing painful has occurred. He chooses the
mean rather than the extremes, and he arrives at moderation of
feeling. He does not resent that nature should be paid the debt
which is its due; he takes the blow quietly and gently.[182]

---

[176] Cf. *In Flaccum*, 17, 29.

[177] *Abr.* 252.

[178] The rabbis aver that Hagar became pregnant after a single effort,
Gen. R. XLV; they do not say specifically that Abraham abstained from her
thereafter, nor do they suggest natural continence as the motivation for such
abstinence. In another rabbinic passage, Abraham reweds Hagar after Sarah's
death and a daughter, Ba-kol, is born; see page 79.

[179] According to Genesis, Ishmael is thirteen when Isaac is born.

[180] *Abr.* 253–254.

[181] The allegory is the substance of *Congress*.

[182] *Abr.* 255–257. Colson, VI, pp. 598–599 and Cohn, I, 148, suggest that
Philo may have known a work of Crantor on moderation in mourning. The
view of the rabbis is the antithesis of moderation. Philo adds a "quickly"
before the "rose" of Gen. 23.3; but they do not suggest that it is "quickly,"

Abraham weeps a little over the corpse, but he quickly rises up from it. He believes that further weeping is out of keeping with wisdom, which teaches him that death is not the extinction of the soul, but its separation and detachment from the body, and its return to the place whence it came, from God.[183] And as no reasonable person chafes at repaying a debt, so he does not fret when nature takes back her own.[184] It is to be noted that Philo is not simply giving his own judgment on death; he is ascribing this judgment to Abraham. Philo undoubtedly felt no sense of incongruity in the rather tortured ascription of his view on death to the sorrowing Abraham. Philo omits from the present account the "mourning and weeping" of Gen. 23.2; had he used them, he would have had to divest them of their usual import in order to substantiate a contention that Abraham bore the blow in moderation.[185] The picture here is a completely hellenistic one, in all its aspects, especially in its standards of proper and improper mourning.

As Philo continues the account, the chief people of the country come to sympathize and to their astonishment they see none of the customs of mourning they expect. Philo lists these for us: wailing, chanting of dirges, and beating of breasts.[186] The thought suggests itself that the list represents Jewish practices of which Philo disapproves because these do not accord with moderation.[187]

Amazed as the people have been before at Abraham's great qualities, they are all the more amazed as they now note in

but only after elaborate mourning. Cf. *Ber.* 18a; *Gen. R.* LVIII; and *Mid. Hag. ad loc.*

[183] Cf. *Opif.* 135. The subject is treated in greater detail in *QG* IV 71–83, see below, notes 379–381.

[184] *Abr.* 258–259.

[185] In *QG* IV, 73, Philo ascribes the mourning and weeping to the loss by the Sage of virtue, the allegorical Sarah. Inferentially, there, too, he denies that Abraham mourns to excess.

[186] *Abr.* 260.

[187] It is impossible to go beyond conjecture that Philo is here dissociating himself from rites of mourning as practiced by his fellow Jews. In context it is the natives of the region to whom he ascribes the rites and not to Jews. Yet the list of rites rejected are mentioned in Scripture, and come into "normative" Jewish practice. But even if the allusion is not to contemporaneous practice of other Jews, nevertheless Philo's formula is unmistakably hellenistic.

admiration his quiet, sober air. They cannot contain their admiration in silence, but declare to Abraham, "Thou art a king from God among us."[188] Philo asserts that the words are true but he proceeds to show in what sense they are true. Other kingships, he says are man-made, and stem from wars, campaigns and numberless ills, inflicted as a result of strife. The kingship of the Sage, however, is a gift from God; such a king brings no harm to anyone but rather the acquisition and enjoyment of good things to all his subjects.[189]

Philo has now completed his demonstration of Abraham's self-control and his moderation, and he has made of Abraham the stoic ideal of the philosopher-king.[190] In conformity with his emphasis on Abraham's piety, he has carefully included the statement that Abraham's kingship is a divine gift.

Philo next turns to the faith of Abraham who "trusted in God."[191] Such faith, Philo tells us, is a little thing if measured in words, but a very great thing if made good by actions.[192] Philo dismisses as unworthy of trust such human accomplishments as high office, fame, honors, wealth, noble birth, or bodily health or capacity of body.[193] He adds a paragraph of scorn for those who trust in bodily beauty: images and statues surpass the human frame in beauty, and Greeks and barbarians set up

---

[188] The verse is LXX Gen. 23.6, and cannot rest readily on MT, which reads נשיא; *Onk.* and *Jon.* read רב. The rabbis, too, make a king of Abraham; they derive this, however, from Gen. 14.17; see *Tan. Be-ha'aloteka* XVII. *Gen. R.* XLIII portrays the survivors of the battle of the nine kings addressing Abraham as *Nasi, Melek,* and *Elohim;* but Abraham replies that the world lacks neither a king nor God; so, too, *SER* 116. This latter pericope seems to me to reflect the knowledge on the part of the rabbis of the pretensions to divinity by hellenistic kings, and it is a denial of the authenticity of such pretensions.

Abraham is conceived of as a king in the traditional Jewish interpretation of Ps. 110, cf. Rashi and Ibn Ezra to verse 1. The "king" in rabbinic literature, however, is a political figure and not the "philosopher" of Philo.

[189] *Abr.* 261. See also *QG* IV, 76.

[190] So, too, Colson, VI, p. 599. Cf. also *Mut.* 152, for a fuller explanation by Philo of this same idea, based on this same text.

[191] Gen. 15.6.

[192] *Abr.* 262.

[193] *Abr.* 263–266.

the creations of painters and sculptors to adorn their cities.[194] What Philo seems to be saying is that beauty is nothing to trust in, and certainly the beautiful icons of the Gentiles are unworthy of trust.

On the other hand, faith in God is the one safe and infallible good. It is the consolation of life, the fulfillment of bright hopes, the death of ills, the harvest of goods, the acquaintance with piety, and the heritage of happiness. It is the all-around betterment of the soul firmly fastened on God.[195] Lack of faith is like traveling on a slippery road, the path of the bodily and the external, and the soul on such a journey is certain to fall. Those, however, who press on to God along the doctrines of virtue walk without falling. Belief in the former is disbelief in God, while disbelief in them is belief in God.[196] Philo, then, has allocated faith as something pertaining to the intelligible world, and he denies that confidence in the perceptible things can be faith. This opposition between the perceptible and the intelligible, as applied to faith, serves to emphasize even more sharply that Philo's thinking inevitably seems to adjust itself to hellenistic modes of expression. Since, in Philo's thought, God is allocated to the intelligible world, true faith operates only in the realm of the intelligible.

Abraham possesses this queen of virtues, faith in God. Moreover, though others (in the Scriptural account) surpass him in years, Abraham is the first to be called an elder.[197] The true "elder" is shown not by his length of days but by a laudable and perfect life. A long life spent among bodily things makes one a long-lived child; he who is enamored of sound sense, wisdom, and faith, is justly called elder, and "elder" is equivalent to "first."

[194] *Abr.* 267.

[195] *Abr.* 268.

[196] *Abr.* 269.

[197] So LXX Gen. 24.1. MT reads זקן. Cohn, *Philos Werke*, I, 151, makes the comment that πρεσβύτερος means old, whereas זקן has the sense of "ehrwuerdig." Both זקן and πρεσβύτερος seem to me to have this sense. In the present context, however, Philo interprets the word as "honorable"; the rabbis deduce from the passage that until Abraham's time the visible signs of old age did not exist, for Abraham is the first to be termed "old," *San.* 107b. See note 296 below, and page 94 above.

The Sage is the first of the human race, like the pilot of a ship, or the ruler in a city, or a general in war, or as a soul in a body, and a mind in soul, or heaven in the world, or God in heaven.[198]

What Philo has been doing has been to contrast Abraham with ordinary men, to show Abraham's pre-eminence. As the first among men, he surpasses them in endowments and in achievements; and his capacities bring benefits to men.[199] These capacities are the result of his possession of faith. Faith makes Abraham the "first" among the human race. Now Philo proceeds towards his climax: God holds Abraham's faith in high esteem, and he repays this faith with divine faith; this consists in God's confirming by an oath the gifts already promised.[200] God's oath is a measure of faith added to that faith which Abraham antecedently possessed.

Moreover, that God utilized an oath is a further token of Abraham's eminence, in that God thereby addresses Abraham not as God usually addresses man, but as a friend addresses an acquaintance.[201] Abraham, then, is not only pre-eminent among men, but his eminence is such that God converses with him in familiar terms.

Philo has now completed his section on Abraham's faith, the last of the four sections. He now comes to the climax of his

---

[198] *Abr.* 270–272. See also *QG* III, 44, based on Gen. 17.6; Philo states that the sage is moreover an intercessor (Marcus supposes that μεσίτης or παράκλητος lay in the Greek) with God, seeking forgiveness for his countrymen, who have committed sins. Philo somewhat similarly treats the circumcision of "those of foreign birth," Gen. 17.27, in *QG* III, 62.

In *V. C.* 31 the true "elder" among the Therapeutae gives a discourse on the Sabbath.

[199] Goodenough, 144, points out that this list of primacies implies the notion of the rule-*soter*. See also *QG* IV, 53, to Gen. 19.27–28. The rabbis and Philo unite in adding that Abraham prayed, Philo being alone in commenting that it was to avert the destruction already begun. *QG* IV, 54, based on God "remembered Abraham" in Gen. 19.29, accords with the wide and usual opinion that Lot's rescue was for Abraham's sake. See also *QG* IV, 70, based on Gen. 20.17–18.

[200] *Abr.* 273. On Abraham's faith see *QG* IV, 17, and below, page 170 f.

[201] *Abr.* 273. As noted above, page 44, Philo alludes to Abraham as the "friend of God." I show in the section on Allegory that "friend of God" is equivalent to prophet; see below, note 347.

treatise: to all the other praises of the Sage, this crowning praise, that "This man did the divine law and the divine commands."[202] The law was not the written law, but that which unwritten nature prompted him to do. When men have God's promises before them, Philo tells us, they should trust in them most firmly. Such a man was Abraham, the founder of the nation. Some, Philo tells us, interpret Abraham as one who obeyed the law; Abraham, however, was more than that; he was himself a law and an unwritten statute.

In summary, the literal Abraham is a man who makes a false start in astrology, but through learning abandons that untrue philosophy in favor of true wisdom. He ultimately achieves perfection, so that he is outstanding in his piety towards God and in the practice of virtue towards his fellowmen.

He is a true Sage, a philosopher-king and a *soter*. He lives by the law of nature, and he is, in fact, a law incarnate and made vocal.

A mystic, he retires from the city from time to time. In the solitude of the wilderness he is able to rise to the best possible sight of God.

The literal Abraham is depicted as perfected. In the allegorical Abraham we shall see how this perfection was achieved.

III

The allegorical Abraham is the record of the process through which Abraham becomes the man of perfect piety and virtue. The spiritual development begins when Abraham, who has been mistakenly absorbed in pantheistic materialism, by divine intervention becomes the first man in history to recognize that pantheism is a wrong conclusion, based on a wrong method. Abraham, therefore, turns away from pantheism, in favor of a new quest which begins within himself. He learns what the body is

---

[202] Gen. 26.5. See below, note 289. Philo interprets the commands as the law of nature; the rabbis use this verse to prove that Abraham observed the whole Torah, *Kid.* 82a, or both the Torah and the words of the Scribes, *Tos. Kid.* V, or even the laws of *Erub*, Yoma 28b.

and what the senses are, and he discerns the peril in them to the rational soul. He therefore conquers his senses and his passions and is able to free himself from domination by bodily matters. He seeks solitude and the opportunity for contemplation. He possesses excellent powers of reason, both of the inner mind and of the outer manifestation of mind, the spoken word. He masters the encyclia, and goes beyond them into knowledge of true philosophy. His virtue is such that his mind has complete ascendency over all the members of the body, and therefore he is able to raise his mind above mundane matters. His mind grasps matters relevant to the intelligible world, possessing as it does a keen sense of discrimination. His gifts are such that he is able to rise to the highest goal of the religious life, the sight of God. As one in control of his body, Abraham is a philosopher-king; as a mystic who achieves the vision of God, Abraham is a prophet through whom divine words and promises are spoken. Abraham's soul is so richly endowed that in contrast to souls which simply disappear at the death of the body, Abraham's soul returns to the divine essence from which it has come.

This is no more than a brief summary of matters now to be presented in detail. Certain other preliminaries ought, however, to be mentioned. First, the allegorical use of Abraham as the figure for the man who progressed is not original with Philo. He heard it, he tells us, from certain "natural philosophers."[203] Second, the context into which Philo fits Abraham is a completely Greek framework. Aristotle had asked the question how happiness and virtue could be acquired, and he had considered, in one passage,[204] three possibilities: by learning, μαθετόν, or by habit, ἐθιστόν, or practice, ἀσκητόν, or by some divine dispensation θεία μοῖρα. In another passage[205] Aristotle mentions as the possibilities teaching, διδαχή, habit, ἔθος, or nature, φύσις.[206] Philo gives us these same categories,[207] and in a number of dif-

---

[203] *Abr.* 99.

[204] *Eth. Nic.* I, 9, 1099b, lines 9–10; Paris, 1883 edition, p. 9.

[205] *Ibid.*, X, 9, 1179b, 20–23.

[206] According to Wolfson, Philo, II, 197, Aristotle accepted only the first two as possibilities, and rejected the notion of virtue by nature.

[207] Direct dependency on Aristotle is not necessarily indicated; the subject

ferent passages he discusses these same possibilities.²⁰⁸ Philo builds his discussion around the patriarchs as allegorical figures for each of the categories; the patriarchs are, allegorically, types of the soul, τρόποι ψυχῆς, all of them worthy, ἀστεῖοι; Abraham pursues the good, τοῦ καλοῦ, through teaching, Isaac through nature, and Jacob through practice. The (literal) patriarchs each possessed all three capacities, but the allegorical quantity which Philo associates with each is that one which most predominatingly characterizes the individual. Each of the patriarchs possesses all these patriarchal qualities or capacities; those capacities can be equated, Philo tells us, with the Graces. That is to say, the capacities, as part of the endowment of the individual, are innate; as "graces," they are the gift of God, or else, Philo tells us, the gift to the reasonable soul from the capacity itself.²⁰⁹

Neither the conception nor the allegorical figure representing the conception is, then, original with Philo. He has absorbed them so completely, however, that almost his every approach to a scriptural mention of Abraham leads him to equate the scriptural verse with some aspect of perfection through teaching, or with the particular incident as a proof that Abraham either assimilates the matter mentioned as a spiritual benefit and advancement, or else spurns it, if by chance the scriptural verse deals with what to Philo is something unseemly.

I divide my discussion into five sections. I derive this division from Philo himself who speaks of five stages in the development of the progressing soul²¹⁰ (based on an allegory of the heifer, the goat, the ram, the turtle-dove, and the pigeon of Gen. 15.9) body, sense-perception, reason, natural philosophy, and the intelligible world. The record of the allegorical Abraham is the manner in which he progresses through such stages to perfection of soul.

---

may well have been a usual one in the various philosophical schools before and after Philo's life-time. Cf. Colson and Whitaker, II, p. 488.

²⁰⁸ *Abr.* 52; *Cong.* 36; *Mut.* 12.

²⁰⁹ *Abr.* 52–54.

²¹⁰ *QG* III, 3.

a. *The Stage of Body*

Abraham is perfected through being taught, in the sense that he makes a false start and has to begin anew. Abraham was born in Chaldean materialistic pantheism, and for a long time was himself an adherent of that creed. The Chaldeans were especially active in the study of astrology (ἀστρονομία) and ascribed everything to the movements of the stars. Thus they glorified visible existence, and they left out of consideration the invisible and the intelligible. They concluded, moreover, that the world itself was God, thereby profaning the Creator by likening him to the created. Abraham, however, did not remain in pantheism; he opened his "soul's eye as though after a profound sleep, and beginning to see the pure beam instead of the deep darkness, he followed the ray and discerned . . . . what he had not beheld before, a charioteer and pilot presiding over the world." Abraham is urged by the Hieros Logos to desist from observing the cosmos, the greatest of cities, and for a time to observe the lesser city, man himself.[211]

Abraham is one of the goodly natures which God promotes without any manifest reason.[212] God has created him in such a way that Abraham merits esteem[213] since his mind, in turning

---

[211] *Abr.* 68–71; *cf. Mig.* 184 ff. Another expression of the view that in departing from Chaldea Abraham departed from astrology is found in *QG* III, 1 and *Heres*, 96 ff., based on Gen. 15.7. The *Ur Kasdim* of MT is rendered by LXX (and in Philo's text) by ἐκ χώρας Χαλδαίων, thereby omitting the Ur, as though reading *'eres* in its place. The peg on which the very frequent rabbinic allusion to Abraham's rescue from Nimrod's fiery furnace is hung is the pun on Ur, either at this verse or at Gen. 11.28. For the legend see Ginzberg, I, 198 ff., and V, 212–214. I have discerned in Philo not one single trace of this legend, and no overtone in his dealing with Nimrod of it. As indicated on page 30, Philo lacks allusions to patriarchal anecdotes; not impossibly he found them somewhat juvenile in comparison with his own theosophical profundities. Indeed, one is struck by a kind of mathematical proportion which can express superficially a possible key to a New Testament problem. The Gospel according to John lacks the anecdotes and pithy sayings of Jesus. The form and manner of the Synoptic Gospels are to John as rabbinic form and manner are to Philo.

[212] *LA* III, 79–84.

[213] Philo in this passage regards "Abram" favorably; elsewhere the name is

away from pleasure and mortal things, soaring aloft, contemplates the universe and its parts, and, going still higher, explores God and His nature, urged to this by the love of knowledge δι' ἔρωτα ἐπιστήμης.[214]

The gifted man, like Abraham, despite a false start, is able by divine help to withdraw from a preoccupation with the visible universe to raise his level of perception to the loftiest of goals, to God. But this process is a long and arduous one. First he must resort to a study of himself. It is, Philo assures us, a wrong method for the mind to plunge into astrology before it learns the senses of the body.[215] Abraham therefore migrates to Haran;[216] this means that Abraham studies his senses.

Terah, Abraham's father, had taken Abraham to Haran (Gen. 11.31–32) where Terah had died. Terah too had known that it was not appropriate for one to try to learn the heavens until he had learned himself. Terah is the figure for the mind which discovers the need of self-knowledge.[217] Terah, however, made the

---

synonymous with our character when still a Chaldean: *Gig.* 62, *Cher.* 4, and *Mut.* 66.

[214] *LA* III, 84.

[215] *Somn.* I, 53.

[216] *Abr.* 72. Philo derives the word "senses" from his etymology of Haran, "holes." The senses are in those organs of the body for which places are dug out in the body. In connection with the injunction of the High Priest to lay aside his usual robes before entering the Holy of Holies (Lev. 16), that is, according to Philo, the robe of opinions and impressions through bodily senses, Philo cites, among others who become similarly naked, Abraham; his proof text is Gen. 12.1. See *LA* II, 55–59.

[217] *Somn.* I, 48. Philo gives the etymology of Terah as (*tar-reah*) "spyer of odor." Terah spies out the odor of virtue while Abraham goes on to taste it. Terah anticipated Socrates, according to Philo, *Somn.* I, 58, in advocating "know thyself." In context this is in the longest passage in which Philo discusses Abraham's migration from Ur to Haran, *Somn.* I, 41 ff. Philo emphasizes that the purpose of the scriptural account is not "that we may learn as from a writer of history that certain people became immigrants, leaving the land of their ancestors . . . ." It is astronomy (astrology) which is abandoned: "Why are you so busy with what you ought to leave alone, the things above?" In the passage Philo cites Gen. 11.32, Terah's death in Haran, as proof that Terah did not possess virtue, but only scouted it out.

mistake of remaining in the world of the senses, while Abraham goes on beyond it.[218]

Abraham learns what the senses are; he makes, in fact, an examination of every component part of the body. He learns about senses and about passions, about pleasures and fears, and he learns how to counteract these.[219] Abraham, accordingly, does not dally with the sense of odor, Keturah, for it is a sensual pleasure; he turns away from her in order to cleave to virtue.[220]

---

[218] *Somn.* I, 48. In *QG* IV, 26, interpreting Gen. 18.23, Philo also discusses a contrast, the man who is a mixture of righteousness and unrighteousness, derived from Scripture that there may be some righteous men in Sodom, allegorically some righteousness in a foolish man. Such a man is in contrast to Abraham who went beyond the senses. The surrounding of the house, Gen. 19.4, symbolizes allegorically the traits of the unproductive soul in surrounding the body with attractions, *QG* IV, 36; cf. *Somn.* I, 122–123 for a description of "Italian" luxury, associated with Sodom. The contents of Gen. 19.5, "bring them out that we may know them," is the effort of the impure to divert the noble from soul to body, *QG* IV, 37. Lot (Gen. 19.7–8) is willing to offer his daughters, his thoughts which serve his bodily needs and are feminine, so as to save those which are masculine, zealous of wisdom and virtue, *QG* IV, 38. Gen. 19.9 is the rebuke to the sojourner who in the territory of the licentious pronounces judgment on evil, *QG* IV, 39. In sum, neither the evil Sodomites nor the wavering Lot paralleled Abraham's achievement of going beyond the senses. While the contrast is not exactly the same as that of Terah and Abraham, it is of the same genre.

Mig. 176 quotes Gen. 12.4, that Abraham was seventy-five when he left Haran. The immediate passage does not treat the "seventy-five," but rather the significance of moving out of the senses, Haran. Philo reverts to the seventy-five in *Mig.* 198 ff.; it is the "borderland between perceptible and intelligible being, between older and younger, between corruptible and incorruptible."

[219] *Mig.* 187–195. See also in *QG* III, 41 the first of Philo's three explanations of Gen. 17.3.

[220] *Sac.* 43–45; cf. *QG* IV, 147 on Gen. 25.1. Philo seems initially embarrassed at encountering Keturah in the Bible, but his allegorical ingenuity enables him to allocate her appropriately. In *Sac.* 43–45, he associates her and Hagar as two transient stages through which Abraham passed. Elsewhere, *Confus.* 74 and *Mig.* 94, her low status is demonstrated by the contrast in the gifts which Abraham gives to her offspring and to Isaac; the latter receives the laws of nature, while Keturah's children receive the enacted laws.

Abraham makes great progress in learning his senses and his passions and in conquering them.[221] Thereby Abraham establishes

[221] Circumcision symbolizes this, *Mig.* 92; see also *QG* III, 46–50 and 52 based on Gen. 17.10–12 and 14, and *QG* III, 61, based on Gen. 17.24–25. Philo also represents the incidents of Gen. 14 as Abraham's conquest of the senses and the passions. Four of the sovereign kings are the passions: pleasure, grief, desire, and fear; the five kings are the senses: sight, hearing, taste, smell, and touch. The passions exact tribute from the senses. When the tribute is rendered, the alliance between the passions and the senses holds good; when it is withheld, discord arises in the body, as when old age or pains beset. Two of the organs, touch and taste, are within the body and are low senses; the other three, the organs of smell, hearing, and sight, are for the most part outside the body and therefore are able to escape complete enslavement by the body; *Abr.* 236–241.

The ten nations of Gen. 15.19–21 are the actions the opposite of wisdom, ultimately destroyed by God. See *Cong.* 119 and *QG* III, 17. The latter, in *Philo Supplement* I, 201, note d, is incorrectly stated to be Philo's only comment on the scriptural section.

Parenthetically, Philo's proof of the holiness of the number ten is buttressed in *Cong.* 91–92, by adding Abraham to the five and four kings, giving us a ten and by citing the "tenth part" of Gen. 14.20.

Philo's thought, at least some of the time, seems to be that in Abraham's progress there was a stage in which the issue of senses and passions versus the soul needed to be fought out. "Lot" is "Abraham" at that as yet indecision stage. As a symbol for indecisive wavering, Lot partakes somewhat of virtue in that he only inclines in the opposite direction, but does not actually get there. Gen. 19.23 f. serves Philo as a basis of indicating a partial affinity in Lot to virtue; the passage that the sun, the divine Logos, went forth upon the earth, and Lot entered into Ṣoʻar (Gen. 19.23–24) demonstrates that the divine logos gives a refuge and safety to those akin to virtue. See *Somn.* I, 85–89; *QG* III, 51 and the fragments in Harris and Lewy, reprinted as appendix A in *Philo Supplement* II. The Sodomites, contrasted with Lot, are one of Philo's several examples of seeking and not finding, based on Gen. 19.11, a just frustration for those seeking unseemly things, *QG* IV, 41. Similarly Philo renders Gen. 19.4, in *Conf.* 27–28. The Sodomites are those who try to bring shame upon divine thoughts; so again somewhat similarly *QG* IV, 36.

Lot, to repeat, is sometimes a different entity, contrastable with Abraham, yet sometimes the Abraham type of progressing mind at the stage at which wavering still abides, ultimately to be passed by, *Mig.* 13. As the antithesis to Abraham, see *Mig.* 148 ff., based on Gen. 12.4.

Lot at the gate of the Sodomites (Gen. 19.1) symbolizes the progressing man who is neither within nor outside virtue, *QG* IV, 31. The wavering man (conjecturing about the lacuna in *QG* IV, 32; cf. Marcus I, 307) receives "appearance" before "truth." The divine powers, which had entered the

democracy within himself.[222] The means of this establishment is the use of chastening reason (σωφρονιστὴς λόγος).[223]

In contrast with Abraham who conquers his senses and passions, there is the mind which succumbs to them, loving them. Such a one was the wicked king of Egypt (Gen. 12.10–20) who pretended, like an actor, to want fellowship with virtue (Sarah, allegorically), so as to have, undeservedly, a good reputation.[224]

Abraham knows true peace.[225] Beyond the mere conquest of his bodily senses and passions, he so controls them that they are

perfect Abraham's home, declined to enter the imperfect Lot's, preferring to remain in the street, *QG* IV, 33, on Gen. 19.2. The MT to Gen. 19.3 reads ויפצר בם, "he pressed them"; LXX reads παραβιάζετο, he "forced" them; the powers turned aside from Lot because of the use of force; the sage desires wisdom willingly, whereas the opposite of the sage needs to be forced!

[222] Colson and Whitaker, VI, p. 118, define "democracy" in Philo as each part of the state having its proper amount of power. Philo speaks several times of democracy as the best constitution, *Conf.* 108, *Abr.* 242, *Spec. Leg.* IV 237, and *Virt.* 180. Philo elsewhere defines democracy as the mean between mob rule and tyranny; it presupposes the presence of a ruler who is neither too cruel nor too yielding. Applied to the individual, democracy is the situation in which the mind rules the body like a goatherd or shepherd; such a ruling mind "chooses for himself and the creatures he tends what is advantageous, in preference to what is agreeable," *Agr.* 45–48. Respecting democracy in the soul, Melchizedek, Gen. 14.18, is the exemplar of the true king, contrasted with the despot; the despot is war-like, but Melchizedek is the prince of peace. Melchizedek is therefore reason which persuades, rather than a despot who orders. The Ammonites and Moabites (Deut. 23.4 ff.) failed to provide bread and water; these, allegorically derived respectively from sense perception and from only their father's mind, take no thought of God. In contrast to them, reason, Melchizedek, did provide bread and wine.

The wine of reason can give to strong souls the sober intoxication, which is another way of describing "prophecy." See *LA* III, 79–82. Melchizedek, like Lot, is the experience of Abraham, but at the stage of "reason," rather than at "wavering."

[223] *Abr.* 242–244. This allegory assumes that nine kings opposed Abraham whereas in the biblical account five kings rebelled against four and Abraham was a by-stander.

[224] *Abr.* 99 f.

[225] True peace is defined in the passage as the state which exists when there is welfare outside, welfare in the body, and welfare in the soul; *Heres* 287.

able only infrequently to arise to challenge the soul.[226] The passions bring afflictions on man in the period of his enslavement to the body.[227] The enslavement consists in the subjection of the intellect to the sway of the passions. Abraham, however, restrains these as a chairman restrains people at a turbulent meeting.[228] When the enslavement occurs it involves (following Gen. 15.16) "four hundred years."[229] The enslavement is not permanent in the case of someone like Abraham, for in the fourth generation (Gen. 15.16) there is a return.[230] The passions, since they are bodily matters, are obstacles to understanding.[231]

[226] Philo interprets the famine of Gen. 12.10 as a dearth of passions, *Heres* 287–289.

[227] Philo is allegorizing the bird(s) of Gen. 15.11, which descend on the segments in the Covenant between the pieces. LXX reads ὄρνεα which Philo takes to mean the passions which descend upon the body. MT reads העיט, a singular, rather than the plural of LXX. The exegesis is possible only on LXX. See *Heres* 268–270.

[228] *Heres* 243; *QG* III, 8. Philo is still interpreting Gen. 15.11 The birds have descended and, according to LXX, συνεκάθισεν αὐτοῖς, as though rendering וַיֵּשֶׁב אֹתָם "sat down with them"; MT, however, reads utilizing the same letters, וַיַּשֵּׁב אֹתָם "drove them off." The LXX reading has forced Philo into the use of the highly artificial picture of the chairman at the meeting; MT would have provided Philo with a readier figure of the overcoming of the passions. It is hard for me to believe, in the light of a passage such as this, that Philo had any direct and personal knowledge of the Hebrew text, or, indeed, any useful knowledge of Hebrew.

[229] *Heres*, 269–270.

[230] The four generations are interpreted as the four periods in the life-time of the individual. The first period lasts for seven years, and the second period is the period of youth. The third period is that at which the individual is tended for his illnesses by philosophy, and the fourth period is that in which the soul, through the aid of philosophy, is firmly rooted in the virtues. In the first period, the soul is like smooth wax on which there is an impression of neither good nor evil; in the second period the body is in its bloom and the passions are fanned into flames, *Heres* 293–298; cf. *QG* III, 12.

[231] *Heres* 268. A strange bit of exegesis is found in *Ebr.* 23–24. As the first in a series of examples of the harm that evils can do to the good soul, Philo passingly cites the "cutting" which Chedorlaomer and his fellow kings had done to Abraham! MT Gen. 14.17 not only reads הכותו "smiting," but there it is clear that it is Abraham who has done the smiting. LXX reads ἀπὸ τῆς κοπῆς τοῦ Χοδαλλαγόμορ κ.τ.λ., that is LXX seems to omit, as unnecessary, the pronominal suffix of the Hebrew. Philo takes the genitive in the LXX as subjective of κοπῆς, where the MT puts these words in the accusative case

The threat of subjection to the body is universal. Every man, Philo tells us, is in some way a slave: outside the body there are cold, heat, hunger, thirst, and many calamities, while inside the body there are pleasures and desires. Therefore when the soul of the wise man, like the soul of Abraham, descends from above, from the sky, and enters a mortal body, it encounters both outside and inside influences. Accordingly, all the while the soul of such a man as Abraham is in the body, it is, because of these considerations, in a land not its own.[232] The earthly nature of the body is quite alien to pure intellect, and tries to enslave it. Freedom from such enslavement can come only after affliction,

(using את) as objects of the infinitive. The German translation of Adler, in V, 15, is greatly superior to the fuzzy rendering at this place by Colson and Whitaker, III, 329–331; these latter miss the point of *Ebr.* 23: the vices destroy the most important inner attribute, the thinking soul. Adler properly cites respecting this latter *Somn.* I 128, *Fuga* 148, and *Opif.* 146.

Piecing together from the incohesive items presented in *QG* IV, 71–83 on Gen. 23.1–19, the death and burial of Sarah, one infers that Philo had not achieved some unified thesis as he has done with Gen. 15, in *Heres* and 16 in *Congress*, both of which chapters are also represented in *QG*. The section is germane to the question of the relation of mind to body. Abraham's mourning for Sarah is the grief of the sage on separation from wisdom. The "possession of a grave" means authority over the body which is the "grave of the soul." The choicest of the monuments (LXX reads μνημεῖοι "memorials" for MT *q'barim*) offered him, is the utmost "recollection" of concern for bodily luxuries. The request to speak to Ephron is Abraham's wish for the people to speak in the council of the soul (cf. *VC* 27) on his own behalf and to discover the worth of reason (the silver). Ephron means "dust" and Hittite "madness of fear"; cf. *Somn.* II, 89. The foolish and the mad give the body the chief rank. The double cave, (Machpelah being rendered by LXX as τὸ σπήλαιον τὸ διπλοῦν) consists of inner and outer ones; they are like the two facets of the body, which responds to external things in lust, and but to inner reason by being controlled. The field, which Abraham had not requested, was offered by the foolish man as equipment for the body for its pleasure. The cave is presumably in the field in verse 9 and 11, but in 17 the field seems to be in the cave; when the body is not ruled by the mind it comes under the power of external things; when it is ruled by mind, it not only does not succumb to external rule, but indeed contains and rules over them. Hebron (verse 19) means "joining," and alludes to the possibility of joining body to soul in such a way that the body ministers obediently to soul, the reigning power.

232 Philo uses Gen. 15.13, that Abraham's descendants would be in a land not their own, as his Scriptural basis.

the discomfort which the individual undergoes in conquering, as Abraham did, the vices inherent in the body.[233]

Abraham then, has controlled his passions, and has thoroughly conquered them. This conquest involves not only a subjection, but also the capacity for using certain bodily properties. Abraham, we shall see, uses sense-perception as a good servant. One example which Philo gives is his discussion of the contrast in the relationship between Abraham and sense perception, and in the relationship of others to it. Eliezer, for example, represents the mind which treats the senses as a master, while Abraham treats the senses as a bondservant. Philo illustrates the contrast by his exegesis of Gen. 15.2 ff. Masek[234] means "kiss"[235] of greeting, in contrast with true love. Masek, the "blood-soul," or lower mind, represents the life in the senses. Her son, Damascus Eliezer, the body and the bodily soul, is the figure for the man who lives on the level of animals.[236] Now every man, Philo tells us, possesses Masek, the senses. The multitude regard her as a mistress and give her genuine and deep affection, but Abraham regards her as a servant and gives her no more than the "kiss" of greeting.[237]

[233] *Heres* 268–270; *QG* III, 10. See *Conf.* 26, based on Gen. 14.3 and *QG* IV, 53, based on Gen. 19.27–28.

[234] Philo follows LXX Gen. 15.2, which diverges from MT in that it regards Masek as a proper name.

[235] The etymology, like the etymology of other names in Philo, is based on the supposed Hebrew. Here *nshq* is identifiable as the root. While it is not strange that etymologies are used for the names occurring in both LXX and MT, it is worthy of note that Masek occurs as a name only in LXX, but is nevertheless accompanied by an etymology. For the question of Philo's knowledge of Hebrew, there is the peculiarity to be noted that he knows a Hebrew etymology but gives no evidence of knowing that in the MT the word was not necessarily a name.

[236] Damascus is made up of the Hebrew *dam*, blood, the "soul as a whole," that is, the soul without the divine, immaterial part; and *saq*, sackcloth, the body. Eliezer, "God is my helper," is the divine gift of breath which animates the mass of clay, *Heres* 40–41; 58.

[237] Masek, representing the blood-soul (the lower mind), is feminine because that lower mind, by which also irrational animals live, has relationship with the female, material line; Sarah, virtue, is of the male line (Gen. 20.12) and is indeed begotten of God. See *Heres* 61–62. Philo's fuller interpretation of the blood-soul is found in *Heres* 54 ff.; see also *Spec.* I, 171 and

b. *Sense Perception*

Abraham uses his senses as a master uses a servant. By their use he is able to make inferences which lead him to a lower knowledge, and then ultimately to a higher knowledge. This lower knowledge, based on the senses, is the stage of sense perception.

Abraham's mastery of sense perception is such that he is able to distinguish between presentations where the object is real and apprehended, and presentations where this is not the case.[238]

Sense perception for Philo is the gate through which the mind goes into the intelligible world.[239] Abraham utilizes sense

Deter. 83 ff. Drummond I, 320–321, discusses the "lower mind" and its affinity with Stoic philosophy; see also Wolfson, I, 386 ff., for Philo's debt here both to Plato and Aristotle. In contrast with Masek, the "blood-soul," or lower mind, which has descent from the female line (Maseq being the "mother" of "Damascus"), virtue stems from the male line, which Philo avers is proved from Gen. 20.12. See *Heres* 61–62, *QG* IV, 68, and compare *Ebr.* 61. One of many contrasts between male and female rests on the names Ammon and Moab of Gen. 19.37–38, treated without much variation from Philo's usual exegesis in *QG* IV, 58.

[238] *Heres* 132. Colson and Whitaker, IV, p. 569, cite from Diog. Laert. VII, 46, a passage illustrating the difference between the two. The apprehended is defined as "that which proceeds from a real object, agrees with that objecti tself, and has been imprinted seal-fashion and stamped upon the mind"; the other is "that which does not proceed from any real object, or, if it does, fails to agree with reality itself, not being clear and distinct." Cf. also Drummond, I, 354–356 and Wolfson, II, 6–7. Philo's basis is part of his allegory of Gen. 15.9, found also in *QG* III, 3.

[239] "... As those who desire to see our cities go in through gates, so all who wish to apprehend the unseen world are introduced to it by receiving the impression of the visible world," *Somn.* I, 188. Philo says, in the same passage, that the irrational soul gathers sensations which the rational soul uses to form conceptions. Elsewhere (*LA* I, 29–30) he gives the same teaching in another form which he derives from Gen. 2.6, the spring which watered the face of the earth. The mind (the spring) waters the senses (the face of the earth), sending to each sense the stream suitable to it. In a chain of three things, mind, sense-perception, and perceived objects, sense-perception is in the middle. Unless there is some object for sense-perception to perceive, the mind does not function in the senses. The mind and the object are always practicing a reciprocity of giving: the object lies ready as the material for sense perception

perception as a means of acquiring knowledge.[240] This lower knowledge is quite respectable; in its domain lies the curriculum of the lower schools, symbolized by Hagar.[241] As a prelude to his union with Virtue, Abraham masters the encyclia.[242] Abraham accomplishes this when his progressing mind is on the borderline between sense perception and the intelligible world.[243] At this point Abraham is already married[244] to Sarah, virtue, and although virtue is the most prolific of qualities, Sarah is barren to

and the mind moves sense perception to produce an impulse towards the object. The capacity of sense-perception marks the superiority of the living creature over the non-living.

[240] *Cong.* 155. The knowledge based on perception is the lower knowledge; the higher is the intelligible knowledge.

[241] Hagar means etymologically "sojourning"; as an Egyptian Hagar was therefore "body." For the good mind the encyclia are a transient phase at the highest aspect of body; they catalogue, arrange, and classify the information which the bodily senses supply, *Cong.* 20–23.

[242] Philo shows the preparatory and limited nature of the encyclia in a number of different ways. In one passage, he speaks of virtue (Sarah) as a great theme which requires these as a great introduction, *Cong.* 11; they are the ornaments of the soul-house fitted to receive God, *Cher.* 99–101. In *Agr.* 18 the encyclia are plants for souls at the stage of youth, before manhood. In *Heres* 275 the encyclia are equipment which Israel takes along on the journey out of the body, Egypt.

[243] Philo infers this by allegorizing Abraham's age; he has been in the land of the Canaanites ten years before his union with Hagar, Gen. 16.3; he had come into Canaan at seventy-five, Gen. 12.4. The decade was a period spent in Canaan, the vices. Philo tells us that every man spends such a period after his initial birth in Egypt, the body, with its passions, pleasures and pains. Seventy-five is the age of adolescence, and the progressing mind, while able to apprehend good and evil, chooses the evil at this time. But after ten years the good mind reaches the desire for lawful discipline; *Cong.* 81–88.

[244] Gen. 11.29. In a laconic, and unclear, passage which cites Gen. 11.29, Philo is attacking the wrongness of taking an allegorical wife for one's self, rather than receiving her for God. Since the verse quoted tells that Abraham and Nahor took wives for themselves, Philo intimates that in Abraham's case (as in the case of Jacob and Aaron) the taking of the wife meant the association with good things. Isaac and Moses, however, do not take wives purely "of themselves"; in the case of Isaac, Gen. 24.67, he first went into Sarah's tent. Philo here seems passingly trying to ward off refutations of his *drush*; the passage, *Post.* 76–77, is not significant for our purposes, nor is its oblique parallel, *QG* IV, 145.

Abraham.[245] At the behest of wisdom he resorts to the encyclia as preparation for the greater things.[246] Abraham recognizes the relationship between the encyclia and philosophy[247] as that of servant and mistress. This relationship must be strictly observed. The encyclia serve the mistress philosophy,[248] and the mistress, in turn, rebukes the servant when, in arrogance, the servant regards herself as the mistress.[249]

[245] Gen. 16 is the basis for this allegory, and its language is to be found throughout this paraphrase of the relevant parts of *Cong.* The passage, XVI, 1, is treated also in *QG* III, 18. See also *QG* III, 20. Philo discusses the allegory of Hagar passingly in *LA* III, 244–245; the passage has undergone textual difficulty, and we get only a beginning with Gen. 16.2 and an ending on Gen. 16.12. The contents can be conjectured as according with Philo's usual views.

Another section which deals with the role of education in the progress of the individual is found in *Heres* 272–274, based on Gen. 15.14. See virtually the same thing, based on Gen. 15.13–14, in *QG* III, 10.

[246] *Cong.* 2–14. The basis is the hearkening to Sarah of Gen. 16.2. Philo finds a shade of difference between the Greek ὑπήκουσε which LXX reads rather than ἤκουσε which it might have read; the former means "hearkened, obeyed," the latter only "heard." It is the LXX which provides the specific distinction Philo is here making; MT reads *va-yishma'*, which could yield the distinction but not, of course, the specific word contrasts. In his allegory it is "virtue" which Abraham obeys. See *Cong.* 63–70.

Philo gives us at least one contrast between Rebecca, who represents perfection, and Hagar, the gradual progress of the encyclia, rather than the usual Hagar and Sarah. In Rebecca's going down to the well, Gen. 24.15–20, she has brought with her a pitcher, whereas Hagar (Gen. 21.19) had with her a leather skin. The pitcher represents the use of reason in ridding one's self completely of the body, while the leather skin is the use of bodily vessels of self-perception, such as eyes and ears. In the passage, *Post.* 130–141, the example of Rebecca, the ever virgin, buttresses Philo's contrast between Sarah, restored to virginity, and Hagar. See also *QG* IV, 98–100.

[247] Philo in *Cong.* varies Sarah as Virtue, Wisdom, and Philosophy.

[248] *Cong.* 79. See also *QG* III, 22, on Gen. 16.4.

[249] *Cong.* 151. The limitation of the mind at the encyclia stage is the ability to be near to wisdom but the inability as yet not to drink from its well, as "proved" by Gen. 16.7; see *QG* III, 27. So somewhat similarly the words of Gen. 16.8 are a rebuke spoken to the imperfected mind running away from better judgment τὴν ἀμείνω καὶ κυρίαν γνώμην; so, too, *QG* III, 28. The verse portrays the angel as questioning Hagar "Whence comest thou and whither art thou going?" It must be a rebuke, not a question, for verse 11 demonstrates the omniscience of the angel, a quality which rules out the need

Abraham understands, as other minds do not, that the encyclia are only preparatory stages, and therefore Abraham is not
abiding with Hagar but only sojourning.[250]

Philo sees in the flight of Hagar (Gen. 16.6) the experience
of Abraham's mind at the level of encyclical knowledge. His
mind becomes ashamed at the margin of difference betwen the
encyclia and true wisdom and therefore wants to flee. The angel
of God encourages "Hagar" to return; the mind involved in the
encyclia is urged to abide in true modesty in the presence of
philosophy, the mistress.[251] Abraham at this stage is still Abram,
"the uplifted father"[252] before his character has changed. He is
pursuing the study of visible matters. His mind, still with the
lower learning, has hastened to flee from the stern and gloomy
life of the virtue seekers.[253] Unable, however, to reach the true
heights, his mind is content for the moment to continue to
sojourn in the encyclia.[254] But now, in its seeking, his mind encounters the angel of God, as did Hagar (Gen. 16.7) at the water-

---

for questioning; *Fuga* 202–205. See *QG* III, 18–38 for congruent explanations
of Gen. 16.1–16, relating to the limitations of "Hagar." Philo sees the encyclia
alluded to in Abraham's discourse with God on the number of righteous who
might save Sodom, Gen. 18.24–25. The fifty, initially set forth, represent
perfection; the residual ten are those who have had school training and start
with a better opportunity for growth than the untrained who have not had it.
See *Mut.* 228–229, *Cong.* 109, *Sac.* 122, and the discussion in Colson and
Whitaker, I, xvi–xvii, especially the problem of rendering μέση παιδεία.
Philo treats Gen. 18.24–32 differently in *QG* IV, 27, limiting himself there to
perfect numbers as salutary harmonies.

[250] See *QG* III, 19 on Gen. 16.1, for Philo's longer explanation of Hagar as
an Egyptian, passingly treated in *Abr.* 251. *QG* III, 21 allegorizes Gen. 16.3
congruently. The afflicting by Sarah, Gen. 16.6, is the discipline by means of
which Abraham is trained to regard the encyclia in the true status, *Cong.*
158–160 and *QG* III, 24–26. Philo shows in the treatise by examples from
geometry and grammar that the arts deal with the perceptible aspects of the
sciences while philosophy defines the intelligible aspects, *Cong.* 139–150.

[251] *Fuga.* 3–6. See also *QG* III, 26, 28–30.

[252] This is Philo's usual etymology of Abram.

[253] Colson and Whitaker, II, 481, point out correctly that Philo here interprets Hagar not as the encyclia but rather as the mind of the sage at the stage
of the encyclia. See *QG* III, 37 on Gen. 16.15 for Philo's clear hint in this
direction.

[254] *Cher.* 4–6.

spring.²⁵⁵ This spring is wisdom. His mind is no more able to drink from wisdom than was Hagar able to drink from the well.²⁵⁶ The progressing mind of Abraham has to return to its proper mistress and to undergo the noble humiliation which philosophy affords, the product of which is the overthrow of the irrational soul.²⁵⁷

At the stage of the encyclia, the best that Abraham can produce spiritually is Ishmael, sophistry, the "child" of the lower learning.²⁵⁸ The sophist differs from the sage in that he loves to argue for the sake of argument; he is therefore the proper target for the attacks of the representatives of the true sciences.²⁵⁹ The mind which has not advanced beyond sophistry

---

²⁵⁵ *Fuga* 177. See also *QG* III, 27.

²⁵⁶ Gen. 16.7 depicts Hagar near the spring, but does not mention her drinking from it. So too, the spring from which Rebecca, "Patience," fills her pitcher, Gen. 24.16, is divine wisdom.

Gen. 14.7, (πηγὴν τῆς κρίσεως) serves Philo as proof that this divine wisdom is both holy and also, as a "sifter" in judgment, just; "the wisdom of God is both holy, containing no earthy ingredient, and is a sifting of the universe, whereby all opposites are separated from each other," *Fuga* 196. For the intent of Philo in the passage, see further *Heres* 133 ff. and note 304.

²⁵⁷ *Fuga* 202–207. Gen. 16.7, "an angel of the Lord found her," portrays the decreeing of a return home to the soul which is going astray. See *Fuga* 119–121 and *QG* III, 27. The irrational soul is the lower mind, symbolized by Masek. See note 237.

²⁵⁸ *Fuga* 208. Ishmael, meaning "hearkening to God," is lower than Israel, "seeing God," because hearing is lower than seeing. See also *QG* III, 23 on Gen. 16.5, and *QG* III, 31–32 on Gen. 16.10–11. The interpretation of Abraham's age, 86, Gen. 16.16, is found in *QG* III, 38. The explanation of the number is clear; the relevance is not. A further deduction that Ishmael is a sophist, or the mind at the sophist stage, stems from Ishmael's being called an archer (Gen. 21.20) "for whatever points he sets forth as a target, at this he discharges proofs like arrows." Cf. *Cher*. 8 ff., which cites Gen. 21.10.

²⁵⁹ *Fuga* 208–211. "Face to face with his brethren," the last part of Gen. 16.12, portray perpetual opposition faced by the sophist, *Fuga* 211 and *QG* III, 33. The iniquities of the Amorites of Gen. 15.16, are also sophistical arguments, destined to be supplanted by the truth. In *Heres*, 302 ff., which cites Gen. 15.16, and in *QG*, III, 13, Philo seems to be arguing against opponents who find in the verse support of the irreligious doctrine that fate (εἱμαρμένη) and necessity (ἀνάγκη), rather than God, direct the destiny of events. *QG* IV, 95 is obscure. It seems to point out some difference between sage and sophist, but the passage is corrupt.

sees the angel of God, but not God himself; it sees only a reflection, but it wrongly thinks it is seeing the true vision.[260]

In conceiving of Abraham as one who has mastered the encyclia, Philo makes Abraham appear to have studied grammar, geometry, astronomy, rhetoric, music, and other branches of study.[261]

[260] *Fuga* 212. Philo allegorizes the locale of the incident of Hagar's flight. Between Kadesh and Bered (between "holy" and "evil") is the stage of the mind when it is on the border between holy and profane things, fleeing from bad things but not yet competent to share the life of perfect goodness; *Fuga*. 213. The meaning of the LXX rendering of *beer lahai roi* of Gen. 16.14 is obscure. LXX reads φρέαρ οὗ ἐνώπιον ἶδον. Philo seems to take LXX to mean that the progressing soul dipping into school-knowledge sees reflected in it, as in a mirror, God, the author of that knowledge. Colson and Whitaker find the passage, *Fuga* 212, difficult, possibly through not noting "reflection in the mirror" of *Fuga* 213 as the key to the passage. The passage means, I think, that the mind at the stage of sophistry sees not God but a dim reflection. Hence, 212 uses the contrast between the freeborn who sees God Himself and the slaveborn which sees only an angel of God but calls it God. The passage is rather well duplicated in *QG* III, 35, to which Marcus adds the correct note that the traditional Jewish interpretation is "the well of the Living One who sees me"; LXX translators, says Marcus, "took Heb. *lahay* as the noun *lehi* 'cheek' in the sense of 'before my face.' " Philo Supplement I, 233, note e.

In the same verse between *Kadesh* and *Bered*, "holy" and "evil," means that he who is in gradual progress is on the borderland between the holy and the profane; so *Fuga* 213. In *QG* III, 36 one reads *Pharan* rather than *Bered*, and there *Pharan* is rendered as "hail" or "dots." As Marcus *ad loc.* notes, hail would accord with *Bered*; but in *Fuga* it is as though Philo read בְּרָע; to this Heinemann (German Translation VI, 103) remarks: "Die Übersetzung 'unter Übeln' möchte man am ehesten so erklären, dass Philos Vorgänger ברד = ברע setzt und den Dental am Schluss so auffasst wie in Elisabeth = אלישבע." *Onk.* renders the names רקם and חגרא, while *Jon.* reads for the last חלוצה; *Onk.* rendered Shur in Gen. 16.7 as Hagro, while *Jon.* rendered Shur of Ex. 15.22 as Haluza; cf. Rosenberg, אוצר השמות, I, 397.

Reverting to the passage in *Fuga* 212, Philo quotes Gen. 16.13 in *Somn.* I, 240, as proof from the experience of Abraham that Jacob also, in his progressing stage though before his perfection, saw not the Supreme Cause but the Logos, while Hagar saw the angel; so, slightly differently, also in *QG* III, 34.

[261] This is the list given in *Cong.* 11. Other lists given by Philo, according to Colson and Whitaker, IV, p. 577, omit astronomy; they suggest that the motive for the omission was the assumption that astronomy was part of

Abraham would not have been a lofty man, if he had lingered over-long, as some do, in the encyclical studies.[262] An affection for sense perception pulls back the human soul from its rise to God.[263] There was a stage at which Abraham was wavering between progress and being pulled back.[264] His mind consisted of two parts, the incorruptible and senior part (represented by the seventy) and the junior part,[265] the five senses. This junior part

geometry. Drummond (I, 263–266) ascribes a conscious motive for the usual omission: astronomers were in Philo's view "only wasting their gifts upon barren speculations. For, in the first place, their inquiries contributed nothing to the true end of life ... In the second place, the questions with which astronomy deals are beyond the powers of human thought"; see *Mig.* 184.

While elsewhere Philo may feel free to omit astronomy, he must include it as an attainment of Abraham for the reason that when we first encounter Philo's Abram he is an astronomer. Yet the inclusion of the subject here does not refute Drummond's view. Philo condemns the Chaldeans as astronomers with considerable force, *Abr.* 69–70. The usual interpretations of these attacks are that they are directed at the Stoics: Goodenough, 138; Wolfson II, 78, and Bréhier, 165; see, however, W. L. Knox's review of Wolfson's *Philo*, in *Journal of Theological Studies*, XLIX (1948), 211–12 for an insistence that this identification is too simple, and overlooks the astral determinism of the period. Philo seems to have believed that the stars could foretell, *Moses* II, 126; *LA* I, 8, and *Opif.* 58. But there is a difference between the ability to foretell and the ability to control. Ascription of ruling power to the stars would be to Philo atheism.

[262] *Cong.* 77–78.

[263] Philo divides men into three kinds: the first looks God-ward; the second looks toward created things; the third is a mixture of the two. The first kind has never submitted to the necessities of the body; Wolfson equates this class with unbodied souls or angels, I, 366–370. The second class does not seek to rise. The third class seeks in its better part, but it is pulled back by the worse; *Heres* 45–53.

[264] Philo's basis is Abraham's age, Gen. 12.4, on leaving Haran. Seventy-five represents the borderline between perceptible and intelligible knowledge, *Mig.* 198–199. (Philo has alluded to the verse in connection with Abraham's age as implicitly eighty-five a decade later, and he has given, as we saw above, a different meaning to seventy-five.)

[265] *Mig.* 198–199, *QG* IV, 30 contrasts the vision, at noon of Gen. 18.1 and evening of 19.1. Gen. 19.17 ff. yield views of the defects in Lot. The injunction of Gen. 19.17 (*QG* IV, 45) are for the wavering man, who has already had ample explanation now to move by himself. The mountain, *QG* IV, 46, is wisdom to which the progressing soul may flee to escape destruction in the death of the body. Philo's exegesis flows from LXX; it would be difficult on

was also represented by Lot.[266] Abraham was on the borderline between the perceptible world and the intelligible, having not yet completely divorced himself from the perceptible. The junior part of the soul[267] was devoted, as was Lot, to herds and material things (Gen. 13.5). The herds of Abraham, however, were the principles of the seperate virtues. These two parts of the soul were in conflict within Abraham, and the conflict remained as long as the higher soul was not purified. The higher soul in Abraham finally triumphs and it bids (Gen. 13.9) the lower part to move off.[268] Abraham prefers to have as his companions "good natural ability" and the "love of vision,"[269] rather than the

the basis of MT. Lot, being imperfect, cannot get to the mountain, Gen. 19.18–20 (QG IV, 47), but must flee to the city "which is small and is not small." See above, note 104. In LXX and MT as Marcus I, 322, note k remarks, the "is not small" is interrogative.

Philo here is greatly removed from the rabbis; cf. Rashi ad loc., Shab. 10b; and see Ginzberg I, 252 and 256 and V, 243. It does not seem to me that Marcus is right (I, 322, note k) in asserting that the allegory in QG IV, 47, is different from Abr. 166; rather, it is more extended and less focused, but still quite similar.

The first part of Gen. 19.22 is, in QG IV, 49, the encouragement to the wavering mind to be steadfast in its progress. The exact intent of Philo in QG IV, 50 to the second part of the verse eludes me. His translation of Zoor as mountain betrays no recognition of the paronomasia in MT; cf. Rashi ad loc.; it can hardly rest on Gen. 19.30, where Philo infers that Lot feared to remain in Ṣoʻar and hence went up to the mountain. The rabbis infer disobedience from the act of Lot; see Kasher, III, 816, note 176. One wonders if QG IV, 50 may not be interpolated into Philo.

[266] The etymology of the name means "inclining"; Mig. 13–14.

[267] Philo does not say so in this context, but he is giving here a contrast between what, as we saw above, he called the "whole soul," which is animal, irrational, and material, and the immaterial, rational part of the soul.

[268] Abr. 217–224.

[269] Eshkol and Aner are so interpreted. Gen. 14.24. Perhaps ability includes memory. The use of memory in learning is touched on several times. One passage gets to the topic rather tortuously. In Abraham's prayer for Sodom, Philo focuses on the ten righteous men who, if found in Sodom, might have saved the city. His discussion is in the context of several related scriptural mentions of ten. First he demonstrates that by Scripture, Gen. 16.3, the ten years which elapsed between the arrival in Canaan and Sarah's gift of Hagar, symbolize the transition from boyhood to adolescence; Egypt is the vice of boyhood, Canaan the vice of adolescence. ". . . Only after a time and

quality personified by Lot. The possession of these good companions leads to the possession of the contemplative life.[270]

Abraham, then, has utilized sense-perception as a servant,
extracting from it the good which it could furnish, but refusing
to remain at this stage. His circumcision, Gen. 17, is his con-
clusive pruning off of the appetites of the body.[271]

c. *Reason*

The instrumentality by which Abraham conquers his senses and
his passions is reason.[272] In going beyond the senses, Abraham
has come to the stage of the mind.[273] The experience of Abraham

---

under the perfect number ten do we reach the desire for the lawful discipline
which can profit us"; *Cong.* 88. The use of ten in scriptural passages is then
alluded to, including Abraham's conquest of the nine kings — the ten resulting
from adding Abraham to the nine! Sodom is the soul barren of good and blind
of reason; Abraham prayed that if in it there was some token of righteousness,
it might receive some remission of punishment. See *Cong.* 109. Thereafter, the
ten camels which Abraham's servant (whom the rabbis, *Yoma* 28b, identify
with the Eliezer of Gen. 15.2) takes as a gift, are interpreted to be the countless memories of his master, *Cong.* 111 and *QG* IV, 92; Rebekkah waters these
camels, that is, virtue emptied all her pitcher, or teacher's knowledge, into the
soul of the learner; the camel is memory because it is a ruminating animal
which softens its food by chewing the cud; moreover, when it has knelt and
has a heavy load on it, it nimbly raises itself with astonishing agility.

In this latter passage, *Post.* 148–152, the allegory has virtually eliminated
the distinction between Abraham and the servant; it discusses memory as
part of the education of the progressing soul; see, similarly, *QG* IV, 94, the
camels of Gen. 24.11 and Philo's discussion there of memory.

[270] Philo interprets Mamre as a place name, deriving it from the root,
meaning "to see." MT and the rabbis take Mamre as a person. Cf. Colson and
Whitaker, IV, p. 227, note c. The passage is *Mig.* 164–165. In *QG* IV, 1,
Mamre means "from sight."

[271] *QG* III, 46–52.

[272] In the allegory of Gen. 14, the five senses and the four passions are
conquered by reason, represented allegorically by Melchizedek, *Abr.* 235 and
244. In another passage, Melchizedek represents "democratic" reason, the
mind which steers a middle course between despotism and lawlessness, thereafter providing, in a priestly fashion, food for an even loftier ascent by the
soul; *LA* III, 81. A similar association of Melchizedek with reason is found in
Cong. 98–99.

[273] Goodenough points out that there is a great variety of descriptions in

was different from that of Adam. Originally Adam had been made of pure material and had been endowed with a copy of divine reason; he associated with divine natures and for a while he passed his time in blessedness. But Adam was fundamentally earth-born.[274] With the appearance of Eve (pleasure) Adam succumbed to the senses, and set mankind off on a downward course that continued for his descendants.[275] These descendants, however, retain some marks of the original forms in which Adam was created; every man, in respect of his mind is allied to the divine reason (Logos), but in respect to his body is allied to the world.[276] Abraham was heaven-born. Originally as an astrologer he had busied himself with the visible world,[277] but once risen to a better nature he becomes an exemplar of the reasoning of the good man.[278]

Abraham's change in name from Abram is a transition from his preoccupation with his lower mind to his use of his higher reason.[279]

Philo of the mind, and some of the descriptions seem contradictory of others. Similarly, Drummond, I, 322–323 and Wolfson, I, 362, enumerate the use of such terms as νοῦς, διάνοια and λογισμός. Goodenough, 383, and Wolfson I, 393, demonstrate that Philo also uses *logos* as a term for the mind. Goodenough is exactly right in saying that "if Philo despaired of an exact knowledge of the νοῦς ἡγεμών, he says many instructive things about it."

In part the variety in terms seems to be due to the variety of allegorical figures by which Philo derives his doctrine. Thus, for example, Laban, the brother of Rebekkah, Gen. 24.29, is for Philo the irrational mind ("whiteness," the symbol of honors given to sense perception) which is the brother to "constancy," the rational mind. See QG IV, 116–119 on Gen. 24.28–31.

[274] *Opif.* 134 ff. and *Heres* 52, 57. See also QG I, 4 for an exposition of Philo's two Adams. Drummond has an excellent discussion, II, 175 ff., of the distinction between "made," generic man, and "moulded," specific.

[275] *Opif.* 151–156.   [276] *Opif.* 145–146.

[277] That is, while he was still Abram.

[278] This is the interpretation Philo gives in one passage to the import of the etymology of "Abraham," as distinct from "Abram," *Gig.* 62–64.

[279] *Gig.* 62–64. The change of name is consistently interpreted by Philo as an alteration in Abraham's character. The basic change is from astrology, with its contemplation of the visible world, to a contemplation of the invisible world. Philo gives a number of slightly different imports in various treatises to the change. The "migration" of Abraham is a series of steps between the Abram phase to the Abraham phase, as we shall see in detail.

This lower reason is human, the higher reason divine. The lower reason dwells among the multitudes, the higher reason seeks out loneliness.[280]

It has been Abraham's experience to go beyond lower reason. He has accomplished this by his migrating from it.[281] Though Abraham rises above speech, into higher reason, his speech is noticeably blessed. He is able to refute the sophist, a capacity beyond Abel, whose speech was so poor that Abel was unable to refute Cain, the poorer mind with the better speech.[282] His speech is definitely not that of the sophist.[283] It is essential for Abraham to have good speech, since poor speech is a bad interpreter of good thoughts.[284] Speech is a derivative manifestation of the higher reason and is not a pure and identical projection of it.[285]

---

[280] *Heres.* 126–127. In another figure Philo speaks of man's mind being in the third position from God, with divine reason (Logos) being in the middle position, *Heres* 230–231. Again, the reasoning power in man and the divine Logos are indivisible from each other, *Ibid.* 235. The figure of loneliness recalls *Abr.* 66, that Abraham departed from Chaldea "with a few or even alone."

[281] Abraham left his father's house. "Speech" (λόγος κατὰ προ φοράν) *Mig.* 2. Philo has to point out the sense in which the mind, the seat of reason, can be called a house; it is as true, he says, for man as it is for God, citing the house of God, Gen. 28.17, as a proof-text; cf. *Somn.* I, 32. In another passage, dealing not with Abraham but with priests, Philo praises these men who cut away (based on Ex. 32.29) the body, the love of passion, the company of senses, and finally "speech." Speech must be excised because it is the medium through which the specious, the probable, and the persuasive implant false opinions; *Ebr.* 69–70. Speech is inconstant with and divisive of the unity of higher reason, *Gig.* 52. Such sentiments are frequent in Philo.

[282] *Mig.* 74–75. The intent of Gen. 24.3, is that speech, the "servant, shall not deceive the perfect mind," Isaac, *QG* IV, 88; such, too, in *QG* IV, 89 is the instruction not to take Isaac back to Chaldean astrology, Gen. 24.5–6. The angel of Gen. 24.7 is the joining of another *logos* to "uttered logos," *QG* IV, 90. Rebekkah might be willing to return with this other *logos*, but not with the "uttered" *logos*, *QG* IV, 91 to Gen. 24.8.

[283] *Mig.* 82–85. Ishmael, as we saw above, is the sophist. He always remains a sophist, *Cher.* 10; cf. *Sob.* 9, *Heres* 302 ff., and *Moses* II, 212.

[284] *Mig.* 72.

[285] *Mig.* 76–79. Philo distinguishes, as noted, in several passages between speech and inner thought, the *logos* προφορικός and the ἐνδιάθετος, a distinction which seems to be Stoic; cf. Colson and Whitaker, II, p. 502. The interpretation of Gen. 24 in *QG* reads as if it is a series of notes out of which an essay might have been written on the relationship of the endiathetos

Abraham passes beyond lower reason, just as he migrated beyond body and sense perception. He rises superior to these, treating them as a king treats his subjects, ruling them and not being ruled by them.[286]

Now that he is in possession of the higher mind, Abraham receives five gifts:[287] first he is able to see the land,[288] "wisdom."[289] Second, he is able to progress in virtues.[290] The third gift is an improvement in uttered word and inner thought.[291] The fourth

and prophorikos. See *QG* IV, 96 to Gen. 24.15. Also, *QG* IV, 85 to Gen. 24.2, in which the "servant" is speech, and Abraham the master mind. So, too, *QG* IV, 120 to Gen. 24.34. In *Moses* II, 127 Philo applies the two aspects to the double breast-plate of the high priest. The *logos endiathetos*, he says, is the source of reason, located in the *nous hegemonikos*, while the *prophorikos* is the stream flowing from it and located in the tongue, the mouth and the other organs of speech. Cf. Goodenough, 100 ff., for his insistence, with Drummond, that the divine *Logos* is singular, against Gförer, Heinze, and Pascher, who think of a double divine *Logos*; according to Goodenough the human *logos* is indeed double, but the divine *Logos* singular.

Philo gives still another example in his interpretation of Ex. 4.14, which assigns to Aaron the task of being the "mouth" of Moses; Aaron is "speech," the brother of "reason," *Deter.* 126–129.

[286] *Mig.* 7–8.

[287] "Covenant" in *Mut.* 52–53, is the symbol of grace which God sets between Himself who offers it and the soul who receives it. Philo alludes to having dealt with the whole subject of covenants in two treatises. Schuerer, II, III, 337 concludes from the absence of these works in Eusebius' list in *H. E.* ii 18.13 that they were by then already lost. Another allusion to the work is found in *QE* II, 34. In one passage, *Spec.* II, 16, scholars propose an emendation which would there eliminate the word covenant; but even for those who want to retain the word, it has in the passage a necessary connotation of will, not mutual contract. There are references in *Deter.* 68 and *Sac.* 57, the latter repeating that "covenant" allegorically is God's grace. In *QG* III, 10 "covenant" is the rational class of possessions which God bestows on the soul; in *QG* III, 40, based on Gen. 17.1–2, they are "incorporeal principles . . . of which this world is made . . ."; so, too, *QG* III, 42, quite similarly. *QG* III, 60, based on Gen. 17.21, contrasts Isaac, the heir to the divine testament (covenant), with Ishmael, not an *heir* but only the recipient of gifts from the heir; Isaac "receives gifts which are bestowed by grace."

[288] Gen. 12.1, is Philo's basis.

[289] *Mig.* 28 and 36. "Seeing," the quality of the wise, is the contemplative life, the most appropriate life for the rational being; *Mig.* 47; cf. *Abr.* 22–24.

[290] The "nation" of Gen. 12.2.

[291] Philo derives this from the LXX rendering of "be thou a blessing," *Mig.* 70–71.

is a good reputation for virtue.[292] The fifth is the gift of actually being that which good reputation reports.[293]

The possession of this higher reason climaxed Abraham's cutting away from himself all material things, and freed his mind to fly upward to God with his understanding stripped of material trammels.[294] Reason teaches him that God is the source of all gifts, and Abraham will no longer accept material things.[295] Abraham is able to reason correctly not only in one direction but in all directions; therefore Scripture terms him an "elder, advanced in years,"[296] whom God blessed in everything. Through

---

[292] *Mig.* 86–93. Philo applies "reputation" to the fulfillment of the literal Mosaic laws.

[293] *Mig.* 106. See also *QG* IV, 7, to Gen. 18.5. In another passage Philo commends the careful examination of "appearance," especially related to the sacred legislation, since appearances can deceive as to vice or virtue; Philo derives this from Gen. 18.21; see *QG* IV, 24. Philo infers from Gen. 12.3 that credit is due to him who praises the good man and blame to him who blames him, *Mig.* 109–119, as his prelude to a view, found often, that a city or country or region has benefited through a single man, *Mig.* 120 ff.

Mig. 107 quotes Gen. 12.2, inferring from *eulogetos*, rather than *eulogemenos*, the difference between praise by God and praise by man. The latter can rest on mere opinion; the former must rest on truth.

[294] *Cher.* 31. Philo so allegorizes the fire and the knife ("reason" and "cutting away") of Gen. 22.6. For the hellenistic background of the notion of rising above corporeality, see Wendland, "Hellenistic Ideas of Salvation in the Light of Ancient Anthropology," in *American Journal of Theology*, XVII (1913), 345–349.

[295] *Ebr.* 105–106. The passage being interpreted is Gen. 14.22–23, Abraham's stretching forth his hand to God that he will take nothing from the king of Sodom. Abraham in the passage has just conquered the four passions and five senses.

The gifts offered, Gen. 14.21–22, by the king of Sodom, things without reason, in exchange for "the men," things with reasons, are refused by the sage. To such a sage, God reveals his secret mysteries, Gen. 18.17. See *LA* III, 23–27 and *QG* IV, 21. Philo reverts passingly to Gen. 14.21–22 in *LA* III, 196–197, adding an allusion to Gen. 25.6: Abraham retains the property which had come to him from God, but gets rid of the horses of the king of Sodom and also the possessions of the concubines. Gen. 25.6 is similarly treated in *QG* IV, 148–149. See also the rendering of αὐτῷ in LXX Gen. 15.10 in *QG* III, 4. The pious soul takes for Him (God), that is, it attributes to God, not to himself (as the natural sense of the verse reads) good and precious ts.

[96] Gen. 24.1. Similarly *QG* IV, 14 interprets Gen. 18.11. *QG* IV, 150–152

the watchful care of God, the rational part of his soul has triumphed.[297]

Abraham walks in the path of right reason;[298] he enters

---

deal with the same idea, though #150 is not intelligible. Elsewhere, *Sob.* 7–9, Philo cites another proof that "younger" and "older" have nothing to do with age. Hagar's ability to carry on her shoulder an Ishmael presumably some twenty years older than Isaac and to allude to her son as a child (Gen· 21.14–16) are his scriptural proof that Isaac is "older" than Ishmael. Isaac was circumcised when Ishmael was thirteen and was weaned from milk when he was seven; ergo Ishmael was twenty-one. Isaac is the heir of wisdom, but Ishmael of sophistry. I have found no parallel in the rabbis to Philo's assumption that the weaning took place at seven years; Kasher (*Torah Shelemah*, III, 845) mentions two interpretations, one of which would make Isaac twenty-four months, the other thirteen years); *PRE* XXX makes Ishmael twenty-four and Isaac ten: *Gen. R.* LIII makes Ishmael twenty-seven, and ascribes Hagar's ability to carry him to his wasting away from an illness induced through an evil eye put on him by Sarah.

[297] *Sob.* 17–18. See also *QG* IV, 83–84, based on Gen. 23.19 and 24.1.

[298] By way of contrast with right reason, Lot ("inclination") is on occasion symbolic of the man with the false idea of his wisdom; he is joined to "custom," which — Gen. 19.26 — is turned to stone (not salt!) and is hostile to truth, for she lags behind to gaze at familiar objects. The elder daughter is "deliberation," the younger "assent"; when the mind has turned to assent, especially to hostile suggestions, then deliberation has ceased. A sober mind would not tolerate this, but the drunken mind does; hence Gen. 19.33, "they gave their father wine to drink." That such a mind does not grasp fundamentals clearly is demonstrated by Gen. 19.35, "he knew not when they slept and rose up." See Philo's complex discussion in *Ebr.* 162–205; the item is presented in shorter form in *Post.* 172 ff.; see also *QG* IV, 52, and, somewhat differently, *QG* IV, 55–56. Philo is discussing the advance made by the soul towards perfection. The enlargement of the mind goes by steps towards perfection, ten from Seth to Noah; a second and better one in the ten from Shem to Abraham; seven from Abraham to Moses; this latter does not "haunt the outer court of the Holy Place as one seeking initiation, but as a sacred guide (hierophant) has his abode in the sanctuary." In contrast to this upward surge, Lot, wavering, went downward, for Deliberation and Consent (*synkathesis*, where *Ebr.* 165 reads *synainesis*) desired to have children by the mind, their father, rather than from God, as was Seth, Gen. 4.26.

Philo in his two allusions to Lot's wife in Gen. 19.26 in the Allegory, *Fuga* 121 and *Ebr.* 164, omits the salt, but uses it in *QG* IV, 52 as a symbol of unproductivity. In *Ebr.* 164 the wife is custom which lags behind and is hostile to truth; in *Fuga* 121 she is the symbol of the laxness in a student which impels him to turn away from the teacher and face backwards. On custom as a "feminine" barrier to truth, see *Ebr.* 54 ff. Philo in other passages virtue's path. He follows God and is mindful of His injunctions. Since the injunctions are right reason, the verse "Abraham did all My law," means that Abraham "did" the divine reason.[299] The actions of Abraham are the *logoi* of God.[300] Abraham governs himself like a father; his mind does not grant to the soul the thing pleasant to it, nor frighten the soul with threats.[301] The mind must so govern because it can only rise above its material component, it cannot be severed from it, for such severance would simply mean death.[302] Similarly, one must not sever himself from the literal law, but should rise above the literal law (the body) to the soul of the law (the allegorical).[303]

commends custom highly (e. g. *Spec*. IV, 149–150). What he seems to oppose is custom when it obstructs truth or right reason.

[299] LXX reads ἐφύλαξε which Philo quotes as ἐποίησε, Gen. 26.5. Of the four items in the verse προστάγματα and ἐντολάς allude to obligations to God, while the δικαιώματα and νόμιμα, to man, *QG* IV, 184, *Heres* 8, and *Mig*. 130. See above, on *Abr*. 275, note 202.

Philo, in an obliquely related passage, comments on Gen. 19.16, about the angels who take the dazed and confused daughters of Lot by the hand, that souls governed by "holy thoughts" can be saved if having taken hold, they continue to hold on, *QG* IV, 44. (On some of the variations between MT and LXX of this verse, see Marcus I, 318, note g. The singular ויתמהמה, is rendered by the plural ἐταράχθησαν, they were confused, as though from √תמה. *Gen. R.* VI plays on the word also inferring confusion (תמהון), or rather confused tarrying, resulting from Lot's regret over the losses of money and jewels soon to occur. In Philo Lot in this section appears favorably; among the rabbis, e. g. Rashi, he is regarded unfavorably, his benefits accruing solely from Abraham's merit.)

Philo points admiringly to the rescue of the progressing man, *QG* IV, 51 to Gen. 19.23–24, at the same moment that evil-doers are being destroyed. In *QG* IV, 101–114 the servant of Gen. 24 is also the symbol of the progressing man who absorbs teaching from "Rebekkah" in proportion to his capacity; the sequence of Philo's view on Gen. 24.18–27 is parallel in content to much of *Cong*. The "progressing mind" is in touch with divine reason; the sage, however, "does" the divine reason.

[300] Philo is interpreting Gen. 12.4, *Mig*. 127–130. He has expressed exactly this same idea in *Abr*. 4–5, where he applied to Abraham the epithet *nomos empsychos kai logikos*. See also the obliquely related passages in *QG* III, 15 and *Heres* 308–312.

[301] *LA* III, 83–84. In *Abr*. 242, Philo calls this establishing democracy in the soul.

[302] *Mig*. 7.

[303] It will be recalled in this connection that the literal laws, the spe-

Abraham has the power of acute discrimination by means of his reason.[304] Since divine reason has separated and apportioned all things in nature, the higher reason is able to participate in such separation and in a subsequent classification and interpretation. Abraham is able to distinguish direct opposites and lesser gradations in both the material and the immaterial world.[305]

Since he has subdued his lower mind, and has freed his higher mind by regimenting his bodily attributes, he is now able to direct himself to the world of intelligible matters.[306]

d. *Speculative Philosophy*

Abraham becomes a speculative philosopher. He has passed beyond the encyclia into the realm of knowledge, as opposed to art.[307] Examples of arts are music and grammar; these use the eyes and the ears. Knowledge, however, utilizes the mind. The arts deal with detached items from nature, while philosophy deals with the whole nature of existing things.[308]

The sense in which Abraham is a philosopher is discernible in the contrast which Philo draws between Sarah and Hagar in *De Congressu*. The encyclia are bodily matters, but prudence and wisdom ($\varphi\rho\acute{o}\nu\eta\sigma\iota\varsigma$ and $\dot{\epsilon}\pi\iota\sigma\tau\acute{\eta}\mu\eta$) are to be found among the reasoning faculties. Abraham accordingly holds wisdom and knowledge to be more honorable than the encyclia.[309] Because he is a philosopher he spends his days in continued well-being

cific ones, are only copies of the natural law which Abraham obeyed; *Abr.* 3–4.

[304] Philo infers that the "dividing" of Gen. 15.10, is a description of the *logos tomeus*, *Heres* 130–136. See also *QG* III, 5–7. Cf. Drummond, II, 168; and Goodenough, "A Neo-Pythagorean Source in Philo Judaeus," *YCS* III, 1932, 115–164.

[305] *Heres* 234–236.

[306] See Philo's interpretation of Gen. 18.10 in *QG* IV, 12, derived from the LXX rendering of חיה כעת. See Marcus' notes, Philo Supplement I, 285, for the different forms of the rendering in Philo.

[307] Art is defined as a system of conceptions coordinated to work for some useful end, a definition which Colson and Whitaker take to be Stoic, IV, 580.

[308] *Cong.* 140–147.

[309] *Cong.* 153–156. On knowledge and wisdom as roads to truth, see *QG* IV, 125 on Gen. 24.48.

(εὐπαθείαις) and gladness (εὐφροσύναις).[310] The transition of Abram to Abraham is a transition from nature study to ethical philosophy; thereby his character is bettered and he yearns to acquire and make use of virtue.[311]

e. The Intelligible World

Abraham has begun as a man possessing specific virtues.[312] He was temperate, prudent, brave, and just. Such virtues, being

[310] *Cong.* 174. Philo tells us in this same passage that the multitude do not recognize the happy lot of the philosopher. It must be remarked that on the surface Philo is considerably less than consistent in his attitude towards philosophy, or else he uses the term in differing connotations. He dismisses as insignificant, for example, the fact that "hardly a day passes but the lecture-halls and theatres are filled with philosophers discoursing at length, stringing together without stopping to take breath their disquisitions on virtue. But what profit is there in their talk?" Some of the audience do not really listen, and some who listen do not truly absorb, and some absorb only an echo of what is said. Abraham, however, really absorbed philosophy, since he hearkened, Gen. 16.2, to the voice of Sarah; see *Cong.* 52–53, 64–66. In another passage he goes further, terming as sophists the philosophers of schools identified as the Peripatetics. Stoics and Epicureans, Eleatics, Sceptics, and non-Sceptics; cf. Colson and Whitaker, IV, p. 574. Bréhier points out that for Philo the knowledge of God is ωomething apart from and above philosophy, p. 294; cf. *Cong.* 79–80. In another passage, *LA* I, 57, philosophy is the road that leads into virtue, and is subdivisible into logic, ethics and physics; some of the ancients likened the physical part to plants, the logical to walls and fences, and the ethical to the fruits of the plants; *Mut.* 73–76. See also *QG* IV, 87 to Gen. 24.3.

[311] *Mut.* 75–76. Philo makes it abundantly clear that true philosophy is concerned not only with information but with morals and ethics. The moral duties are the specific virtues and copies of the generic virtues. These generic virtues, planted in the soul, lead to specific activities, *LA* I, 56–57.

Abraham's fear of being childless, Gen. 15.2 refers to his soul, that its moral excellence might not come to naught, *Heres* 34 ff. Philo interprets Abraham's speech as a question, not as a statement. The passage seems to veer between the literal and allegorical.

[312] *Cher.* 5 and frequently. Sarah, like Lot and Hagar, varies in Philo's exposition. She is sometimes philosophy, as in *Cong.* She is, as Sarah, generic virtue, in contrast to Sarai, specific virtues. Like Lot and Hagar she often seems, allegorically, not to be a person in her own right, but to be merely a quality or characteristic of Abraham. Lot, we saw, at times was Abraham's lower mind; Hagar was Abraham's progressing mind; Sarai is Abraham's

specific, are perishable.[313] The change of name from Abram to Abraham means a change in the nature of the patriarch; he is no longer concerned with the visible world but with the intelligible world.[314] Specific virtues are part of the perceptible world, being the property of men and perishing with men; generic virtue belongs in the intelligible world, the immaterial world, since it is imperishable. The change in Sarah's name[315] represents the ethical change in Abraham. His concern is no longer simply the observable virtues of different men, but the intelligible virtue of which these specific virtues are only the copy.[316] Generic virtue is an idea.[317] As a possession of Abraham, his generic virtue is bound to have a "nation" of virtues in the perceptible

specific virtues, and Sarah, Abraham's generic virtues. Isaac, in part, is Abraham's joy.

In taking Sarah to himself (Gen. 11.29) Abraham took a good thing, in contrast with worthless men who take to themselves evils, men such as Lamech, *Post.* 75–76.

[313] *Cher.* 4–6; *Mut.* 77 ff.

[314] Abram means "uplifted father"; uplifted, in that Abraham dealt with astrology; father, in that astrology in a limited sense yields some results. Abraham means "elect father of sound"; "father of sound" is the mind, "elect" connotes that it is a wise mind; *Mut.* 66–71; *Cher.* 4; *Gig.* 62–64, *QG* III, 43.

[315] From Sarai, specific virtues, to Sarah, generic virtue. See *QG* III, 53.

[316] *Mut.* 79–80. Philo has several figures for virtue in addition to Sarah. It is the tree of life, *LA* I, 59; it is, Gen. 2.10–14, the river flowing from Eden, dividing into the four specific virtues, *LA* I, 63–64; see *QG* I, 12. It is the Tent of Testimony, *Deter.* 160 ff. Philo gives this schematization in *LA* I, 63 ff.: generic virtue issues out of the Sophia of God; specific virtues issue out of generic virtue. The Sophia of God, Philo tells us, is the Logos of God. Generic virtue is goodness ἀγαθότης. The four rivers are prudence, φρόνησις, concerned with things to be done; courage, ἀνδρεία, with things to be endured; self mastery, σωφροσύνη, with things to be chosen, and justice, δικαιοσύνη, with things to be rewarded. The first three of these belong each to a part of the body: prudence belongs to the head, the seat of reason; courage belongs to the breast, the seat of passion; self-mastery belongs to the abdomen, the seat of lust. When these three are in harmony in the soul, the fourth, justice, appears.

[317] *Mut.* 148. Since generic virtue is within the intelligible world, and by virtue of being intelligible is archetypal, it is natural that Philo regard it as an idea. For a discussion of Philo's view of ideas, see Bréhier, 152–153.

world.[318] Abraham's possession of the four cardinal virtues[319] of the perceptible world is the direct result of his possessing in his mind generic virtue.

The possession of such virtue leads Abraham to become the best kind of king, the philosopher king, appointed not by men but by Nature herself.[320] The transformed Abraham, then, is no longer the "atheist" of his Chaldean days. He is now completely transformed into the Sage, in possession of archetypal virtue. As a result of the change in his nature, he is now in full possession of piety.[321]

Abraham's faith in God, the mark of his piety, is firmly established.[322] That a doubt passed through his mind momentarily

---

[318] Philo is interpreting "she shall be for nations," Gen. 17.16, *Mut.* 148 ff. and *QG* III, 44.

[319] The theme of the second half of *De Abrahamo*.

[320] *Mut.* 151. Philo adds that the teaching that the Sage is the only true king stems from Moses. This sceptre is a gift of God to Abraham, *Sob.* 57. Wisdom is the true kingship and is impossible while one lingers among bodily things; *Mig.* 197. Virtue is a rulership and kingship whose authority is final, *Somn.* II, 244. The epithet for Abraham, with a similar explanation, was noted above in *Abr.* 261. The verse which serves Philo is Gen. 23.6 (*QG* IV, 76) a verse which in MT reads נשיא rather than the βασιλεύς of LXX. The notion of the kingship of the sage seems to be intimately associated with Philo's notion of democracy in the soul, though Philo does not, to my knowledge, make this association directly. Democracy, as we saw above, meant a regimentation of the passions and the senses by the mind, which acted neither as a tyrant, abusing his subjects, nor as a weak sovereign, capitulating to the wishes of the mob. The connection between democracy and the sage as king is that "reason" is the means by which the members of the body are regulated; when this regulation takes place, democracy has been established, and the soul has become the sage and king. Cf. Goodenough, *Introduction to Philo Judaeus*, 154 ff.

[321] *Mut.* 76. We saw above, in the literal Abraham, that piety is regarded by Philo as the outstanding characteristic of Abraham. Philo derives Abraham's piety primarily from LXX Gen. 17.1, "Be well-pleasing before me." "Before" means that the one who practices piety towards God loves his fellowman, *Mut.* 39–40.

[322] Philo dwells at length on Abraham's faith in God and his concomitant distrust of created things. He derives this from Gen. 17.18, "Let this Ishmael live before thee." Ishmael, elsewhere the sophist, is here the mind which hears creature wisdom rather than divine wisdom. See *Mut.* 201 ff. and 216 ff., also *QG* III, 57. As the son of Hagar, Ishmael is the progenitor of the early branches

distinguished Abraham's faith from divine faith.[323] Even though Abraham's faith so swerved, the doubt was, in accord with his nature, short and momentary.[324] The transformation which occurs is a divine gift in the form of betterment of soul; God has called

of learning (Gen. 17.20 f.), but is contrasted with "joy" whom virtue (Sarah) bears, *QG* III, 59. The "season" at which "joy" is to be born is God Himself, *Mut.* 264–266; "in another year" is not an interval of time but archetypal time, that is, eternity; virtue in general is to perceptible virtues as eternity is to perceptible time, *Mut.* 267–269. See also *QG* III, 59, the last phrase of which is lost on me. Possibly some corruption in the text, from the Greek into the Armenian, occasions the unclarity.

[323] *Mut.* 177–178. The doubt is inferred from Gen. 17.17, Abraham's laughter at the promise of a son in view of his and Sarah's advanced age.

On the other hand, however, Philo, having eulogized Abraham's faith based on Gen. 15.6, treats the substance of Gen. 15.8 as if in no way modifying that high faith. The question, "By what shall I know?" expresses no doubt at all, but only curiosity as to the manner of eventuation of God's prediction‘ *QG* III, 2. In *Nedarim* 32a, Gen. 15.8 is interpreted as expressing doubt, and it is the ultimate reason for the enslavement of Abraham's descendants in Egypt; the interpretation here is quite at variance with Philo's. The same passage quotes another sage who ascribed the punishment to Abraham's forced impressment of disciples of the wise into his "army," based on a fanciful interpretation of Gen. 14.14B. In *Gen. R.* XLIV, there is a denial that Gen. 15.8 expressed doubt; rather, it inquired, "through what merit?" But most rabbinic interpretation assumes that the verse expresses doubt; see Kasher, III, 644-645.

Having justified Abraham, Philo proceeds to show that Gen. 15.9, "take for Me," is the proof that there is no doubt expressed in the verse; these words are the injunction for the sage to use God's gifts as a trust (which man may take for himself); see *Heres* 90 ff. Philo next proceeds to show that Gen. 15.10, "Abraham took all these things for Him," means that "the man of worth guards the sacred trust . . . of soul, sense, and speech, of divine wisdom and human knowledge, . . . not for himself, but solely for Him" — that is, the "Him" (αὐτῷ) is God, *Heres* 129.

[324] *Mut.* 186. See also *QG* IV, 86 to Gen. 24.2, the allegory of the "thigh." Gen. 15.4, והנה דבר יהוה אליו is rendered by LXX καὶ εὐθὺς φωνὴ θεοῦ ἐγένετο πρὸς αὐτὸν λέγων. Philo's text differs only very slightly, cf. Ryle, 54. From *euthus* Philo infers that God hastens to forestall the questioner, anticipating his speaking. See *Heres* 66–67.

Philo infers "constancy" from Rebekah. She is ὑπομονή, *Somn.* I 46, or ἐπιμονή *Fuga* 45 and *Cher.* 41. As the daughter of Bethuel, she is the "daughter of her god," that is wisdom, *QG* IV, 97 to Gen. 24.15. See similarly *Fuga* 50–51. It is the "self-taught" Isaac with whom Philo associates "constancy," as in *QG* IV, 127–146, based on Gen. 24.50–67.

Abraham to a partnership in virtue and has made him both in fact and in name a Sage.[325]

Abraham differs from Enoch who was also a Sage. The earlier Sage did not abide among men, but, inspired with heaven-sent madness, went out into the wilderness.[326] Abraham, however, follows a tame and gentle piety[327] and accordingly practices both piety to God and friendliness to men.[328]

Abraham's constancy[329] is the result of his virtue having been acquired by teaching, something different than the acquisition by practice which marked Jacob. Abraham has been endowed with a happy nature which, with the cooperation of memory,[330] assures retentiveness; he has a tight grip and firm armhold on what he has learned and therefore he remains constant.[331] The "Practicer," on the other hand, relaxes after a strenuous exercise while he collects and recovers the force which has been enfeebled by his exertions.[332] It was God who improved Abraham's nature, while Jacob's was improved by the divine Logos.[333] The

---

[325] *Mut.* 71.

[326] That Enoch "was not," Gen. 5.24, means that the Sage is usually not recognized among men and they shun his company. This might lend support, Philo suggests, for the notion held by some (cf. *SVF* III, 32) that there is no such thing as a sage, but Philo declines to enter into this question, simply asserting that there are in existence both wisdom and sages. He infers further from the "translation" of Enoch that Enoch left human society.

[327] In *Heres*, 127 Philo distinguishes between divine and human wisdom; the former is a lover of solitudes and the possession of the solitary God; the latter is gentle, tame, and sociable, and pleased to dwell with mortals.

[328] *Mut.* 39–42, based on Gen. 17.1. See also *QG* III, 40.

[329] "He remained in his place," Gen. 18.22; *QG* IV, 25. See *QG* IV, 29, on Gen. 18.33, "Abraham returned to his place," which is interpreted without contradicting "constancy"; indeed, it buttresses it. Compare last part of note 324.

[330] On memory, see Philo's interpretation of the ten camels of Gen. 24 in note 269.

[331] Philo's contrast between Abraham and Jacob rests on the observation that though the name of each was changed, Jacob is still frequently called Jacob even after the alteration, while Abram does not recur once Abraham is mentioned.

[332] *Mut.* 83–84.

[333] Gen. 32.25, tells that a "man" wrestled with Jacob. Philo interprets the man first to be an angel and next to be the *Logos*, *Mut.* 87.

Logos can perfect the mind, but it cannot, as God can, produce a mind which is constant and unswerving.[334]

The perfection attained through teaching ultimately equals perfection by nature;[335] this, Philo tells us, is the sense of "journeying together, they came to the place of which God had spoken."[336] Both Abraham and Isaac prove capable of carrying off virtue's prizes.[337]

Abraham, to summarize, is now perfected. He possesses not only the (four cardinal) specific virtues, but generic, ideal virtue itself.[338] Abraham has attained to this intelligible virtue by stripping himself, as it were, of the wordly bond imposed by the body and bodily requirements.

Virtue now guides Abraham, not like a slave, but a perfect administrator.[339] Abraham achieves the highest kind of joy and

---

[334] *Mut.* 85–87.

[335] See *QG* IV, 143: ". . . For when Abraham and Isaac are analyzed (they are) one and the same thing . . ."

[336] Ryle, *op. cit.* p. 86, and Wendland, *ad loc.*, cite the verse as Gen. 22.3. Colson and Whitaker cite it as 22.8. "They journeyed together" is indeed 22.8. The remainder of Philo's citation is 22.9, words which are quite similar to 22.3.

God as place, both near and far, based on Gen. 22.3–4 is found in *Somn.* I 63 ff. and *Post.* 17 f. Gen. 22.3 is treated a little differently in *Mig.* 139 f.: when the mind has passed the divisions of time and has quit them for timeless existence, then it "will sacrifice his only son, no human being (for the wise man is not a slayer of his offspring), but the male progeny of . . . the soul."

[337] Philo compares them with painting and sculpture, which, before perfection, create only inanimate copies of nature; but Abraham (and Isaac) now become embodiments of nature itself, *Mig.* 167. This notion seems to be related, though not directly, with the notion that the patriarchs were the embodiment of natural law (the *nomos empsychos*). What is lacking in the connection is an explicit mention of law. When it is recalled, however, that Philo insists that the lives of the patriarchs are legal matters and not simply biographical, then the connection seems to me to be beyond doubt; cf. *Abr.* 5.

[338] This possession comes late in a man's life, Gen. 15.17, *Heres* 307–308. Marcus conjectures, probably correctly, that *QG* III, 14 lacks the expected interpretation, *Philo Supplement*, I, 198, note c.

Humility as the precursor to coming before God is derived from Gen. 18.27. See *Heres* 30, *Quod Deus*, 161, and *QG* IV, 28. On the sage's humility, in the light of "joy," see *Mut.* 154, based on Gen. 17.17; see also *QG* III, 41.

[339] The basis is Gen. 18.10 in *QG* IV, 13. In *MT*, the *hu 'aḥarav* is vague. *Tar. Jon.* tells that *"hu"* was Ishmael, eavesdropping. Rashi follows older

gladness.[340] This joy is a divine gift to him, stemming from his

authorites in taking *hu* as "it," that is, the door was behind the angel. LXX
renders the *hu*, Sarah "being" behind him (Abraham).

[340] See *QG* IV, 18–19 on Gen. 18.14–15. Philo also infers this from Gen.
15.18 in one allegory by a play on Εὐφράτης and εὐφροσύνη; *Heres* 316; cf.
QG III, 16 and *Somn*. II, 255 ff. In another and frequently repeated allegory,
Isaac represents the joy begotten by God out of Sarah, virtue, and given to
Abraham. Further on Isaac as joy, God's offspring, cf. *Mut*. 130 f. based on
Gen. 17.16; see also, passingly, *QG* III, 54.

Gen. 21.6 is the principal source (though not the only one) for Philo's
view of the allegorical Sarah as impregnated by God with the "joy," Isaac, to
be presented to the Sage. The longest discussion of what Philo describes as a
saying not for all to hear, so strongly does the evil of superstition flow, is
Mut. 137–141. Philo cites the verse in *LA* III, 219, with the advice to initiates
to open their ears wide and take in holy teachings; Philo here precedes his
esoteric interpretation and the warning about it with a more literal, though
still allegorical, statement of the Sage begetting out of virtue, based on Gen.
17.15–16. The esoteric here is buttressed by assuming that the *kyrios* (אדני) of
Gen. 18.11–12 is the divine Logos, and the "old" means "great"; *LA* II, 82 is
only a passing mention; *Deter*. 124 has the same notions expressed with less
reservation: "God may, with perfect truth, be said to be Isaac's father."
Philo in *Cher*. 45 ff. has no more than an allusion to the same verse in the
midst of two other instances of portraying God as the impregnator (of Leah
and Rebekkah); what he dwells on is the mystic nature of his interpretation
and his injunction to the initiates not to babble about it. One despairs of
adequately interpreting exactly what Philo means in his reference to seeing
Jeremiah; possibly it is no more than an expression of Philo's delight at
finding in Jeremiah's book a verse which lent itself to this esoteric twist. If the
passage means more than that, the plus eludes me.

The exposition of the allegory of the birth of Isaac utilizes the sexual
imagery of the biblical passages. Other relevant Philonic passages are *Abr*.
99–102; *Cher*. 43–50; and *QG* IV, 14–18. The point that Philo makes in this
elaborate exegesis can be summed up as follows: When a man possesses true
virtue as Abraham did, God gives that man joy which God begets out of
virtue. Generic virtue in turn begets out of the mind (and therefore in the
man) specific virtues. Philo's utilization of the sexual imagery is what Goodenough has in mind in speaking of the great Female Principle of nature, *BLL*,
22 ff. Philo makes a good many verses accord to this sexual allegory with
persistent single-mindedness. God visits Sarah, Gen. 21.1 — to procreate joy
out of virtue, *Cher*. 45. Sarah has "ceased after the manner of women,"
Gen. 18.11 — the virtue which God will deal with is virginal, *Cher*. 50; *LA*,
III, 217 (which explains similarly Gen. 17.16–17, and Gen. 21.6;) *Det*. 28;
Post. 134; *Ebr*. 59–62; *Fuga*. 128; and *Somn*. II, 185. Note also *QG* IV, 15.
See *QG* III, 55–56. "My Lord is 'old' " (*ibid*.) is an allusion to God or the

virtue which has fathered it.[341] True Sage that he is, Abraham is prepared, in his piety, to offer this joy to God.[342] God, however,

---

Logos and not to Abraham, *Mut.* 166 and *LA* III 217. Isaac as joy, or pure thought, is the product of a virgin (derived from Gen. 18.11), and is timeless, for Gen. 21.2 seems to allow no interval, and hence no time factor, between Sarah's conception and giving birth; see *Fuga* 167. The allegory can be found worked out in a good many ingenious and even far-fetched details in *Mut.* 130–174.

[341] The interpretation of Gen. 21.7 in *Mig.* 140 bothers the commentators both as to Philo's sense and as to the syntax of the Greek; cf. Colson and Whitaker, IV, 563. The difficulty does not seem to me to be too great; rather, the high involvement of Philo's exegesis, in this case confounded by a parenthetical clause, occasions the problem. As I see it, Sarah does not know how she bore Isaac; he ("joy") is a divine growth; Gen. 21.7 expresses the idea of the soul's ignorance of having produced joy. At this point, hearkening back to Aristotle's doubt, namely, that perfection through being taught and through practice are discernible in the world, but perfection through nature not so, Philo tells us that Sarah, as though like Aristotle, assumed that Abraham did not believe in the appearance of a breed like Isaac; to reassure us that Isaac is indeed the example of this type, Philo points out that the verse does not occur in the passive ("a child is being suckled by Sarah"), but in the active, ("Sarah is suckling") that is, he is arguing that virtue produces joy actively. Next, as though fearing that the production of Isaac might compromise his natural perfection, he reverts to a restatement of the natural perfection: the autodidact is not nourished by anyone, but is the nourishment of others, being able to teach and not needing to learn. It seems unnecessary to me to follow Cohn, V, 189 and Colson and Whitaker in taking *Paidion* as the subject of Philo's sentence; there is nothing that I have encountered in Philo's writings which accords either literally or allegorically to it. Variation occurs in Philo's thought; the difficulty with the interpretations here argued against is that they imply matters as if Philo is directly reversing himself.

[342] Philo so interprets Gen. 22, *Abr.* 200–204 and *LA* III, 209; cf. *Somn.* I, 193–195 and *Quod Deus*, 4. The paradox of "the place," reached in Gen. 22.3, but still three days distance in verse 4, seems crucial in the allegory. On God as "place," a common rabbinic title too, see Wolfson I, 247 ff. The "binding" itself, which gives the rabbinic name עקדה to the incident, is virtually ignored by Philo.

A passage, *Mig.* 125–126, which is in itself obscure because of its brevity, alludes to Abraham, Isaac and Jacob as the three divisions of eternity. Colson and Whitaker IV, 563 note the obscurity and offer in explanation, based on *Mig.* 154, which alludes to Gen. 22.3 "they came to the (P)lace on the third day, as entering upon the inheritance of virtue by a threefold light, memory of things gone by, clear sight of things present, and the expectation of things to come"; they point out, however, that on the surface the allegory of Abraham rewards Abraham by returning joy to him, because Abraham travels the road of virtue.[343]

does not fit in here as well as would those of Isaac and Jacob. But it seems to me that a comparison of the contents of this passage with *Mut.* 267–269 can disclose Philo's intent. There Philo sets forth the proportion that eternity is to time, that is, eternity is to its divisions, as generic virtue is to perceptible virtues. As for the difficulty of aligning all this with Philo's allegorical quantities, perhaps Colson and Whitaker are expecting an undue measure of precision from Philo. See also *Plant.* 113–116, in which Philo discusses the fruits of instruction as the three-fold aspects of eternal virtue, but without reference there to the patriarchs. A note by Heinemann in the German translation, V, 193, denies that the three days of *Mig.* 154 is an allusion to Gen. 22.3; Heinemann suggests other Scriptural possibilities, probably on the basis that in context we deal in *Mig.* 154 with Israel going out of Egypt, not with Abraham; but none of his suggestions seem persuasive. It does not seem to me that it does violence to Philo to attribute to him a mixing of his metaphors. Heinemann's citation of Rashi to Deut. 1.2 does not seem to me felicitous.

[343] *Abr.* 204. Philo takes Gen. 18.9, "where is Sarah, virtue," as a prelude to the answer, "it is in the soul" (the "tent"); *QG* IV, 11 and *Deter.* 57–60. Philo alludes once again to God's impregnating virtue with joy, thereafter born out of her to the Sage.

His all too frequent preoccupation with numbers leads Philo in *Mut.* 188 ff. to align Abraham with other worthies whose virtue-joy must harass and destroy injustice, all this under the aegis of a perfect number. This is to be discovered in Gen. 21.33, in the *'eshel* which Abraham planted; Philo's text reads ἄρουραν which Philo interprets "in the technical sense of a piece of land of 100 cubits square" (Colson and Whitaker, V, 239 note). There is in Philo no reflection of the wondrous rabbinic exegesis of *'eshel*, such as its being an abbreviation for אכל שתיה לויה, *Mid. Psalms* 110, and elsewhere. Philo discusses the same passage in Genesis in *Plant.* 73 ff.; he has there the same data about the size; he tells us that the text does not tell us what Abraham planted but only the size of the plot of ground. Philo goes on to explain how the details of the rest of the verse, the well of the oath (Beer Sheba) and the invoking of the name of God fit into the passage. Briefly, the expression "planted" presupposes attention to the appropriate trees, that is, a spiritual tree, planted in the mind (διάνοια) of the one beloved of God; the 100 cubits square yields a total of 10,000 square cubits, and 10,000 is to 1 as the end of a race-course is to the beginning; hence the *aroura* is the symbol of proclaiming God as the beginning and final goal of all things! "Well-diggers" are those who search for spiritual water which nourishes the soul; for some the search, whether for real or spiritual water, is unsuccessful. This particular well is known from Gen. 26.32 f., to have yielded no water; it is impossible to attain perfection in any of the sciences; it is appropriate to call such a well "the oath" because when God is called in on disputed points, there is nothing on which a surer

A second result of Abraham's virtue is his steadfast apprehension of the wisdom of God.[344] Vice leads the thoughts downwards, but virtue leads upwards.[345] Because his thoughts lead upwards, Abraham experiences the highest form of *ecstasis*, prophecy.[346] He is inspired and God-possessed, a prophet, and a friend of God.[347] Abraham, as a prophet and friend of God, passes

oath can be taken that no perfection is reached in studying the sciences; the true power of apprehensions springs from the seeds of certitude sown on the organs of perception by God. The fruit of the *aroura* is "the name of the Lord, as God eternal; Lord is the ruling power, God the beneficial power" — as so frequently in Philo, especially in connection with Gen. 18.

In contrast with Abraham, the laughter of Lot's sons-in-law (*QG* IV, 43 to Gen. 19.14) is the short-lived joy achieved through the body, rather than virtue.

[344] *Heres* 313–315.

[345] *Heres* 241. In *QG* IV, 93 to Gen. 24.10 Philo allegorizes Nahor as "rest of light." His intent is quite elusive. He seems to be saying that Nahor — rest and quiet — is not profitable, but that wisdom must move the sage towards things suitable and related. Marcus I, 376, note i, hazards a guess, a commendable effort to solve an obscure and possibly corrupt passage; but I do not agree that Philo means that "the wise man seeks the quiet of light."

[346] Philo derives the notion from ἔκστασις of LXX Gen. 15.12, for which *MT* reads *tardema*; the exegesis is possible only on the LXX. See *QG* III, 9. Philo lists four kinds of *ecstasis*; delusion, consternation, passivity, and prophecy; *Heres* 249–258. He adds that the notion is not only derivable from his verse, but explicitly stated, Gen. 20.7, which terms Abraham a prophet; *Heres* 258 and, passingly *QG* IV, 66; cf. also *QG* IV, 90, based on Gen. 24.7.

[347] *Ecstasis*, Philo tells us, is the regular inheritance of the race of prophets beloved of God; it consists in the "setting" (Gen. 15.12, in which the sun becomes allegorically human reason) of the human mind and the entrance of divine reason. The prophet himself does not speak (as proved by the passive, "it was said to Abraham," Gen. 15.13), but God speaks through the prophet; *Heres* 263–266. The "race of prophets" constitutes, as it were, a synhedrion of God's friends, whom God addresses by name, as he did Abraham, Gen. 22.1–2, 9–12; *Somn.* I, 193–195. The man who is not a sage perceives God through his senses, and to him God is "master and benefactor"; but God is not a master, but rather a friend to the Sage, as proved by "shall I hide anything from Abraham, my friend," Gen. 18.17; on this verse, see above, II, note 130. The passage is *Sob.* 55–57; see also *QG* IV, 21.

That Abraham is God's friend is proved by the familiar language which God uses, "by Myself have I sworn," Gen. 22.16, *Abr.* 273; this oath brought with it an abundance of good things to the perfect Abraham, *LA* III, 203.

Philo summarizes briefly the treatment of *ecstasis* based on Gen. 15 in beyond the bounds of human happiness. He becomes nobly born, registering God as his father and becoming by adoption His only son; he is the possessor not merely of riches, but even of all riches, of the good things which do not grow old but continually renew their youth; he has not only a good reputation, but he is truly good, since his praise is not the flattery of men but praise ratified by truth. He is the sole king,[348] having received from God

LA III 40 ff.; he quotes Gen. 24.7 as another Scriptural basis for his contention that only he whom God rescues out of the prison of the body can attain to being with God.

In *Heres* 258–263 Philo quotes Gen. 20.7, in which Abraham is expressly called a prophet. That is to say, Philo buttresses his exegesis with a clinching proof-text. His continuation, however, is significant: "The Holy Word assures prophecy to every worthy man" (*panti asteio*). Not only is there in Philo no hint of the rabbinic view that prophecy ceased at the time of Ezra, but to the contrary, it is a continuing possession of the human race. See Frank Young in *JBL*, LXVIII (1949), p. 297.

Wolfson II, 52, offers a somewhat long discussion at the termination of which he concludes that Philo's view of continuing prophecy is akin to the rabbinic *bat kol*, and that Philo presumably also believed that the older Scripture-creating prophecy had ceased. Wolfson is hardly to be followed here, Marginal Jewries, if one can judge by the continuing apocalyptic tendencies and their literary expressions, did not share the rabbinic view of the cessation of prophecy. Prophecy is assumed to be extant in Paul's letters, especially Galatians frequently, and in I Corinthians XII, 10 and XIII, 2. See also Ephesians, IV, 11. See Didache XI–XIII, wherein the distinction between apostle and prophet becomes blurred; presumably the prophet is an apostle but not every apostle is a prophet. The dates of the *Apocalypse of Abraham* and the *Testament of Abraham* are uncertain; see *JE* I, 674; they get their points of departure from the same Scriptural section, Gen. 15. Wolfson's horizons here seem quite limited.

[348] Philo has several passages in which he alludes to Abraham as king: *Mut.* 152, *Abr.* 261; *Virt.* 216 (cf. *ibid.* 207 for his pleasureless mating). The most striking passage is *Somn.* II 244, where Philo declares that those who recognized Abraham as king "laid down the doctrine for students of philosophy that the Sage alone is a ruler and king, and virtue a rule and a kingship whose authority is final." *Sob.* 57 does not directly make this same identification; it is there only allusively, and ensues on Philo's interpretation of Gen. 18.17, which we have noted supplied Philo with "friend" rather than LXX "servant"; cf. note 347 and *LA* III 27 and *QG* IV, 21. See, too, *QG* IV, 121. In the present passage, Philo goes on to say that one who has such a portion (that is, of being God's friend) has registered (ἐπιγεγραμμένος) God as his father and become

the sceptre of universal sovereignty which none can dispute. He is the sole freeman, for God has released him from the tyranny of vain opinion.[349]

As a prophet, Abraham enjoys the vision of God. This occurs when Abraham has dispelled the bodily mist and comes into the clear atmosphere of the higher verities.[350] When a soul comes into God's presence, He does not turn away, but in His love of mankind comes forward to meet the soul and, in the measure that the beholder is capable of seeing, reveals His nature. A man cannot by himself apprehend the Truly Existent, but he requires His revelation and manifestation.[351]

The sight of *To On* is the ultimate. Philo insists that Abraham receives this best possible vision, as we shall see below. Before that, however, he "still stood near" (Gen. 18.22) to the Power of God.[352] He does not, like Cain, hide himself from God, but both sees and is seen.[353] While he rises from time to time to the supreme heights, he abides between these ascents among the

by adoption his only ($\mu \acute{o} \nu o s$) son. The language here brings to mind Romans VIII, 14–15 and Eph. I, 5. See also *Conf.* 145 ff. for Philo's discussion of Deut. 14.1 and related expressions equal to "sons of God"; Deut. 14.1 is also discussed, in the same way, in *Spec.* I, 318. In Philo's writings expressions such as, son of God, friend of God, family of God, and prophet are nearly interchangeable.

[349] *Sob.* 55–57. For the Sage as a freeman, see Colson IX, 2–3, part of the introduction to *Probus*, which is, of course, Philo's lengthy exposition of the doctrine. Cf. *Probus* 42, where Philo tells us that the "friends" of God are free. Cf. also *Probus* 158–160: freedom is not a question of citizen or slave but of the capacity of the soul to rise above bodily hindrances, and to live agreeably to nature.

[350] In another passage Philo makes the oak of Gen. 18.1, equivalent to Sophia. Abraham sees the vision of God as incorporeal rays of light while seated under the oak; *QG* IV, 1. The prediction of Gen. 24.7 shows also that Abraham was a prophet, *QG* IV, 90. That the vision of God results after freedom from the bondage of the body is treated laconically by Philo through citing Gen. 12.1 and 7 in juxtaposition, in *Deter.* 159–60.

[351] *Abr.* 77–80. The use of the passive, "God was seen by Abraham," LXX Gen. 12.7, $\H{\omega} \varphi \theta \eta$ proves that God must reveal himself for man to be able to see him.

[352] *Cher.* 18–19, *Post.* 27, *QG* IV, 25.

[353] *LA* III, 6, *Somn.* II, 226.

divine *Logoi.*[354] As a follower of God he travels along with
the divine *Logoi,* or angels, as they are called.[355]

Abraham, however, progresses to the final, climactic sight.
It is not the eyes of his body which receive this vision. Bodily
eyes require light as a means of seeing, while the soul sees by its
own agency without any intermediary light. Just as conceptions
become intelligibly visible without light, or put forth their own
light, so God puts forth pure rays intensely bright and free from
shadow which are discernible to the soul.[356] Initially, before he
had become perfect, Abraham had not actually seen God. He
had seen one of the Powers, the Royal Power.[357] While Abraham
is progressing, his God is spoken of as *Theos,* the Creative or
Beneficial Power, because *Theos* is the maker of the virtuous
soul, the soul stripped of the body.[358]

---

[354] *Somn.* I, 70. God's going up from Abraham, Gen. 17.22, is not the
separation of God from the sage, but rather an opportunity now for the pupil
to exhibit his own powers, *Mut.* 270.

[355] Gen. 18.16 is the basis. The verse reads "Abraham travelled with them,
joining with them in escorting them on their way." Philo adds: "What a
glorious privilege to be put on a level with them! The escort is escorted; he
gives what he was receiving . . . For as long as he falls short of perfection he
has the Divine *Logos* as his leader," *Mig.* 173. See also *QG* IV, 20.

[356] *Mut.* 3–6. On this "light-stream" and its probable Persian antecedents,
see Goodenough, 12–14. Philo tells us again in this passage, *Mut.* 7–15, that
To On is never apprehended by man, since there is neither an organ in sense
to envisage him nor in mind to conceive Him, and even Moses fails in this
quest to know God. It is sufficient for mortals to know the things, material and
immaterial, below God. Because God appears to have a name does not mean
that God is known. In truth, God has no name, but men need a substitute for
it in order to be able to address their prayers. Even *His* Powers (the wrestler
with Jacob Gen. 32.29) cannot reveal God's name.

[357] *Mut.* 7–15. *Kyrios* and *Theos* are the Powers of God. *Kyrios* is the
ruling Power; *Theos* is the creative Power. Neither of these is actually God,
except in a loose way of speaking; they are only the senior Powers of *To On,*
Abr. 120–121. See *QG* III, 39 and *Mut.* 28–30. That it is *Kyrios* who appears
in the first part of Gen. 17.1 is explicable by the fact that, as Abram, our
protagonist requires a master, the Royal Power; while the *Theos* of the second
part of the verse indicates that Abraham is on his way to betterment, and
therefore he is associated with *Theos.* The exegesis, depending on LXX Gen.
17.1, would not be possible on *MT,* which reads *Yahweh* in the first of the
verse, but *El Shaddai* in the second part.

[358] *Mut.* 27–34.

God appears to men in either a triple vision, if the mind is only partly purified,[359] or in a single vision if the mind is completely purified.[360] This can be stated, Philo tells us, in still another way. There are three classes of temperaments which get the divine vision in different ways. The lowest class sees the Power on the left, κύριος, the ruling Power. The intermediate class sees the Power on the right, θεός, the beneficial Power. The best class sees the form in the middle, To On. Temperaments of the best[361] kind worship only To On, and nothing can make them swerve from this.[362]

Another proof that Abraham saw God is to be inferred from the zeal and speed with which he bade virtue (Sarah) to knead three measures of meal and make "buried cakes."[363] God has

---

[359] QG IV, 5, based on the reversion from singular to plural in Gen. 18.4; and QG IV, 6 to Gen. 18.5, in which the comment stems from the unexpected "I will take," rather than "take you."

Philo infers from the use of the singular in the Decalogue that they are addressed to each single person; when he is law-abiding and obedient to God, he is equal to a nation, or nations, or indeed the whole world. This, too, says Philo, is the intent of LXX Gen. 17.1, in which God says, "I am thy God," even though He is the God of the whole world. See Decal. 37–38. To the righteous, He is a beneficial deity; to the unrighteous, He is a stringent master; see Mut. 18 ff.: "His will is to be called the Lord and Master (Κύριος καὶ Δεσπότης) of the bad, the God (Θεός) of those on their way to betterment, but of the best and most perfect at once God (Theos) and the Lord (Kyrios)."

[360] Abr. 122; QG IV, 2, based on Gen. 18.2.

[361] It is undoubtedly a typographical error which produces a contextually impossible rendering of ἄριστος as "last" in place of "best" in Colson's translation, Abr. 125.

[362] Abr. 125. See also QG III, 41 to Gen. 17.3 and QG IV, 4 to Gen. 18.3. The LXX of Gen. 15.2, in which אדני אלהים is rendered by Δέσποτα κύριε, leads Philo into an explanation of δεσπότης and its supposed Greek etymology, utimately from the root meaning "fear," by way of the word for "bond." See Heres 23 ff. Wolfson does not list Δεσπότης in his section in which he enumerates other titles used by Philo or suggested by LXX, I, 39–40; Wolfson does not discuss the present passage. It also fails to appear in the list which Drummond, II, 63 acknowledges to be incomplete, but he cites the passage in II, 85–86. On God as the bond, a frequent item in Philo, see Bréhier, 85, who properly notes that more usually, as in Plant. 8 ff. (incorrectly cited in Bréhier as Plant. 10) it is the Logos which is actually the "bond."

[363] Gen. 18.6. The LXX adds ἐγκρυφίας for which MT provides no basis. The word is crucial to the allegory. See QG IV, 8, end. Note also QG IV, 35,

come into Abraham's "soul-eye" attended by His two highest
Powers, rulership and goodness. God called up before the eye
three separate visions or aspects. Each of these aspects is the
measure of all things, the rulership of its subjects, the goodness
of all good things; and God Himself is the measure of all things
corporeal and incorporeal. The Powers serve God by assuming
the functions of rules and standards, and measure what lies in
their province. While God who overtops his Powers is visible
apart from them, it is well that the three (measures) be kneaded
and blended in the soul, so that the soul can receive the impression of God's sovereignty and beneficence.[364]

That Abraham is a temperament of the best kind and that
he saw the triple vision as a single object is clear, Philo tells us,
not merely from allegory, but from the use of the singular in the
literal text.[365] As a prophet, Abraham seems to be speaking when

to Gen. 19.3; the sage knows things hidden from the multitude; Lot, not a
sage, offers other food, i. e., the things the multitude knows.

[364] *Sac.* 59–60. Philo terms this a teaching of the higher mystery, like a
similar teaching in the lower mystery, the baking of Matzoth, Ex. 12.39. The
lower incident represents the kneading of passion with reason; this higher
incident represents a vision of God. The "buried" aspect means that this
higher mystery must not be blabbed or babbled about by those admitted to it;
Sac. 60–62. On the greater and lower mysteries, cf. Goodenough, 95–96, and
Wolfson I, 47–48; while these commentators seem opposed to each other on
the significance of the mysteries, they agree that the lower mysteries are the
level of perception and the higher, the level of the intelligible.

[365] *Abr.* 131–132. As explained above, page 120, Gen. 18 varies from the
singular to the plural and back, giving Philo (and later Christian trinitarians)
a point of departure for equating God with a tri-partite form. Philo infers a
number of different conclusions from the association of a particular divine
name with one or more of the patriarchs, and his inferences do not always
agree with each other. We saw above that Philo declared that Abraham ultimately equalled Isaac in perfection. Elsewhere Philo comments on Gen. 28.13,
"I am the Lord God (*kyrios theos*) of Abraham thy father and the God (*theos*)
of Isaac." Philo first explains that Jacob, having attained virtue through
practice inherited God under both titles. Abraham needs two tending powers
so that he might be directed and graciously benefitted; Isaac needed only the
gracious benefaction and not the direction since he was born perfect and needed
no improvement. Jacob, as their offspring, inherited both *kyrios* and *theos*;
Abraham is spoken of as his father, instead of grandfather, because practice
stems from instruction; and Jacob can be spoken of as the son of Isaac, Gen.
46.1, only when he becomes Israel, the seer of God; *Somn.* I, 159–170. In

delivering the prophetic message, but he is really holding his peace; his organs of speech are wholly in the employ of God.[366] Ecstasy is, however, not a permanent state, but only an incident which recurs to the qualified individual. The created being is not able to contain God forever but only from time to time, and then must return to itself.[367]

Abraham abides in the state from which the ascent to the divine vision can take place. He remains immutably in wisdom,[368]

recognition of the virtues of the patriarchs, God, insofar as He has a name, is associated in that name with the patriarchs as the God of Abraham, the God of Isaac, and the God of Jacob, an eternal name, Ex. 3.15; *Abr.* 50–51. It would seem that on the one hand Philo can regard the biblical word used for God as only a Power of *To On*, or, if it suits his purpose, as *To On* Himself.

[366] *Heres* 266 ff. and *QG* III, 10, Philo's biblical basis is the passive ἐρρέθη of LXX Gen. 15.13, for which *MT* reads the active *wa-yomer lo*. The exegesis can rest only on the LXX. The inference accords with Philo's notion of *ecstasis*. The mind, having been led out of itself, is no longer the agent directing speech. It has been led out of the prison-house of the body; it is therefore ministering to God; it is not a human mind but now a divine one; *Heres* 84–85. Elsewhere Philo describes the process as akin to persons possessed and corybants (κατεχόμενοι καὶ κορυβαντιῶντες) who are filled with inspired frenzy (βακχευθεῖσα καὶ θεορηθεῖσα), or, like the mind under divine afflatus (ἐνθουσιώσης) and no longer in its own keeping, but stirred to its depths and maddened by heavenward yearning, drawn by *To On* and pulled upward to Him; *Heres* 68–70. Another Philonic term is "sober intoxication," a phrase which Philo apparently invented (cf. Lewy, *Sobria Ebrietas*), as a description of the union of the purely spiritual side of man with the divine. The phrase is to be found in connection with Samuel in *Ebr.* 143 ff.; in connection with Abraham, Philo asserts that the wine brought forth by Melchizedek brought on the sober intoxication, *LA* III, 77 ff. Bréhier believes that the conception of prophecy is Greek and Egyptian (p. 185); Wolfson, on the other hand, believes that Philo's views on prophecy are derivable and derived from Scripture, and then adjusted to Platonic terminology regarding frenzy (II, 10 ff.). I incline to the view of Bréhier. It seems to me that Philo's process is to begin with a hellenistic view and then to justify it on a biblical basis; Wolfson's view would suppose that Philo began with a series of biblical views of prophecy and fortuitously found a Platonic equivalent.

[367] *QG* IV, 29. The basis is Gen. 18.33, "The Lord departed when he ceased speaking with Abraham and Abraham returned to his place." In another passage, Philo uses this verse somewhat differently: God Himself has withdrawn and Abraham is now meeting with His "place," divine *Logoi*; *Somn.* I, 70.

[368] *QG* IV, 53, based on Gen. 19.27–28.

since he has virtue as a sister through inherent kinship, rather than through the accidental relationship of marriage.[369]

In his Ishmael phase, Abraham has been still in sophistry.[370] The sophist hears God.[371] Abraham has wanted to hear God profitably, and therefore he prays (Gen. 17.18) that "Ishmael"— hearing God — may live, but he still hopes for Isaac, joy,[372] the stage beyond hearing, that is, the sight of God.[373]

Abraham's joy is not visible, corporeal laughter, but the invisible joy of the mind. This is the best and most beautiful of all good states, the one by which the soul is filled entirely with contentment.[374] The joy is not confined within time, in the sense of intervals perceived by sense and sight, but in eternity, the intelligible archetype of time.[375]

The gift of this joy[376] marks the end of the process of the perfection of Abraham. Before, as Abram, he had been devoid of

---

[369] *QG* IV, 68. Abraham's dwelling in the "south," *QG* IV, 59, is interpreted as his abiding in virtues. See also *QG* IV, 60.

[370] *Fuga* 209.

[371] *Mut.* 202.

[372] *Mut.* 202, 218. In interpreting Gen. 15.5, Philo notes that the text does not say "so many" will be your seed, but only "so"; God suggests not merely number, but a multitude of other things which make happiness complete. Ultimately, that seed will be like the visible ether (on which see *Heres* 283), the very likeness of the stars. The Sage is a counterpart of heaven, or rather a heaven on earth, possessing here the qualities of "ether." Colson and Whitaker do not render the Greek of *Heres* 87 as happily as does Joseph Cohn in the German; indeed, the passage, which is not too difficult in Greek, is in the English involved and obscure. The verse is interpreted correspondingly, but yet differently in *LA* III 39 ff.: as elsewhere Philo focuses here on the pleonastic *hexo*, inferring the *ecstasis* that goes far beyond mere stand-out from sense-perception.

[373] Philo does not directly equate "Isaac" with the sight of God. I do not believe, however, that I have gone beyond his intent in making this equation. The natural step in Philo's gradation would be from hearing God to seeing God; Scripture does not provide Philo such a natural step and he must therefore proceed from hearing to joy, rather than to seeing.

[374] *Praem.* 31–35. See, similarly *QG* IV, 122, to Gen. 24.36.

[375] *Mut.* 264–267, based on Gen. 17.21: God is the "season" at which Sarah bears joy.

[376] These gifts are prepared by nature for the one perfected by teaching, *QG* IV, 123 to Gen. 24.36.

wisdom; now he is filled with immortal thoughts. The words of Gen. 17.22, "When God completed talking with him, he went up from Abraham" do not mean that Abraham is parted from God; they only show that the learner arrives at the stage at which he becomes independent of the teacher, and, as one completely taught, he is ready, in his perfect state, to proceed on his own powers.[377]

Abraham's body, of course, dies.[378] His mind, however, purified of both body and of the material irrational soul is incorruptible.[379] Abraham has been promised such incorruptibility of his immaterial soul long before his death: Abraham would go to his fathers, nourished in peace, in a goodly old age.[380] The fathers, Philo tells us, can be interpreted variously. One view identifies fathers with the sun, moon, and stars. Another view interprets fathers as the world of ideas in which the mind of the Sage, after the death of the body, makes its new home. A third view identifies fathers with the four elements of the material world, earth, air, water, and fire, and with the fifth element, of the immaterial world, ether; by this latter view, the human soul is a fragment of the fifth essence.[381a]

---

[377] *Mut.* 270.

[378] *QG* IV, 152: "Death is the most glorious life of the . . . soul."

[379] *Quod Deus*, 45–46; *QG* IV, 152–153; *Sac.* 5.

[380] Gen. 15.15, where LXX reads τραφείς, "nourished" for תקבר, equivalent to ταφείς. See *QG* III, 11. The exegesis ignores the Hebrew.

In connection with this verse Philo quotes Gen. 12.1–2 to demonstrate that the soul having once departed from the "father's house," would scarcely be returning to it; hence "thy fathers" must mean something else, *Heres* 277.

[381a] *Heres*, 280 ff. See note 380. The literal fathers of the verse would be the ancestors buried in Chaldea; Philo sneers at this notion in the passage. Wolfson I, 400, would have it that Philo actually denies the soul's return to the fifth essence: Philo "could not accept the view that souls become stars for to him the stars are made of the element fire, whereas the immortal souls are immaterial. For the same reason he could not accept the view that the souls are resolved into the primary fire or ether." However, Philo has insisted that the fifth essence differs from the other four in its superior quality; it is, according to Philo, the purest of substances; *Heres*, 283. In Philo's view, ether, the fifth substance, is immaterial; that stars and the whole heavens are made of this substance would mean that these were immaterial to Philo, and not, as Wolfson suggests, the material, primary fire; the stars, Philo tells us, are

V

We saw that the literal Abraham was an exposition of the events of the physical life of Abraham, arranged as to depict his piety towards God, and his possession of the cardinal virtues. We saw that the allegorical Abraham was a record of the spiritual side of Abraham, of his false start in pantheistic materialism, of his retracing his steps and through learning becoming a Sage, a king, and a prophet. It is necessary to point out what the differences between the two conceptions amount to, and what the similarities are. These similarities and differences can be seen most clearly against the total background of Philo's thought. Philo's message is essentially a very simple one: man represents a mixture of the material and the immaterial. Man can separate himself from the material only at death. But even while alive man can rise above his material aspect, can live by immaterial reality, can unite himself from time to time with God, and ultimately, at death, rejoin the immaterial world which he left when his soul entered a physical body. The religious life which

souls divine and without blemish, and each of them is mind in its purest form; *Gig.* 7. Wolfson may be influenced here by Drummond's effort, I, 273, to deny Soulier's affirmation that Philo believed in the fifth substance. After disparaging Soulier's method of assembling passages to prove the point, Drummond proceeds himself to assemble passages in the same way. The question of whether or not ether was material may be left for another occasion; for our purposes, in the passage under consideration, Philo gives no evidence of rejecting the view that the soul returns to the fifth essence. That Philo is vague on the destiny of the soul after the death of the body is recognized by Goodenough ("Philo on Immortality," *Harvard Theological Review*, XXXIX, April, 1946, 101): "Clearly the soul or higher mind returns at its death to its source ... But it is impossible to say whether for Philo that meant what we call 'personal immortality' or was a spiritual absorption into the Source by which the individual spirit became an anonymous part of the universal spirit." Philo is vague, again, on the question of whether the patriarchs abide in heaven after death as, in Christian doctrine, Christ does. Philo speaks of three paracletes, connected with the patriarchs but not identical with them; these are, first, God's clemency, third, the reformations worked by virtuous men, and second, "the holiness of the founders of the race," *Praem.* 166; cf. *Spec.* IV, 181. Philo, following views derivable from the Bible, seems clearly to assert that the merits of the patriarchs abide, but he does not go as far as suggesting that the patriarchs themselves abide as separate entities.

Philo urges is that man should act by his ability to rise above his material nature, that he should walk on the king's highway which leads to God. The historical Abraham is an example of a man who does just that. This Philo proves primarily from episodes in the life of Abraham. Episodic treatment lends itself to topical divisions. Thus, *De Abrahamo* moves from "piety" to the four cardinal virtues.

The allegorical Abraham is not presented in incidents or episodes, but in minute details, based on a painstaking appraisal of a verse, clause, phrase, word, or even a part of a word, of the biblical text.[381b] Often a sequence of details adds up to a topic. The literal Abraham disclosed his piety in obeying the divine oracle to migrate from Chaldea. The piety of the allegorical Abraham is revealed by interpreting the words of Gen. 12.1, as departure from body, sense-perception, and speech. That Abraham conquered the kings and rescued Lot proves his literal courage; allegorically, the incident proves that he conquered his warring senses and passions by the use of reason. The literal Abraham and the allegorical differ primarily in literary form, and not in substance. The two Abrahams of Philo are congruent with each other.

Philo's separation of the two Abrahams is no more than his literary device. It enables him to choose whether to present a summary topic or, instead, exegetical details.

The almost universal agreement among scholars that *De Abrahamo*, the primary source for the literal Abraham, was written for Gentiles must not lead incorrectly to a notion that Philo has in the interest of apologetics given a distorted view of his Abraham to the outside world. Whether Gentiles or Jews were intended as the audience, it must be insisted that apologetic nuances do not affect Philo's conception of his Abraham one whit. The Abraham of the *Exposition* is exactly the same as the Abraham of the *Allegory*.

This identity may possibly be concealed, at least on superficial notice, by reason of the fact that the Abraham of *De*

[381b] This is true as a generalization even though Philo cites individual verses in *De Abrahamo*.

Abrahamo is regarded virtually throughout the treatise as the perfected Abraham, whereas in the scattered verses of the Allegory we are confronted with an Abraham usually on the way towards perfection and only occasionally perfected. In only ##68–84 of *De Abrahamo* does Philo allude to the process of Abraham's perfection; he is concerned almost exclusively with the end result. In the *Allegory*, however, the preoccupation with single verses or parts of verse leads Philo into detailed expositions of the process.

The topical arrangement of *De Abrahamo* permits Philo to summarize in briefest forms matters which he discusses in the *Allegory* at great length. For example, he discusses Abraham's kingship most briefly;[382] and he fails to make specific mention of Abraham as a prophet (although this notion lies behind Abraham as a friend of God in *Abr.* 273). In the *Allegory*, however, these matters are dealt with in considerable detail. The detail is present for apparently two reasons: first, the consideration of scriptural texts in all their peculiarities seems to obligate Philo to enumerate all the matters to be inferred; and secondly, Philo is interested in "proving" that all of tenable Greek philosophy is implicit or explicit in the Bible. While in *De Abrahamo* he is able to content himself with the brief statement that Abraham migrated from Chaldean astrology, in the *Allegory* Philo considers in elaborate detail the significance of every single scriptural word describing the call to migration and Abraham's obedience, always deriving philosophical explanations from the fortuitous wording of Scripture.

But the *Allegory* too is in a sense topical, in that each treatise is on some subject. In that pursuit Philo very often finds a contextual reason for citing from the Abraham part of Genesis as a device for buttressing an argument begun in some other connection but strenghtened by citation and explanation. For example, Philo begins *Cherubim* by considering what banishment is; he promptly recalls the incident of Hagar, so that *Cherubim* 3–10 is occupied with Philo's explanation of Hagar's flight and banishment. The result of the sporadic citation is to furnish the collator

---

[382] *Abr.* 261.

with an abundance of Abrahamic passages which give much more elaborate detail than the topical arrangement of *De Abrahamo* could possibly afford. Moreover, context can prompt Philo to emphasize at one point a facet of the exegesis of a verse which elsewhere is scrutinized for some different facet.

That is to say, the laconic, topical treatment in *De Abrahamo* has behind it the richness of the multi-faceted material of the *Allegory*. What is stated for once, and without adornment, in *De Abrahamo*, is often repetitiously and complexly to be encountered in the *Allegory*. Accordingly, Philo omits from *De Abrahamo* all mention of his allegory of Hagar, but there can be no doubt that his allegorical understanding of her is implicit. Hagar appears, though namelessly. Philo, indeed, has no need there to allegorize Hagar. Dealing with the end result, Abraham, the perfected sage, Philo need not specify that Abraham mastered the encyclia.

The topical arrangement, again, leads Philo to discuss general characteristics with a polished rhetoric and marked completeness: for example, he writes at some length on faith, in *Abr.* 268–273. The proof-text, Gen. 15.6, is cited by Philo in no less than seven other places;[383] but only in the topical arrangement does Philo follow the topic rather than the biblical verses.

The difference, then, between the literal Abraham and the allegorical is one of method and not content. The literary form of *De Abrahamo* has led Philo to follow an arrangement which differs only in form from the congruent conceptions expressed in other forms in the *Allegory*.

Two conclusions follow. First, the commentator who makes inferences from *De Abrahamo* alone, without searching out Philo's fuller view, can inadvertently distort Philo's intent. Second, the apologetic cast of *De Abrahamo* is limited to literary form. The Abraham there is not conceived or moulded apologetically, but is in all verity Philo's genuine conception of Abraham. To put it in another way, while Philo may in *De Abrahamo* be presenting Abraham to Gentiles, he is not altering his essential view of Abraham one whit.

[383] *Mig.* 44; *LA* III, 228; *Quod. Deus*, 4; *Heres*, 94–95; *Mut.*, 177 and 186; and *Virt.*, 216.

The early Graeco-Jewish writers, including Josephus, out of an apologetic motive, depicted Abraham as a philosopher and mathematician, whose achievements were a benefit of a universal character. The Abraham of IV Maccabees was portrayed as a model who through pious reason overcame his passions, and lived by the four Greek cardinal virtues.

The Abraham of Philo is the mystic philosopher, a resident of some city like Alexandria. He has a thorough grounding in the lower learning and in philosophy. Through reason he conquers his bodily passions and rises above his senses. His life demonstrates that he lived by the four cardinal virtues, which are the by-product of his piety.[384] Indeed, Abraham penetrates beyond the specific virtues to generic virtue itself. He lives in the realm of the intelligible world; accordingly, he abandons city life from time to time for sojourns in the wilderness. There by contemplation he rises to the best possible vision of God. Abraham is thus a perfected man, despite a false start in pantheism. He lives by the law of nature, and he is himself a law made vocal and incarnate. His contemporaries and his descendants benefit from his achievements.

These three views just described represent three different measures of hellenization. The first is little more than surface. The second exhibits a partial concession to Greek norms. The third shows the process carried through to the greatest possible degree consistent with Jewish loyalty.

Abraham is only part of Philo's hellenization of Judaism. While Philo defends the Law, the truly religious man is, to him, no longer only an observer of the Law, but, in conformity with hellenistic notions of salvation, such a man must rise above corporeity, to use Wendland's phrase, into communion with incorporeal and immaterial reality. Like IV Maccabees Philo regards the Law as divine; but unlike IV Maccabees, which does not in reality discuss the question, Philo believes that there is a higher law of which the Law is only a copy. The Law leads to the higher reality, but is not identical with it.

---

[384] IV Maccabees and Philo accord in some measure regarding piety, on the one hand, and the four virtues, on the other hand, as the ability to control the passions, and as characteristics of Abraham.

Both for Philo and for the rabbis Abraham is the first true believer. The rabbis infer from this biblical datum that Abraham observed piously all the details of the particular laws; Jubilees portrayed Abraham as an observer of the Law of Moses, and the rabbis add that he observed also the Oral Law. They accordingly bring Abraham into relationship with details and minutiae of the two Laws.

To Philo the observance of the Law is a lower aspect of religiosity; we may conjecture that he would have denied indignantly the notion that Abraham was preoccupied with only the copy of the law of nature. Philo has so metamorphosed Judaism that no matter how much he wants to exalt the Law, he can raise it only to conformity with the law of nature and never to identity with it.[385]

Philo's approach to the Law, in such treatises as *De Decalogo* and *De Specialibus Legibus* is that of a defender rather than that of an exhorter; his exhortations are reserved for the higher law. A particular of the Law is never considered by Philo as an end in itself, but an illustration of an underlying principle. Bréhier[386] points up this Philonic view of underlying principles in noting that Philo divides the Decalogue into two groups of five laws, the first five centering on piety towards God and the second set centering on justice, a division similar to what we have noted in *De Abrahamo*.[387] It does not overstate the case too much to draw the contrast that Philo is somewhat passive in defending the Mosaic Law, but active and aggressive in exhorting his hearers to the higher law.

Philo's view that the written Law is secondary accounts for his linking Abraham with the higher law. It is the conviction that there is nothing higher than the Law which impels the Jubilees and rabbis to make a halakic observer of the patriarch in advance of the Law. Abraham is to the rabbis and to Philo (as well as to Paul) the foremost example of the man who did what each is urging; but each is urging a different thing.

---

[385] I give a fuller comparison of Philo and the rabbis below, page 199 ff.
[386] *Op. cit.* 30.
[387] Cf. *Decal.* 50–51 for Philo's division of the Law into the two sets of five.

The rabbis were interested in an abundant depiction of Abraham observing specific laws. In the case of Philo, however, the concreteness is inevitably lacking in that the laws of nature, being ideal, are not specific. Philo gives us not one single example of Abraham's observing some specific biblical or halakic item.

Philo rather asserts that Abraham practiced piety towards God and the cardinal virtues toward his fellow men. There is a lack of concreteness in such matters which may well have raised for Philo and for his audience a question of this sort: It is very well to urge men to live by Immaterial Reality, or by these metaphysical abstractions; but is it truly feasible?

That such questions were raised is explicit in the treatise *Mutatio* 36–37: "Indeed are there not still among the disciples of philosophy some who say that a wise man is non-existent and therefore wisdom also? None, they say, from the beginning of man's creation up to the life of today has been held to be completely free from fault, for absolute happiness is impossible to one imprisoned in the mortal body. Whether these statements are true we will inquire at the proper occasion. At present we will accept the text and say that wisdom is indeed something which exists, and so too is the lover of wisdom, the Sage, but, though he exists, we who are evil fail to see him, for good cannot keep company with bad."

Philo, then, is concerned to demonstrate that it is feasible for a man to be a sage, that is, to rise above the body and to live by metaphysical principles. He gives demonstrations both from the present, and from the past, of his affirmative conviction. Thus he "proves" his point by describing two sects of his own time, the Essenes and the Therapeutae. Discussing the true freeman, Philo tells us, in *Probus*, that there are people who judge only from appearance, who ask "who have there been in the past, and who are there living now of the kind that you imagine? An excellent answer is that in the past there have been those who surpassed their contemporaries in virtue, who took God for their sole guide and lived according to nature's right reason . . . . Also in our own time there are still men formed as it were in the likeness of the original high excellence of the sages." The exemplars from his own day do not appear herded in throngs, Philo tells us, because they avoid the crowd. They pray that they may work a reformation in the lives of others; this is impossible in the cities, and therefore these exemplars go out into the lonelinessess.[388]

The Essenes are, according to Philo, a group which, in accordance with the meaning of the name, holiness, sanctify God not by offering sacrifices but by resolving to sanctify their minds.[389] They live in villages and avoid the city dwellers, this in order to escape the contamination inherent in cities. They pursue simple trades and crafts and cooperate with each other. They do not try to acquire more physical wealth than is required for the necessities of life; they stand alone among men in having become moneyless and landless deliberately. Peace lovers, there are no manufacturers of weapons of any kind among them. They reject the institution of slavery, and denounce slave owners for doing violence to the law of equality and annulling, impiously, the law of Nature. They leave the study of logic to quibblers and sophists, and the study of the physical world to babblers, while they themselves retain that part of philosophy which treats of the existence of God and the creation of the universe. This ethical part they study industriously, taking as their trainers the laws of their fathers which could not have been conceived by the human soul without divine inspiration.[390] Philo adds several more details[391] which need not here concern us, since the outline above indicates adequately how Philo regards them: they are the example of his own way of living by the Higher Reality.[392]

The similarites of the Essenes and of the career of the patriarchs are not set forth by Philo, beyond his laconic statement that

---

[388] *Probus*, 62–63.

[389] Bréhier points out (p. 52) that in his description of the Essenes Philo is being an apologist and not an historian. I should not hesitate to express the judgment that much if not most of what Philo has to say about both the Essenes and also the Therapeutae is fanciful, and congruent rather with Philo's *Tendenz* than with facts.

[390] *Probus*, 75–80.

[391] *Probus*, 81–91.

[392] The various problems about the Essenes, especially the slight variations between the account by Josephus in *B. J.* II, 8, 2–13, need not be treated here. Cf. Colson IX, pp. 514–516.

the Essenes are formed in the likeness of the great sages. But
Philo's description of the Therapeutae, on the other hand, reads
almost as though it was constructed out of the phrases and
conceptions which Philo uses in tracing the career of Abraham.

Philo begins his treatise, *De Vita Contemplativa*, by alluding
to his previous work which depicts the Essenes as exemplars of
those who led the active ($\pi\rho\alpha\kappa\tau\iota\kappa\delta\nu$) life, and then proceeds to
describe, in contrast, the exemplars of the contemplative life.
As we shall see, the contemplative life accords in many details
with the career of Abraham; it seems likely that Philo conceived
of a similar accord between the Essenes as exponents of the life
of perfection through $\check{\alpha}\sigma\kappa\eta\sigma\iota\varsigma$ of which Jacob is his exemplar.
Philo does not make these associations explicit; it is the more
readily discernible in the case of the Therapeutae and Abraham
than in the case of the Essenes and Jacob. Nevertheless, the
contrast between the Therapeutae and the Essenes is the same
as the contrast between Abraham and Jacob; perfection by
meditation and contemplation as distinct from perfection through
action.

The name Therapeutae, as derivable from the root meaning
to cure, alludes, Philo tells us, to the cure of the soul; the sickness
of the soul consists of those things inflicted by the passions and
the vices. This is reminiscent, in general effect though not in
language, of Philo's interpretation of Abraham's conquest of
the nine kings of Gen. 14.[393] The name, as derivable from a root
meaning to worship, means that the Therapeutae were taught
by nature and the sacred laws to worship *To On*.[394] They did
not revere the elements, for these are lifeless; nor the deified
beasts of Egypt. Like Abraham, the Therapeutae are taught
by nature; like Abraham they reject the "pantheism" represented
by Chaldea, as well as the other "false" religions of Philo's day.[395]

---

[393] *Abr.* 236–244.

[394] *VC* 1–2. In the passage Philo contrasts the worship of $\tau\delta$ $\check{o}\nu$ which is
purer than the $\dot{\epsilon}\nu\delta\varsigma$ and more primordial than the $\mu o\nu\acute{\alpha}\varsigma$. Colson IX, 114–115
cites Zeller, *Presocratics* (English translation) vol. I, 309 ff., for this type of
distinction in Pythagoreanism. What Philo is saying, for our purposes, is that
the Therapeutae worshiped what is God, the ultimate reality, rather than
some intermediate entity.

[395] *VC* 3–9.

Like Abraham, the Therapeutae want the vision of *To On*, and they therefore rise above sense perception; they too are carried away by a heaven-sent love, and they too become rapt and possessed like bacchanals or corybants until they see the object of their yearning.[396]

Like Abraham, the Therapeutae leave their homes and their kinfolk.[397]

The Therapeutae, like Abraham, do not migrate simply from one city to another city; instead they pass their days outside the walls.[398] The Therapeutae include many who give utterance, when asleep or dreaming, to the verities of their holy philosophy. What Philo seems to be saying indirectly is that there are prophets among the Therapeutae.[399] At sunset the Therapeutae want to relive the experience of Abraham and be wholly relieved of the press of the senses.[400]

The Therapeutae are allegorists, who penetrate beyond the literal texts to antecedent "nature."[401]

The πρεσβύτατος among the Therapeutae gives a discourse on the Sabbath. The discourse is not clever rhetoric or sophistry, but is a careful and exact expression of the meaning of the thoughts.[402]

---

[396] *VC* 10–12; cf. *Abr.* 68 ff.: Abraham departs from those who glorify visible existence; he opens his soul's eye; the mist of sense is dispelled and Abraham receives the vision of *To On*. Cf. also *Heres* 69–70, for an almost identical passage on heavenly love, divine possession, and yearning for *To On*.

[397] *VC* 13 and 18; cf. *Mig.* 1 ff.

[398] *VC* 19. Cf. *Abr.* 85: Abraham migrated "not . . . from state to state but into a desert country."

[399] *VC* 26; cf. *Heres* 264–266.

[400] *VC* 27; cf. Philo's interpretation of "about sunset there fell upon him an ecstasy," Gen. 15.17, *Heres* 263.

[401] *VC* 28. The essence of Abraham, it will be recalled, is that he lived according to nature. The Therapeutae, then, are interested in the life which accords with nature. They possess the writings of men of old which point out the way to allegorical interpretation.

[402] *VC* 31. Abraham was called the "elder" in Gen. 24.1, an epithet which according to *Sob.* 17–18 has to do with one's soul and not with one's age. Abraham passed beyond the stage of Ishmael, sophistry, *Sob.* 8. Abraham was blessed with both good thoughts and good speech, *Mig.* 70 ff. Philo gives this explanation of "elder" later on, in *VC* 67.

Philo's contrast of the banquet of the Therapeutae with Greek banquets, as exemplified in the *Symposium* of Plato, leads him to describe the Platonic banquet in terms almost identical with those he uses in denouncing the Sodomites: cities are desolated, the best kind of men become scarce, sterility and childlessness ensue, and the like.[403]

The Therapeutae contemplate nature, and live in the soul alone.[404]

The Therapeutae, then, are those who lived the life of which Abraham was the exemplar, as the Essenes are those who lived the life of which Jacob was the exemplar.

Reverting to the matter discussed earlier, the Essenes and the Therapeutae serve Philo as his proof that it is possible in his day for men to live by metaphysical principle. Philo's use of Abraham seems, in its way, to be Philo's calling upon antecedent history for attestation that such a life was possible in the past.

In this light, some of the introductory phrases of *De Abrahamo*

[403] *VC* 60–62; cf. *Abr.* 135–136. Philo seems to equate by implication the "Italian expensiveness and luxury" with the wealth of the Sodomites and their gluttony; *VC* 48 and *Abr.* 133–134.

[404] *VC* 90. I have been led to wonder if the title "contemplative life" gives the true import of the Greek βιὸς θεωρητικός. The Greek means basically "seeing," a connotation that seems to me inevitably lacking in the term "contemplative," though the word does have the dictionary meaning of "looking upon." This meaning, however, has become secondary to something like "consider with attention or thoughtfulness." The point to be made is that for Philo the highest religious experience is the seeing of God, and in the measure that "The Contemplative Life" fails to connote that it is the life which concerns itself with "seeing" God, the phrase is unintentionally deficient. The Therapeutae, like Abraham, are those concerned with the life of the "sight" of God. Philo makes this clear about Abraham in a number of passages: there is, he says, *Mig.* 165, an intimate connection between seeing and contemplation (τῷ δὲ θεωρητικῷ τὸ ὁρᾶν συνῳδόν τε καὶ οἰκειότατον). The change in Abraham's nature implicit in his change of name is his passing from concern for the sight of his eyes to concern for the sight of his soul. The sight of the soul is the "contemplative" life; and Abraham is for Philo the chief exponent of contemplation, for the reason that the Bible records that Abraham received the vision of God; cf. *Abr.* 84 and *Mut.* 3–6; 66–76.

Philo's allegory of Abraham, we saw, was his demonstration that Abraham rose above the body to live by his soul.

cease to be mere rhetorical devices and become living and important words to Philo: the lives of the patriarchs appear in the books of the Law not only because such men lived good and blameless lives. But Moses wants to do more than to sound their praises; he wants to instruct the reader and to induce him to aspire to be like these men. Since these men were ἔμψυχοι καὶ λογικοὶ νόμοι, Moses mentions them for two reasons: first, he wants to show that the enacted ordinances are not inconsistent with nature; and second, that those who wish to live in accordance with the laws as they now stand have no difficult task, because the first generation followed the unwritten law of which the written is only a record.

It seems unmistakable that Philo has attributed to Moses Philo's own desire: to instruct the reader and to induce him to be like the patriarchs. Abraham, then, is one of the models after whom a man can in a later generation model his life.

The study of Abraham, then, clearly reveals what to Philo is the true and significant religiosity. It is not only the observance of the particular laws, the Law of Moses. Beyond them true religiosity is the living in accord with nature, the rise of the soul above the obstacles of the body; the determination not to be contaminated by the evils inherent in the city, but to live in a pure state as though one were in heaven, and to receive the divine afflatus as the end result of the proper life.

In the way that Philo's Abraham differs from the rabbinic Abraham, in the same way the essential religiosity of Philo differs from that of the rabbis. No matter how much Philo exalts the Law of Moses, no matter how consistent he proves it to be with the Law of nature, the Law of Moses is at best a copy, and thereby inescapably secondary.

Philo concedes to his environment what the rabbis never felt need of conceding, or if they felt the need, would never have been willing or able to do: Philo admits that there is something more basic than the Law of Moses, something antecedent to the Law. Only in a thoroughly hellenistic environment, with the implicit dualism of the material and the immaterial, and with the echoes of Platonism everywhere ringing, however faintly, in the ear, is such a concession at all admissible.

The allegorists who do not observe the literal law[405] are those who have succumbed entirely to the Greek spirit. However much Philo, who abides by the Laws of Moses, denounces them for their lack of observance, his admission that they are right in seeing beyond the literal[406] seems to doom his own position. He will defend the Law of Moses to the best of his abilities, but what he is defending against the allegorists is the body of Scripture, the second best, and he is defending it against, as it were, the soul, which he must concede is the "first best." Philo is so thoroughly hellenized that his loyalty to Judaism is everywhere shaped by his simultaneous agreement with the contentions of the extreme allegorists. The Greek cast of his thought is so germane to him that he truly believes that the religious and philosophical system which his thought inhabits, is a Jewish creation, stemming from Moses, and that Plato and other Greek worthies were latter-day imitators and plagiarists. Philo seems to believe this implicitly; his hellenization is so thorough and so complete that undoubtedly he himself was unaware of how Greek his Judaism is. His Abraham, whom he exalts as an example of Jewish perfection, achieves that perfection in terms of Greek salvation. Philo himself is as hellenized as is his Abraham; his Abraham is portrayed in the author's image.[407]

Respecting Philo's Abraham and the Abraham of the Apocrypha and Pseudepigrapha, we are again struck with the absence of connection and relationship. I have been able to discover not one single item of any substance which would bind Philo's view to the views in the other literatures. The single possible exception is the common motif that Abraham was the first man to discover the existence of God; but even in this item in which some community of view might be alleged, Philo's explanation of the manner of Abraham's discovery again separates him.

---

[405] *Mig.* 89 ff.   [406] Cf. *Conf.* 190.

[407] There are several passages in which Philo makes a personal application of the scriptural lesson he has inferred about Abraham. He urges his own soul to imitate Abraham's migration, *Heres* 69 ff. Philo, too, wanted to beget out of virtue, Sarah, *Cong.* 6, cf. *Mut.* 255 ff. The mating with the encyclia is Philo's experience also, *Cong.* 88. The *ecstasis* of Abraham, *Heres* 68, is paralleled by Philo's own *ecstasis*, *Mig.* 34–35.

It is only with Josephus and with the rabbis that there are random overlapping items. With Josephus these are extremely occasional and of no telling significance.

It remains now to assess the alleged overlappings, and their, to me, distorted significance in some of the scholarly writings.

VII

Two different matters now concern us. First, it will be contended that there are significant and decisive contrasts between the Abraham of the rabbis and the Abraham of Philo, and that these contrasts accord with the contrast in the fundamental religiosities of the rabbis and Philo.

Second, it will be contended that the alteration which Philo makes of the biblical patriarch is not a re-writing of "normative" traditions and views of Abraham, but that Philo creates his Abraham independent of the rabbis.

There are these contrasts to be noted as preliminaries. The Abraham of the rabbis is arrived at through exegesis of the Hebrew Bible, the Abraham of Philo from the Septuagint. Therefore Philo's exegesis will follow what the Septuagint offers and not the Massoretic Text. Philo as we saw, interprets his Abraham in Gen. 12.9, as going into the desert, instead of going southward.[408] To Philo this is a commendable act of the philosophic mystic; the desert and not Palestine is, in fact, the goal of Abraham's migration.

Gen. 14.21 portrays the king of Sodom as offering to Abraham what MT describes as רכוש and LXX as ἵππον Philo's exegesis draws a contrast between the irrational animal and rational man. In Gen. 15.11, the Septuagint renders the singular *ayit* by the plural *ornea*; it renders "drove them away" by "sat down with them." In both cases Philo's allegory is based on the Septuagint; in the first case, he renders the birds as the passions, and in the second case, he portrays Abraham as sitting down with the passions like a chairman, and calling them to order. The use

---

[408] The rabbis read into "southward" the notion that Abraham headed towards the site of the Temple; *Gen. R.* XXXIX.

of different versions of the Bible leads to different conclusions where the versions differ.

Second, the rabbinic exegesis is a totality of legends and utterances stemming from many centuries and countless individual interpreters, whereas the exegesis of Philo, however variegated it may occasionally be, is single-minded and, within limits, consistent. The rabbinic Abraham however must be pieced together from countless disparate and occasionally dissonant passages.

Third, the rabbinic Abraham is couched in terms of the popular mind, while the Philonic represents philosophical and mystical meditation, and the Philonic view, especially of esoteric allegory, is suitable only for the few and not for the many.

Fourth, the comparison between the Philonic and rabbinic Abraham can be made only in the light of basic exclusions. Philo, as stated, gives us not even one legendary narrative. On the other hand, the allegorical quantities assigned by Philo and his associates are not found in the rabbis. It is therefore necessary for one who draws a contrast to bear in mind that while Philo and the rabbis apply exegesis, it is a different mode of exegesis.

Philo's Abraham is depicted in only those incidents which occur in the Bible. The rabbinic Abraham is provided with an early youth. Philo alludes only passingly to Abraham's youth; he lacks the stories of the iconoclasms and Nimrod. Philo shows no knowledge of Abraham as a missionary; rather, his Abraham is an exemplar of the proselyte. The rabbis portray Abraham as coming to the knowledge of God through an observation of astronomical phenomena. Philo knows such a tradition; it is found in his hellenistic predecessors; he rejects, however, astronomical observation as being equivalent to atheism, and he insists that the proper recognition of the existence of God comes from one's turning inward and by deducing the existence of a Mind in the universe from the existence of a mind in man.

The rabbis portray Abraham's victory over the kings in extravagant, miraculous terms, especially focused on the phrase (Gen. 14.15) *wa-yeḥaleq 'aleyhem layla*, "he divided the night against them"; Philo gives a most naturalistic picture of a sudden night attack.

Mamre in the rabbis is the name of a person; Mamre in Philo

is the name of a region and not a person, even in the occurrence of the name with Aner and Eshkol in Gen. 14.24.

Philo pays no attention to the "test" of Abraham in Gen. 22.1; he shows no knowledge of the tests expanded by the rabbis and by Jubilees into ten. Philo shows no knowledge of the atoning power of the *shofar* on Rosh Hashanah as a reminder of Isaac's binding.

The rabbis interpret the three visitors of Gen. 18 as Michael, Gabriel, and Raphael. Philo interprets the chapter as the manner in which the vision of God presents itself to different minds.

The rabbis infer from the exegesis of Gen. 14.17, *'emek ha-melek*, that the surviving kings, in appreciation of Abraham's military might, proclaim him a king. Philo, too, knows Abraham as a king, but this rests not on exegesis but on a direct statement: LXX Gen. 23.6 renders נשׂיא by βασιλεύς. The context establishes that for the rabbis Abraham's kingship rests on his military prowess; Philo expressly denies that Abraham was a king of this type, and he insists that Abraham was the "philosopher-king."

In specific details, then, the connection between the Abraham of the rabbis and the Abraham of Philo is demonstrably negative. A consideration of the over-all conception of Abraham reveals that this disparity in details abides thorough-goingly.

The Abraham of the rabbis is basically an exemplar of the ancestor who lived in accordance with Jewish law, both the Law of Moses and the developed Oral law, commended by the rabbis to his descendants. The Abraham of Philo lived by the natural law of which the Mosaic law was only a copy. Philo in no place suggests that Abraham had anything to do with the Oral law; indeed, the greatness of Abraham was his capacity for living by the higher law, and to have made him an observer of the details of law would have removed for Philo Abraham's uniqueness. The Laws of Moses are for Philo the record of what Abraham did; the Laws of Moses conform to the laws of nature; but the greatness of Abraham was his capacity for actually living by nature. Philo is not interested in portraying Abraham as an observer of the Law, even though Philo admires such an observer. Abraham is Philo's proof that there is a law antecedent to the Laws of Moses, and that it is possible for a man to live by that law.

The Abraham of the rabbis is a "folk-character"; the Abraham of Philo is a deep and profound philosopher, educated in the various disciplines of the university; a philosopher, and a mystic. Philo's Abraham is not the rabbi who is busy with the details of exegesis as discussed in the Academy, learning daily from God a new halaka; Philo's Abraham is the mystic who periodically must forsake the busy city and its contaminations for a quiet retreat in the wilderness and for the contemplation there of the nature of God that leads to the vision of God.

The rabbis, not dividing man into opposing aspects of soul and body, have no need of portraying Abraham as one who rose above body into living in conformity with the intelligible world. The banquet which the rabbis describe Abraham as giving for Isaac at the time of the weaning reveals exactly those aspects of sensual pleasure which Philo denounced as Italian and which he associated with the wealth of the Sodomites. The religiosity of the rabbinic Abraham is that of conformity with divine law, enjoined through Moses and his legitimate successors, and Abraham's greatness was his pious obedience to these commandments, and his subsequent rewards, both in this world and in the world to come. The religiosity of Philo's Abraham is his rejection oj the body and of everything sensual, his conformity with the unwritten laws of nature, and the reabsorption of his mind, at his death, into the divine Mind. The religiosity of the rabbinic Abraham, despite his being a prophet, is the religiosity of the pious observer of objective laws; the religiosity of Philo's Abraham is the successful attainment of salvation by rising above bodily contaminations into mystic union with God.

Insofar as the role of Abraham is decisive, it can be said that the religiosity of the rabbis and the religiosity of Philo differ substantially.[409] Their common base, the Bible, provides a deceptive similarity; that both Philo and the rabbis were "loyal Jews" adds to the deceptive quality of the apparent similarity In essentials, however, the religiosities are markedly diverse.

---

[409] Moore's words respecting the destiny of the soul after death are appropriate to the respective religiosities of Philo and the Rabbis: "What to Philo would have seemed the greatest imaginable evil was to the Pharisees the highest conceivable good." (II, 295).

Those who insist that Philo's essential religiosity is no different from the rabbis go on to aver that Philo inherits the rabbinic tradition. Wolfson, we remember, calls Philo a member of a collateral branch of Pharisaic Judaism. Apparently on a basis suggested by Ginzberg, Wolfson would explain the nature of Philonic Judaism as that of turning popular religion into philosophical religion. Ginzberg[410] speaks of utterances of Philo as revealing on close scrutiny sound rabbinic doctrines, the philosophical tinsel of which can easily be removed.

The assertion made above, that Philo's essential religiosity differs from that of the rabbis, does not depend for its justification on demonstrating that Philo is independent of rabbinic tradition. Philo might have come to his philosophical mysticism from the doctrines of the rabbis. The case that Philo's religiosity is different can be strengthened by a demonstration that Philo is independent of the rabbis; but the case can stand without this item.

It is in order, however, to examine some of the matters presented by Ginzberg and Wolfson in contention that it specifically is rabbinic doctrines which Philo is turning into philosophy.[411]

Ginzberg[412] implies a relationship between the rabbinic notion that Abraham was a king, and the Philonic. It was shown above that the rabbinic notion derived from scriptural exegesis of Gen. 14.17 while the Philonic was directly stated in the Septuagint, Gen. 23.6. Ginzberg cites in support of the notion that the rabbis did not really conceive of Abraham as a political king a passage in *Gittin* 62a; this passage simply states on the basis of Proverbs 8.15, that scholars are called kings. The passage makes no mention of Abraham; it specifies no details of the nature of the kingship of the Sage, such as Philo gives abundantly. The implied parallelism seems completely lacking.

Ginzberg does not directly state that Philo's elaboration of

---

[410] V, p. ix.

[411] I limit myself to those matters associated by Philo with Abraham. The frequency with which Wolfson equates some rabbinic doctrine with a Philonic notion makes it necessary to adopt this limit.

[412] Ginzberg V, p. 216.

Abraham's departure from home is dependent on the rabbis; he only mentions it as a parallel. In detail the views of the departure have nothing in common (as a comparison of *Abr.* 62–67 with *Gen. R.* 39 will reveal). The expansions are quite dissimilar; they are based on the Bible, not one on the other.[413]

Again, the agreement of the rabbis and Philo that Abraham was a blessing and that the good man is a blessing, is rooted in the Bible,[414] in Gen. 12 and elsewhere.

Ginzberg speaks of Philo as paralleling the rabbis in portraying Sarah, in Egypt, in prayer to God. The rabbis quote her prayer.[415] Philo says, to give a literal translation of *Abr.* 95, that Sarah "fled with him (*sc.* Abraham) to the last championship, that of God." Philo does not specifically say that Sarah or Abraham prayed. But even if Philo had mentioned prayer specifically, it would not imply that Philo is dependent on the rabbis; Gen. 12.17, is a sufficient basis for its natural inference.[416]

Ginzberg sees parallelism in the rabbinic and Philonic portrayal of the battle against the Kings. While the rabbis imply and Philo states explicitly that Abraham trusted in God, the parallelism ends there. Beyond this matter, readily deducible from Scripture, Ginzberg does not seem to notice that Philo portrays Abraham as dividing his home-born servants into three centuries (ἑκατονταρχίας) and advancing with three battalions;[417] Ginzberg errs in attributing to Philo a view that Abraham possessed only home-born servants; Philo speaks also of the ἀργυρωνήτοις. Philo here seems to me to be as far as possible removed from the rabbis.[418]

Ginzberg[419] believes that the statement in *Abr.* 71 is an almost literal rendering of the Hebrew expression צא מאיצטגנינות. This expression occurs in *Gen. R.* 44 as a comment on Gen.15.5; Abraham is portrayed as informing God that he has seen by the planets

---

[413] Ginzberg V, 218–219.
[414] *Ibid.*, 219.
[415] Ginzberg translates it, I, 223.
[416] Ginzberg V, 221.
[417] *Abr.* 232.
[418] Ginzberg V, 224.
[419] *Ibid.*, 227.

that he will not have any offspring. God therefore tells him to "come out from astrology." In the passage in Philo astrology is not to be equated merely with forecasting, but with pantheistic materialism. Colson renders the passage in Philo: "Dismiss, then, the rangers of the heavens and the science of Chaldea, and depart for a short time from the greatest of cities, this world, to the lesser, and thus you will be better able to apprehend the overseer of the All." In the Philonic context, the departure from Chaldea is a spiritual experience; Abraham, made perfect by instruction, abandons pantheism with its method of sensible observations for a method which is to lead to intelligible knowledge. In terms of context, the two passages have at best only superficial resemblances, and they do not require the necessary dependence of either Philo on the rabbis or the rabbis on Philo.

Ginzberg suggests that an identical view is "very likely" expressed in Philo's statement that Abraham desisted from Hagar after her pregnancy and in the rabbinic view, *Gen. R.* 45, that Hagar became pregnant from a single effort. However, the Abraham of Philo who, in accord with Philo's view, has sex relations only for procreation, is hardly the same as the rabbinic Abraham who succeeds after only one effort. Philo's motive is to show Abraham's freedom from sensuality; the rabbis were not concerned with sensuality; they may have been interested in Sarah's honor, or in diminishing Abraham's unions with an Egyptian, but it is to be doubted that it is their motive to prove abstemiousness. I see no reason for supposing the two motifs to be related.[420]

The rabbis tell that Abraham's three guests were very courteous. Philo also speaks of their courtesy.[421] Philo derives this courtesy from the fact that although they were three only one spoke; hence, it was courteous of them not to speak all at once. The rabbis infer the courtesy in a different way; the chapter Gen. 18 begins: God appeared to Abraham at *elone Mamre*; it continues "he raised his eyes and saw three men." The rabbis infer that two different visits took place almost simultaneously,

[420] Ginzberg V, 231–232.
[421] *Abr.* 110–132.

one by God and one by three angels. Since the Shekinah permitted the visitors first to speak, Abraham knew they were worthy; by observing that they respected each other Abraham knew that they were distinguished. The rabbis do not specify in what way they showed respect for each other. There is insufficient data here to indicate borrowing on either side.[422]

Philo's comment that Abraham himself ran to the cattle is not paralleled in the otherwise lavish compliments the rabbis pay his hospitality.[423]

The statement that the angels did not really eat is found in the rabbis, Philo, and Josephus. The matter is hardly, however, an expansion of this story, but is part of the more general question ("docetism") of whether or not angels ate.

Ginzberg describes *Abr.* 142 as a haggadah similar to the rabbinic legends of Gen. 18 that the three visitors were Michael, Gabriel, and Raphael. Of these only Gabriel and Raphael went on to Sodom, the former to destroy the city, the latter to save Lot. These haggadahs have some similarity to each other, but they both rest on the same scriptural basis. The Rabbis solve the problem of the discrepancies in number in Gen. 18.1–12 by equating the three visitors with Michael, Gabriel, and Raphael. Philo solves the problem by considering the variation between one and three to be the manner in which the Divine potencies appear to men, either in the form of one or of three. In Wolfson's discussion[424] he makes by implication an identification of the visitors in Philo with the angels of the rabbis, though he concedes that Philo does not ever name any angels. Wolfson does not go as far, in this instance, as to term Philo's discussion of the Powers a conversion of a popular motif into a philosophical one, but this quite clearly seems his intent.[425] To my mind, the similarity of the explanations is so easily accountable by the

---

[422] Ginzberg V, 234.

[423] Ginzberg V, 235.

[424] *Ibid.* I, 126 and 378–381.

[425] Wolfson seems to be misinterpreting Goodenough; he seems to infer that Goodenough, 79–80, denies to Philo the existence of angels. All that Goodenough is denying is that to Philo the angels have fixed personalities, names, and distinct functions.

common scriptural account that dependence of Philo on the rabbis is not indicated. Philo's interpretation is readily derivable from Scripture; to require a rabbinic legend as an intermediary would be to imply that he was unable himself to expound Scripture. Ginzberg, in limiting himself to terming the haggadahs similar, has remained within the realm of the plausible. Philo's explanation accords so well with his numerous comments, in very many passages, on the Powers of God, that one need not be surprised that he turns this handy passage into a quite typically Philonic interpretation.[426]

Philo's ascription of licentiousness and gluttony to the Sodomites is not paralleled in these particulars in rabbinic literature. Scripture specifies the homosexuality of the Sodomites, and the wealth of the region. Philo's ascetic strain leads him to stress their sensuality. The rabbis stress the injustice and the sexual irregularity, but not the gluttony.[427]

The rabbis and Philo accord in the view that the punishment of Sodom did not come directly from God. The rabbis ascribe the punishment to God's court of justice. Philo says that although *To On* gives benefits through his own hand, punishments come at the hands of the Powers.[428] Ginzberg[429] believes that this is an example of Philo's tendency: "To give a philosophic turn to a popular conception is one of Philo's chief merits." But Gen. 19.13, portrays the two angels saying, "We are going to destroy, etc.," while verse 24 says, "God rained down sulphur and fire." Hence the Bible can be the source of Philo's explanation; there is no reason to assume that a popular rabbinic conception stands between Philo and the Bible.

Ginzberg[430] suggests that since all creation rejoiced at the birth of Isaac, this is an explanation of the name similar to Philo's allegory of Isaac as joy. The rabbis do not ever explain Isaac's name as other than "laughter." Philo explains this "joy," as the Sage's spiritual joy, transcending ordinary laughter.

[426] Ginzberg V, 237.
[427] Ginzberg V, 238.
[428] *Abr.* 143–145; cf. *Cong.* 168 ff., *Fuga* 68 ff.; and *Op.* 72 ff.
[429] Ginzberg V, 5, and 241.
[430] *Ibid.*, 245.

That the explanation of the repetition of the calling of Abraham by name, Gen. 22. 11, is paralleled in Philo,[431] need not presuppose dependence, since it is a rather obvious inference from a common biblical basis.[432]

Ginzberg[433] declares that "diffuse comments of Philo on the 'Akedah, which he explains as a protest against the sacrificing of children, show that Alexandrian Judaism, no less than Palestinian, attached great importance to this episode in the lives of the patriarchs." It was indicated above[434] that Philo refrains from attaching to the Binding narrative either the motif of the testing of Abraham or the atoning power of the act as symbolized by the ram. It seems to me that Ginzberg misses entirely the point of Philo's remarks. Philo is polemical and apologetic about the incident; his "diffuse" comments are his reply to the malignity and bitterness of the critics of Abraham; the reply does no more than assert that Abraham's action proved his piety. The chief impression made on me in reading the passage was not any sense at all that the Binding was important to Alexandrian Jews, but rather that it was a somewhat embarrassing story which needed defense.[435]

Ginzberg paraphrases a comment by Philo respecting the mourning of Abraham for Sarah, and adds that "this last remark of Philo is often met with in Jewish writings." The remark which Ginzberg attributes to Philo is that Abraham mourned a short time only, for the wise do not feel sorry when restoring to God the deposit entrusted to them. Philo, however, has said something entirely different: Philo says that Abraham neither grieved overly bitterly as at a new and unheard of misfortune, nor did he assume an indifference as though nothing painful had occurred; he chose the mean between extremes and aimed at moderation, not resenting that nature should be paid the debt which is its due.[436] The rabbinic comment is completely different from what

---

[431] *Abr.* 176 and *Pesiqta Rabbati* XL.
[432] Ginzberg V, 251.
[433] *Ibid.*, 254.
[434] Pages 124 ff. and 173 ff.
[435] See especially *Abr.* 184 and 191.
[436] *Abr.* 257.

Philo says: it is a narrative of the inconsolability of Johanan ben Zakkai after the death of his son; a succession of rabbis try in vain to comfort Johanan until ultimately Elazar ben Azariah tells him the parable of the king who came to claim a deposit entrusted to him.[437] Ginzberg's paraphrase of Philo inadvertently distorts what Philo is saying; there is little in common between these alleged parallels.[438]

Similarly, Ginzberg's paraphrase of *QG* IV, 74, that the Sage is a stranger among bodily things, seems to me to do considerable violence to what Philo says both in this passage and in many other passages. Ginzberg's paraphrase reads, "The pious feel like strangers in this world, they are at home in the other world only." The contrast which Philo is drawing is between material and immaterial things, a contrast quite foreign to rabbinic thought.[439] It is quite startling to read a paraphrase of Philo which implies a contrast between this world and the future world; I have not encountered this rabbinic contrast in Philo.[440]

Ginzberg suggests, though only tentatively, that in Philo's view Gen. 26.5, refers to the Torah which Abraham observed before the revelation on Sinai.[441] The passage says nothing about the revelation on Sinai; as above, Philo does not teach that Abraham observed the Torah, but that the written Torah is the record of what Abraham did. The verse is also expounded in *Mig.* 130, with reference to "doing" the Logos, and nothing is specified about what "law" was involved. Again, when Philo quotes the verse in *Heres* 7–14, he makes no mention of what law is referred to. It can be stated confidently that Philo is not of the opinion that Gen. 26.5, refers to the Law of Moses.[442]

Both the rabbis and Philo call Abraham an elder; the epithet, however, has a biblical basis, Gen. 24.1, and dependency is not necessarily indicated.[443]

---

[437] *ARN* XIV.
[438] Ginzberg V, 255.
[439] Cf. Moore II, 292–295.
[440] Ginzberg V, 256.
[441] *Abr.* 276.
[442] Ginzberg V, 259.
[443] *Ibid.*, 260.

That Philo and a rabbinic comment coincide on the Hebrew etymology of Keturah is hardly surprising. It is not, however, indicative of borrowing. The rabbis seem to know only this of the many etymologies which Philo knows and which the Bible does not itself give.[444]

The case seems then to be that the parallels, on examination, are not nearly as crystal-clearly parallel as Ginzberg (and Wolfson) imply. One who looks into them is struck immediately by the reduced measure of commonness and the striking measure of diversity.

An effect of pointing up the parallels and alleging dependency is to imply that Philo and the Alexandrians were incapable of interpreting the Bible on their own. It overlooks the fact that interpretation of ancient books, by the allegorical method, was by no means unknown in the hellenistic world.[445] It seems to allege that Philo and his associates could approach Scripture only through the medium of developed rabbinic Judaism. It would deny to Philo a capacity to do what Gentile Christians were gifted at, but without the Christians requiring a rabbinic basis.

I should not be ready to deny that some Palestinian traditions are in Philo's possession. But I have seen no evidence in many alleged parallels either that persuasive parallelism occurs in any measure, or, where similarities are superficially present, that Philo is giving a philosophical turn to a rabbinic popular sentiment. Indeed, as one notes the wide differences in details along with the bits of Philonic and rabbinic similarities, he tends all the more to see in Philo someone outside the ultimately dominant rabbinic Judaism. And as one concerns himself with larger aspects, such as the significance of Abraham, he sees a hellenization that is thoroughgoing and complete.[446]

---

[444] *Ibid.*, 264.

[445] Cf. Wolfson I, 131–133.

[446] Cf. Lewy, *Philo Selections*, 1946, 20–21: "Philo received a double education: as a Jew and as a Greek philosopher. The extent of his Jewish learning was very small . . . Of Rabbinical interpretation of Law (Halakah) and Bible narrative (Haggadah) he had very dim notions; he owed both his

Insofar as the limited study of Abraham is decisive for the entire Philonic corpus, these conclusions seem to be in order. First, Philo either has little knowledge of or else rejects the characteristic content of rabbinic exegesis. Second, Philo's view of Judaism differs from that of the rabbis as philosophical mysticism based on the Bible differs from halakic legalism. Three, Philonic Judaism is the result of a hellenization which transcends mere language; it is as complete a hellenization as was possible for a group which retained throughout its loyalty to the Torah, and the separateness of the group. Fourth, as contrastable with normative, rabbinic Judaism, Philo and his associates reflect a marginal, aberrative version of Judaism which existed at a time when there were many versions of Judaism, of which ultimately only Rabbinism and Christianity have survived to our day.

exegetical training and his actual knowledge in matters Jewish to that school of Alexandrine commentators whose methods were perfected by himself . . . We must remember that in Philo's environment there did not exist anything like an authorized, canonized tradition of religious learning . . . It is true that in Philo's time the so-called Oral Teaching . . . began to take definite shape; this development, however, occurred in Palestine and exercised, at that time, no sensible influence on the hellenized Dispersion."

INDEX OF
PHILONIC PASSAGES

KEY TO ABBREVIATIONS OF PHILONIC
TITLES USED IN THIS INDEX

Figures in (   ) indicate volume in Loeb
Classical Library edition

Abr.	*De Abrahamo* (VI)
Agr.	*De Agricultura* (III)
Cher.	*De Cherubim* (II)
Conf.	*De Confusione Linguarum* (IV)
Cong.	*De Congressu Quaerendae Eruditionis Gratia* (IV)
Decal.	*De Decalogo* (VII)
Deter.	*Quod Deterius Potiori Insidiari Solet* (II)
Ebr.	*De Ebrietate* (III)
Flaccus	*In Flaccum* (IX)
Fuga	*De Fuga et Inventione* (V)
Heres	*Quis Rerum Divinarum Heres* (IV)
Gig.	*De Gigantibus* (II)
L. A.	*Legum Allegoriae* (I)
Mig.	*De Migratione Abrahami* (IV)
Moses	*De Vita Mosis* (VI)
Mut.	*De Mutatione Nominum* (V)
Opif.	*De Opificio Mundi* (I)
Plant.	*De Plantatione* (III)
Post.	*De Posteritate Caini* (II)
Praem.	*De Praemiis et Poenis* (VIII)
Probus	*Quod Omnis Probus Liber Sit* (IX)
QG	*Quaestiones et Solutiones in Genesin* (Supp. I)
QE	*Quaestiones et Solutiones in Exodum* (Supp. II)
Quod Deus	*Quod Deus Immutabilis Sit* (III)
Sac.	*De Sacrificiis Abelis et Caini* (II)
Sob.	*De Sobrietate* (III)
Somn.	*De Somniis* (V)
Spec. Leg.	*De Specialibus Legibus* (VII)
Virt.	*De Virtutibus* (VIII)
Vita	*De Vita Contemplativa* (IX)

—   *indicates a reference to a work as a whole.*

Index to Philonic Passages Quoted

SUBJECT INDEX TO PHILO

No index to Philo can be simple or completely consistent. Synonyms, both in Philo's Greek and my English, have here complicated matters. For practicality, and to make the index useful to foreign scholars who can readily read English but whose control of our capricious synonyms is limited, I have generally listed the subjects in Greek, even when the particular Greek term does not appear in my English text. Yet since Philo varies his terms, these Greek entries are to be regarded as general clues to the subject and not as exact reflections of Philo's broad and varying vocabulary. Moreover, while occasionally he distinguishes as between *psyche* and *pneuma*, and among *logos, nous, dianoia,* and *logismos,* he is apt to abstain from abiding even by such distinctions. I give in parentheses, after the Greek, the English term or terms which appear in my text. Some English entries, even beyond the names of biblical characters, have seemed inevitable.

*   *   *